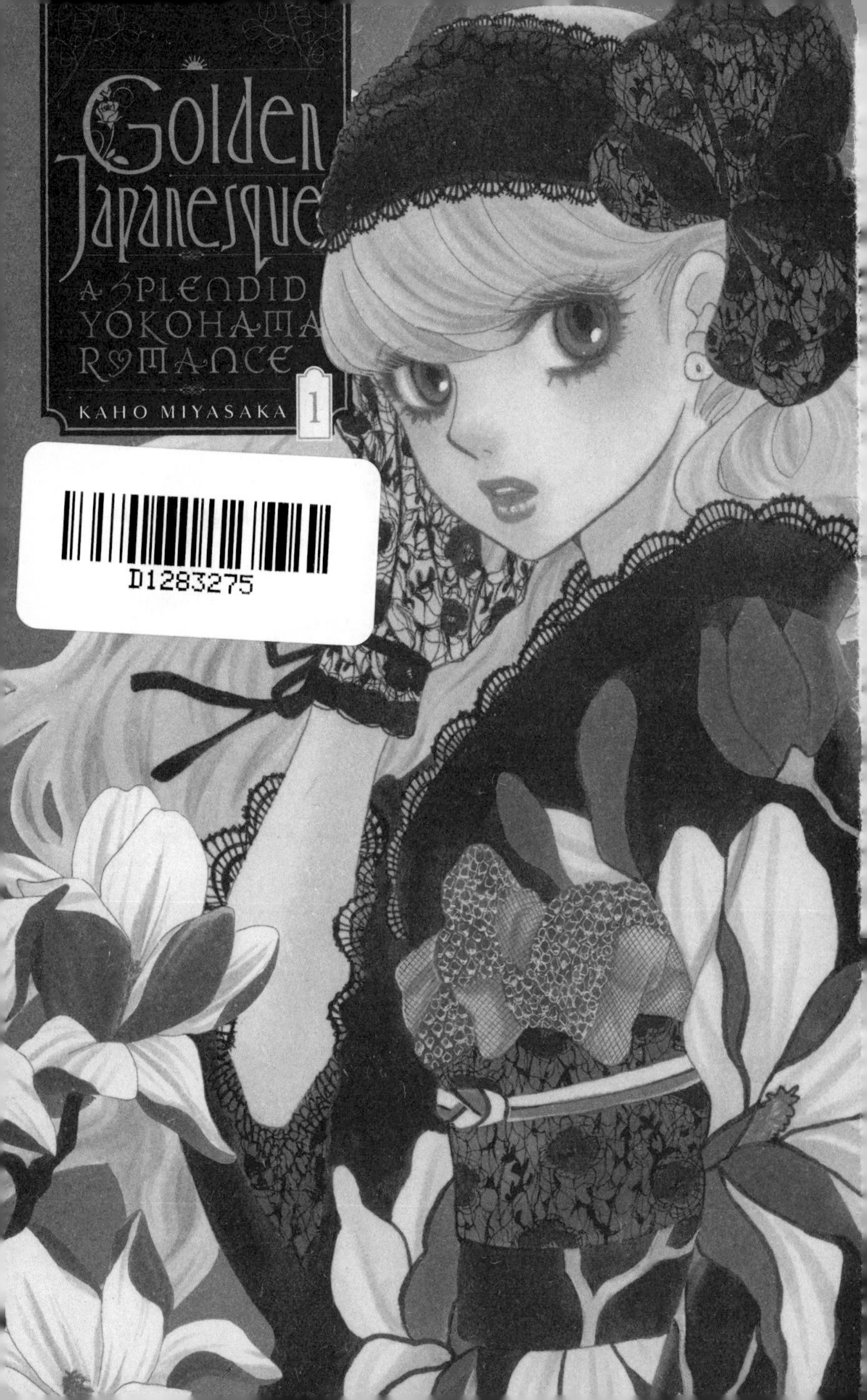
Golden Japanesque
A Splendid Yokohama Romance
KAHO MIYASAKA
1

Golden Japanesque

A Splendid Yokohama Romance

1

Contents

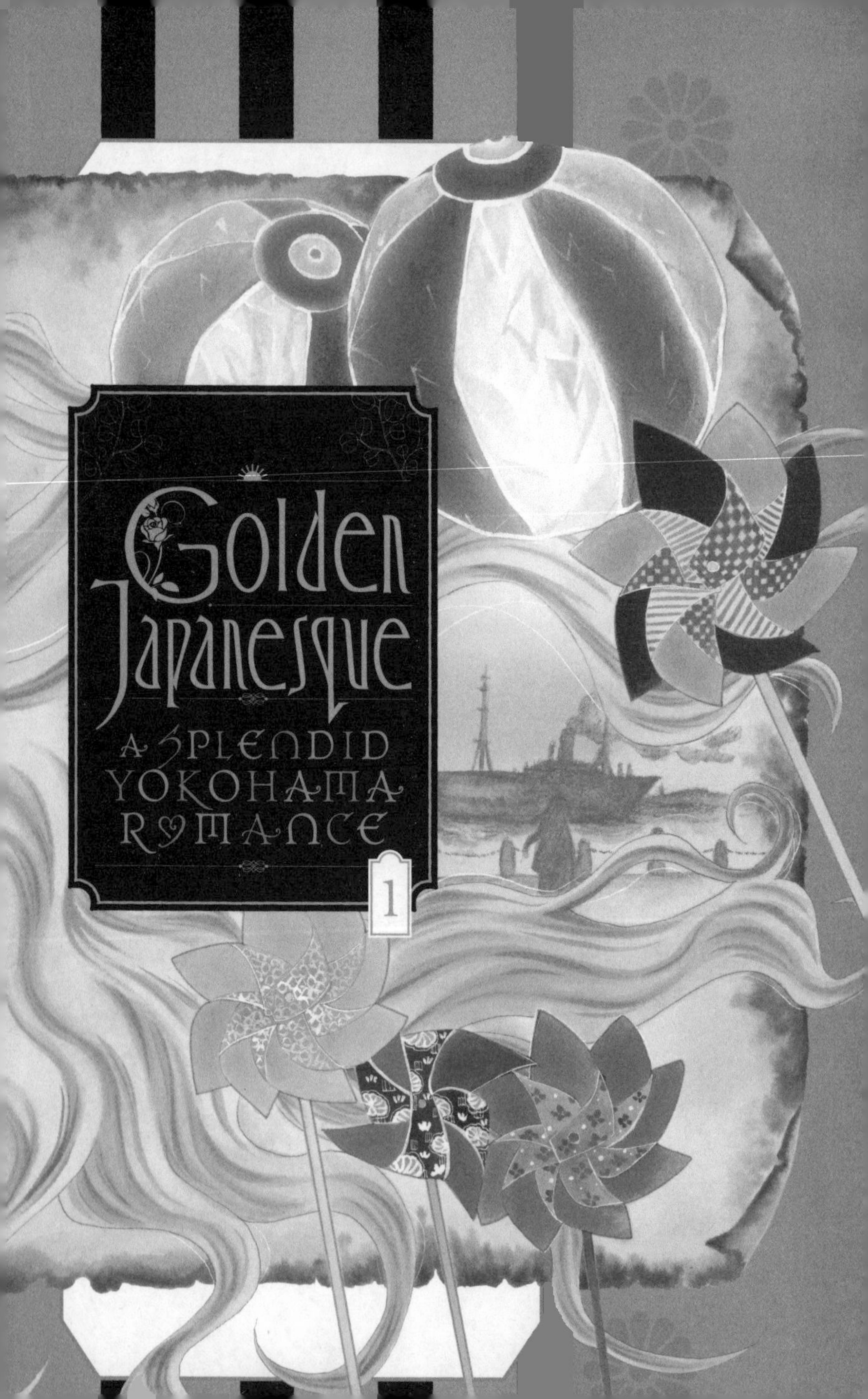
Golden Japanesque
A Splendid Yokohama Romance
1

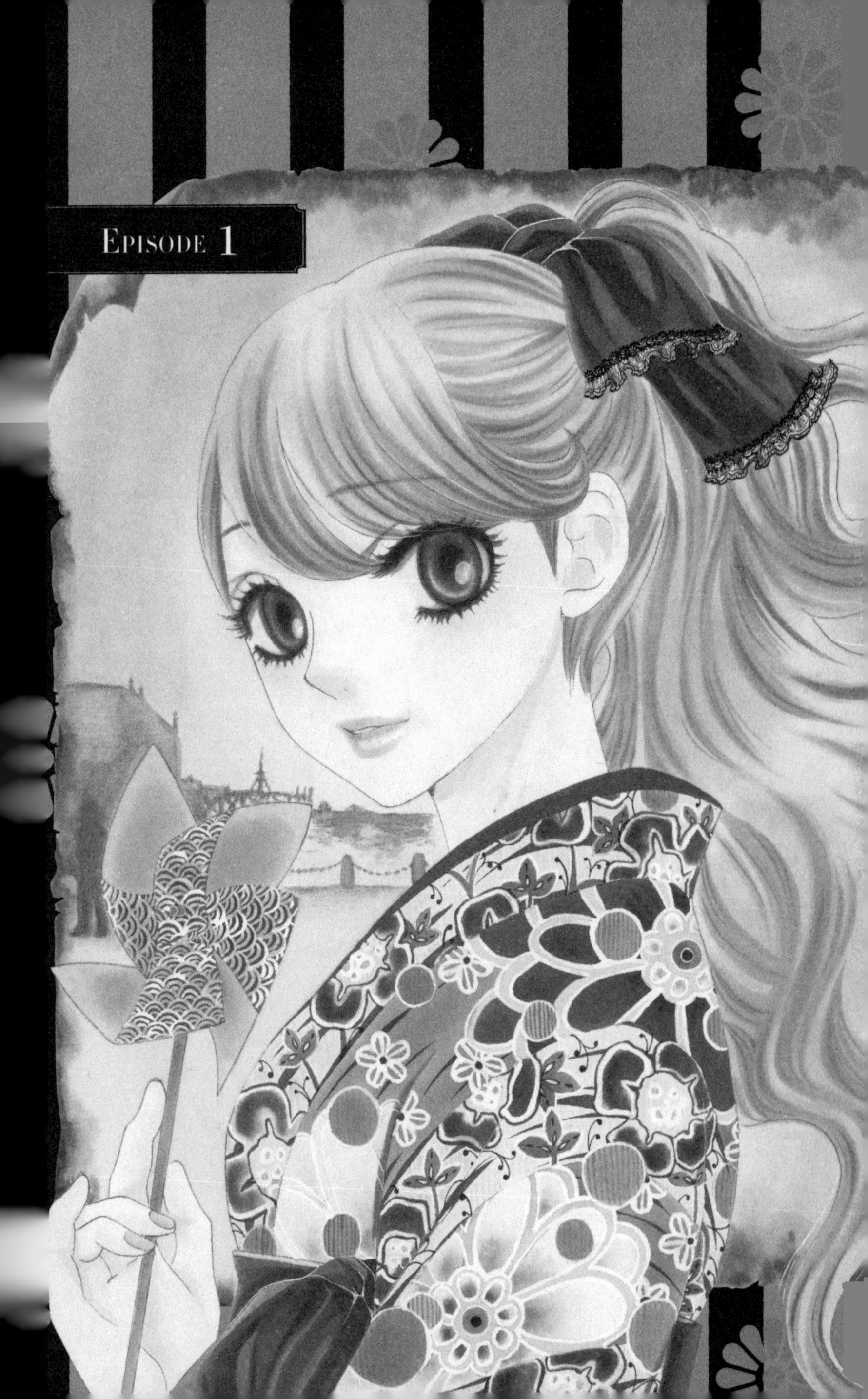
EPISODE 1

I ALWAYS LOOKED DOWN WHEN I WALKED— HOLDING MY BREATH, COUNTING PEBBLES— SO THAT NO ONE WOULD NOTICE ME...

...UNTIL THAT DAY—

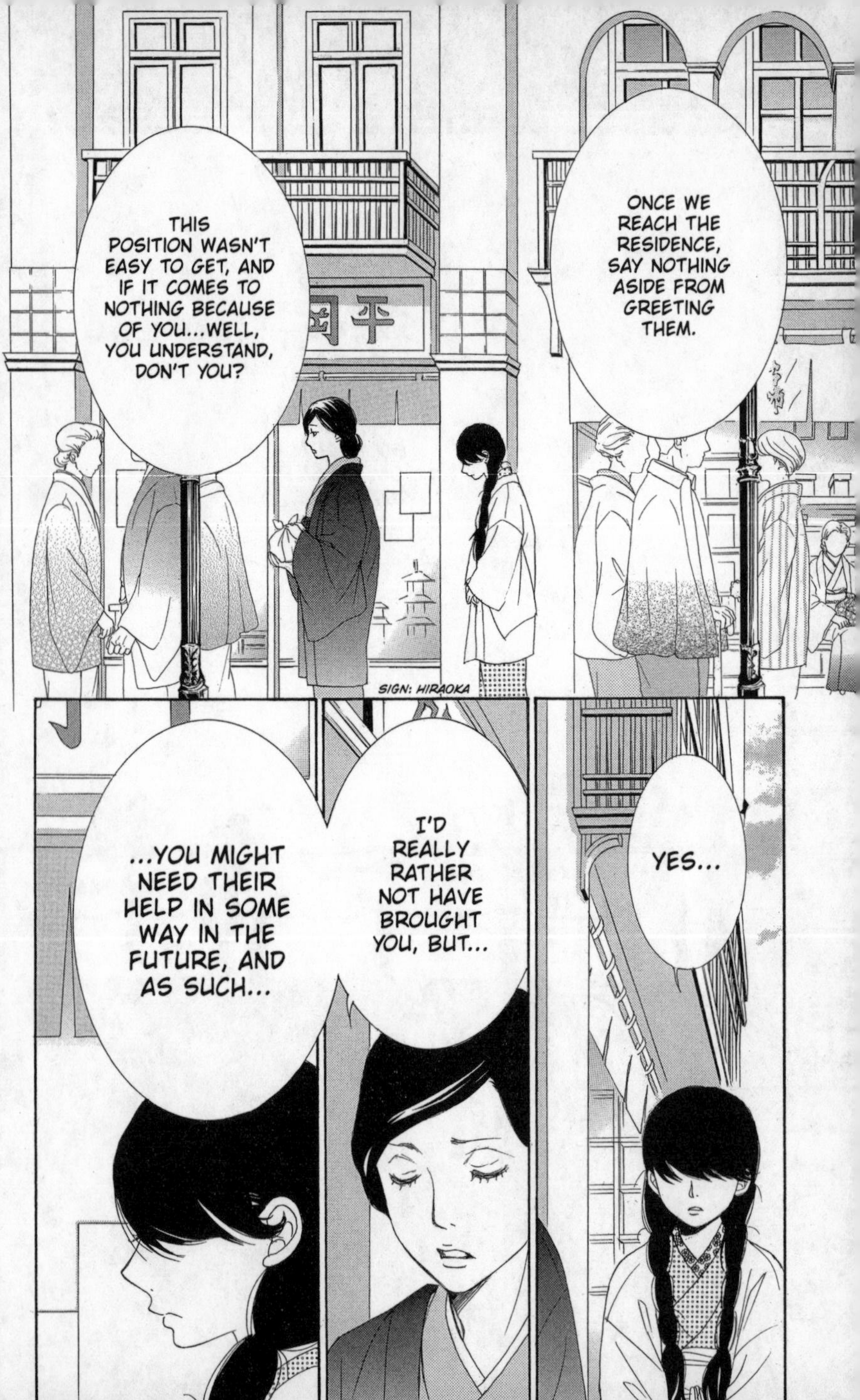
ONCE WE REACH THE RESIDENCE, SAY NOTHING ASIDE FROM GREETING THEM.
THIS POSITION WASN'T EASY TO GET, AND IF IT COMES TO NOTHING BECAUSE OF YOU...WELL, YOU UNDERSTAND, DON'T YOU?
SIGN: HIRAOKA
YES...
I'D REALLY RATHER NOT HAVE BROUGHT YOU, BUT...
...YOU MIGHT NEED THEIR HELP IN SOME WAY IN THE FUTURE, AND AS SUCH...

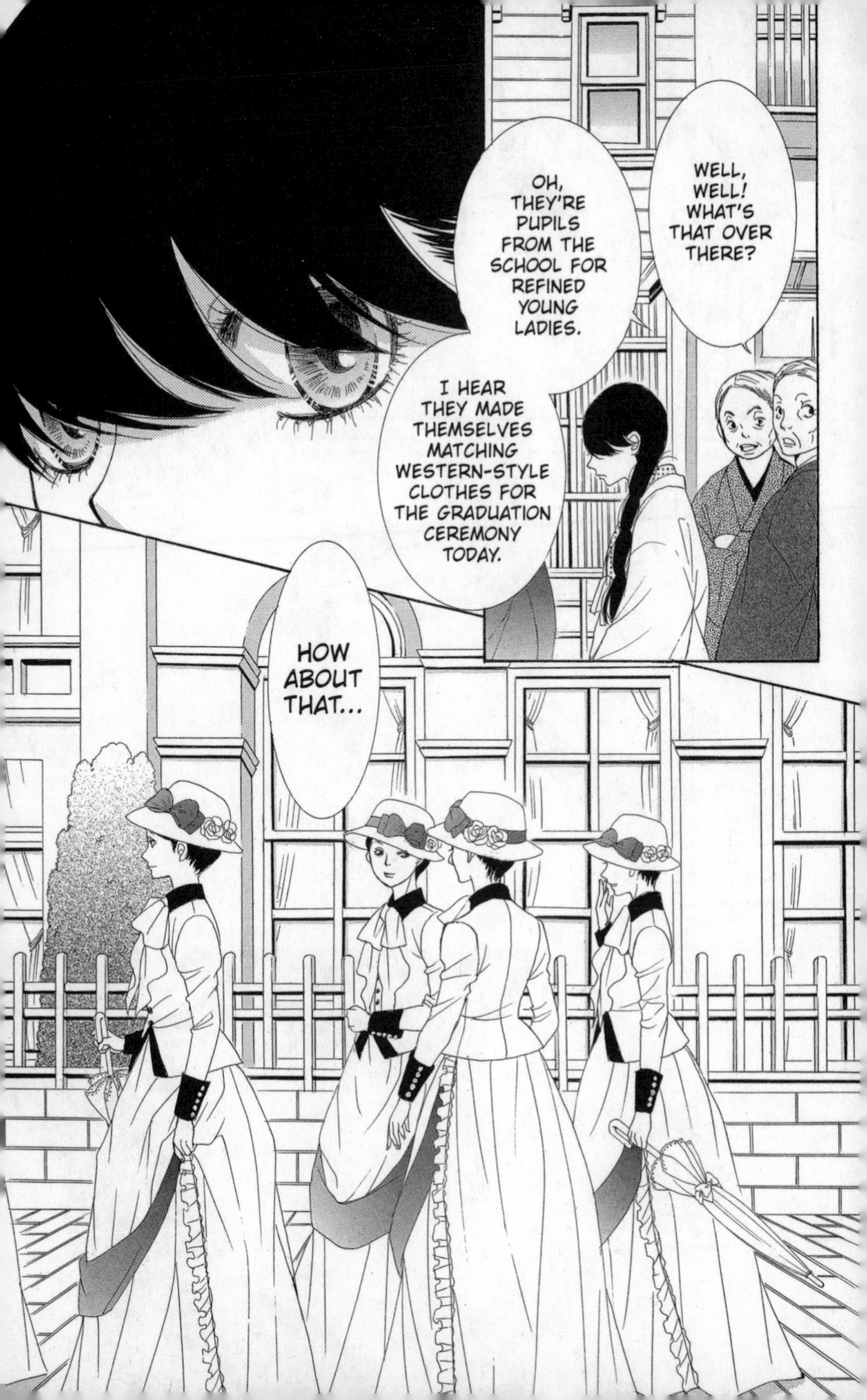
WELL, WELL! WHAT'S THAT OVER THERE?
OH, THEY'RE PUPILS FROM THE SCHOOL FOR REFINED YOUNG LADIES.
I HEAR THEY MADE THEMSELVES MATCHING WESTERN-STYLE CLOTHES FOR THE GRADUATION CEREMONY TODAY.
HOW ABOUT THAT...

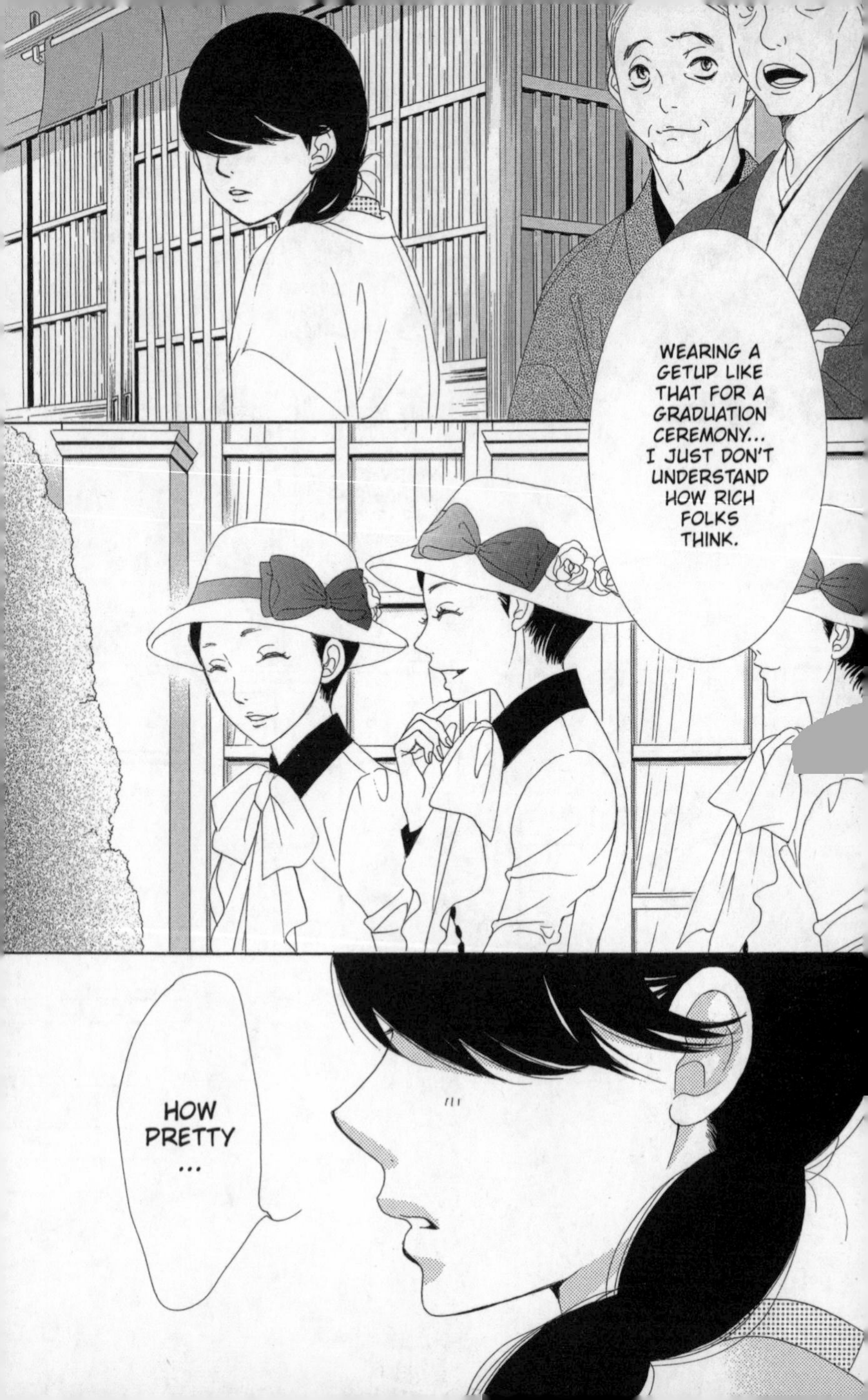
WEARING A GETUP LIKE THAT FOR A GRADUATION CEREMONY... I JUST DON'T UNDERSTAND HOW RICH FOLKS THINK.
HOW PRETTY ...

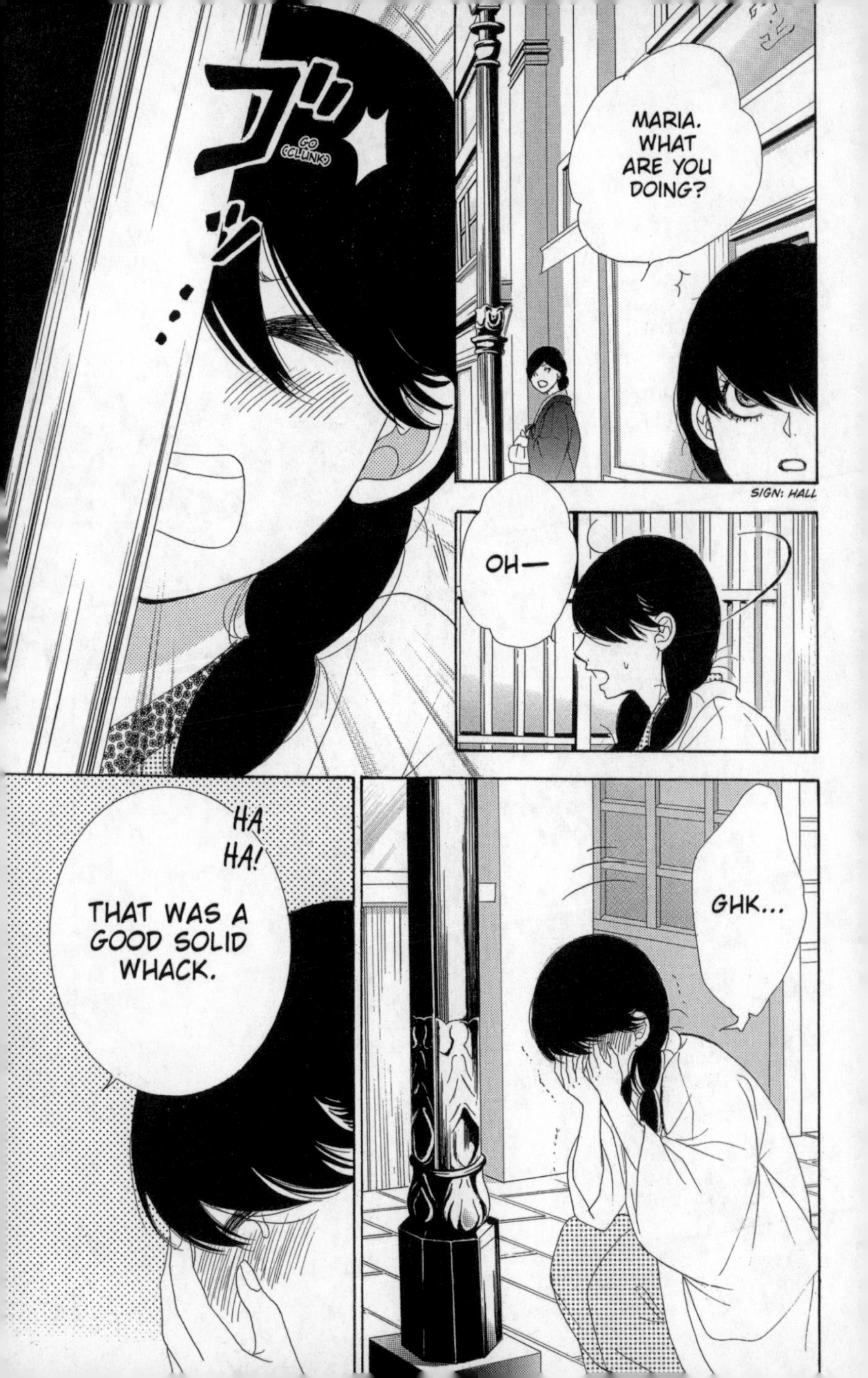
MARIA. WHAT ARE YOU DOING?
SIGN: HALL
OH—
ゴッ
GO (CLINK)
...
GHK...
HA HA!
THAT WAS A GOOD SOLID WHACK.

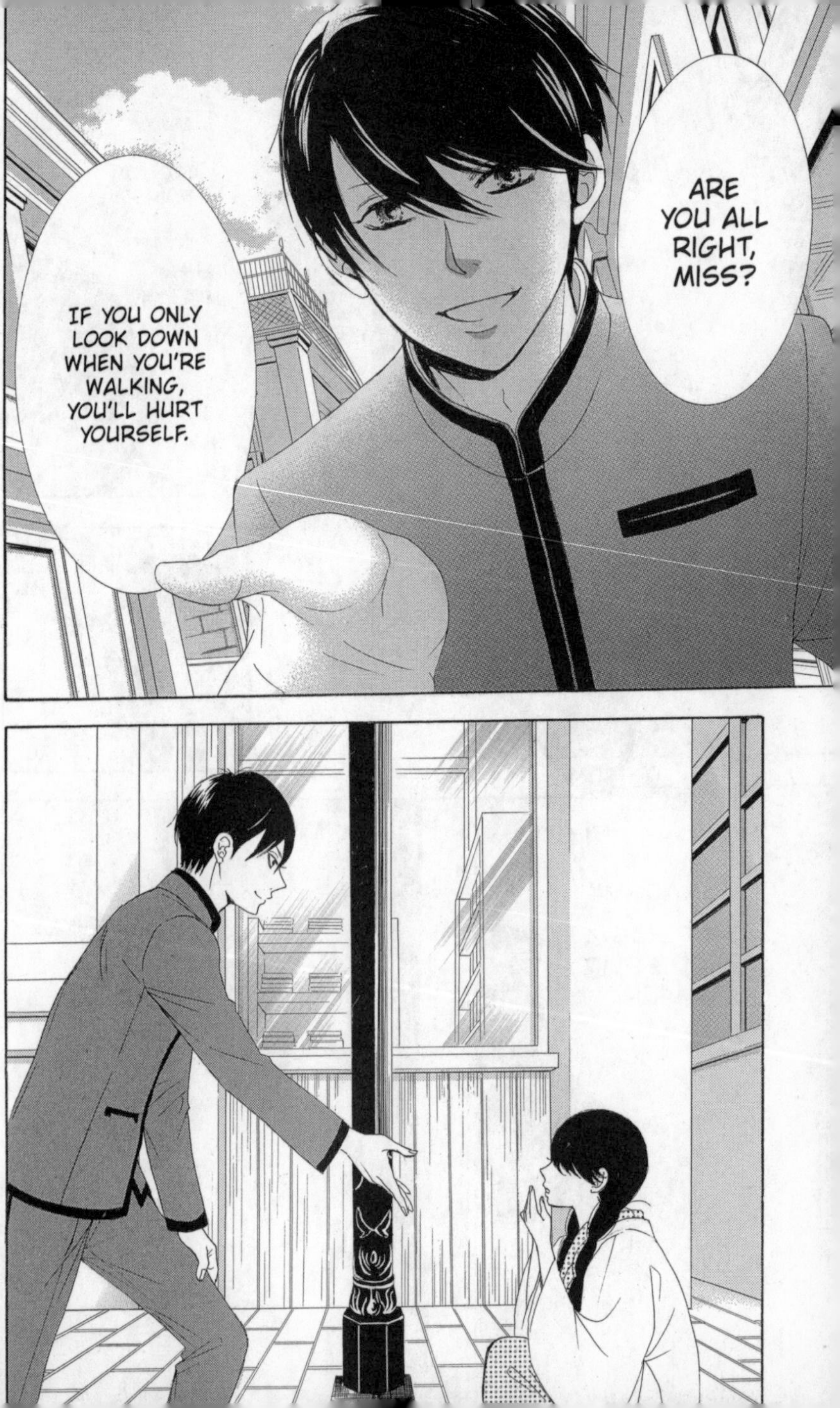
ARE YOU ALL RIGHT, MISS?
IF YOU ONLY LOOK DOWN WHEN YOU'RE WALKING, YOU'LL HURT YOURSELF.

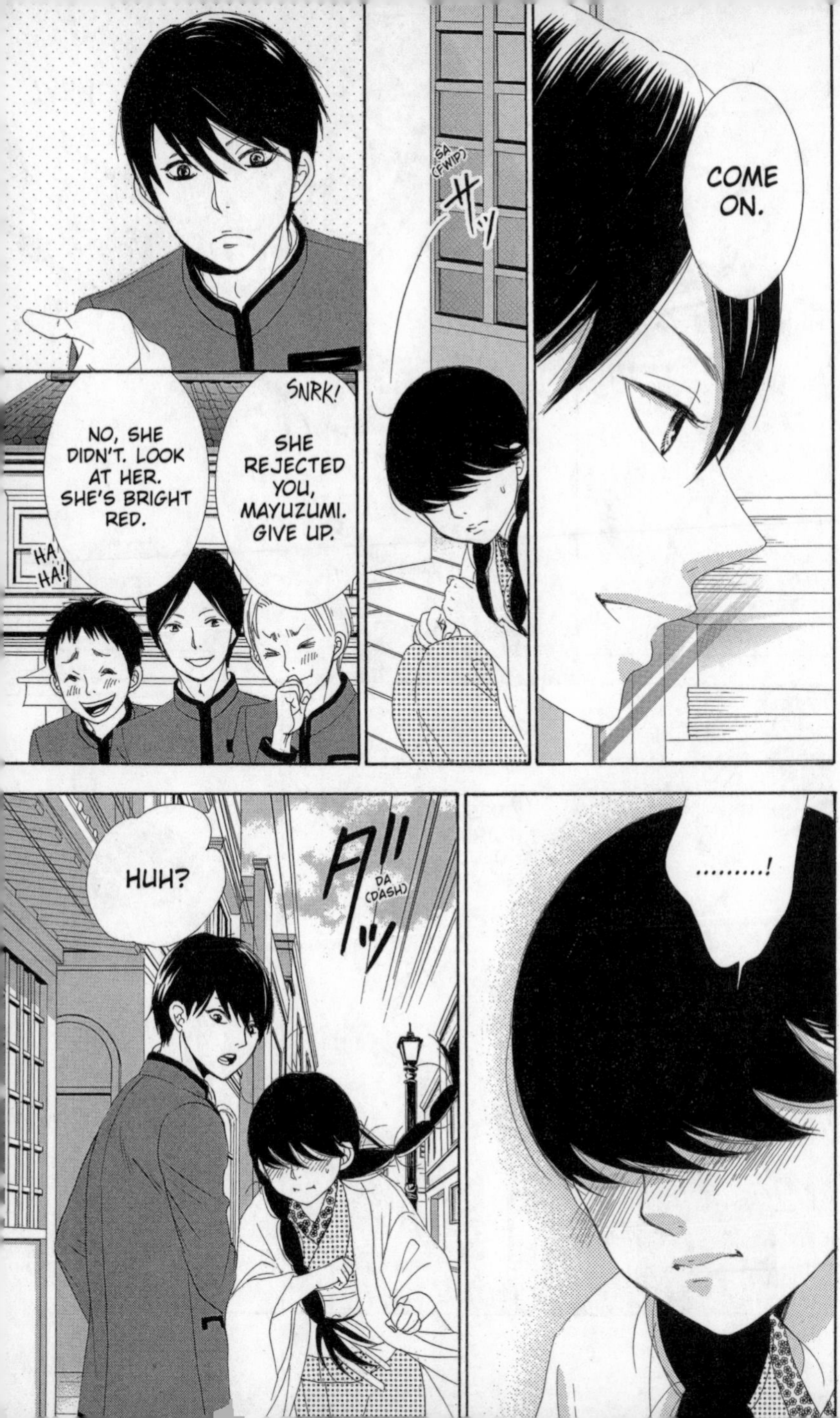
COME ON.
SA (FWIP)
SNRK!
SHE REJECTED YOU, MAYUZUMI. GIVE UP.
NO, SHE DIDN'T. LOOK AT HER. SHE'S BRIGHT RED.
HA HA!
.........!
DA (DASH)
HUH?

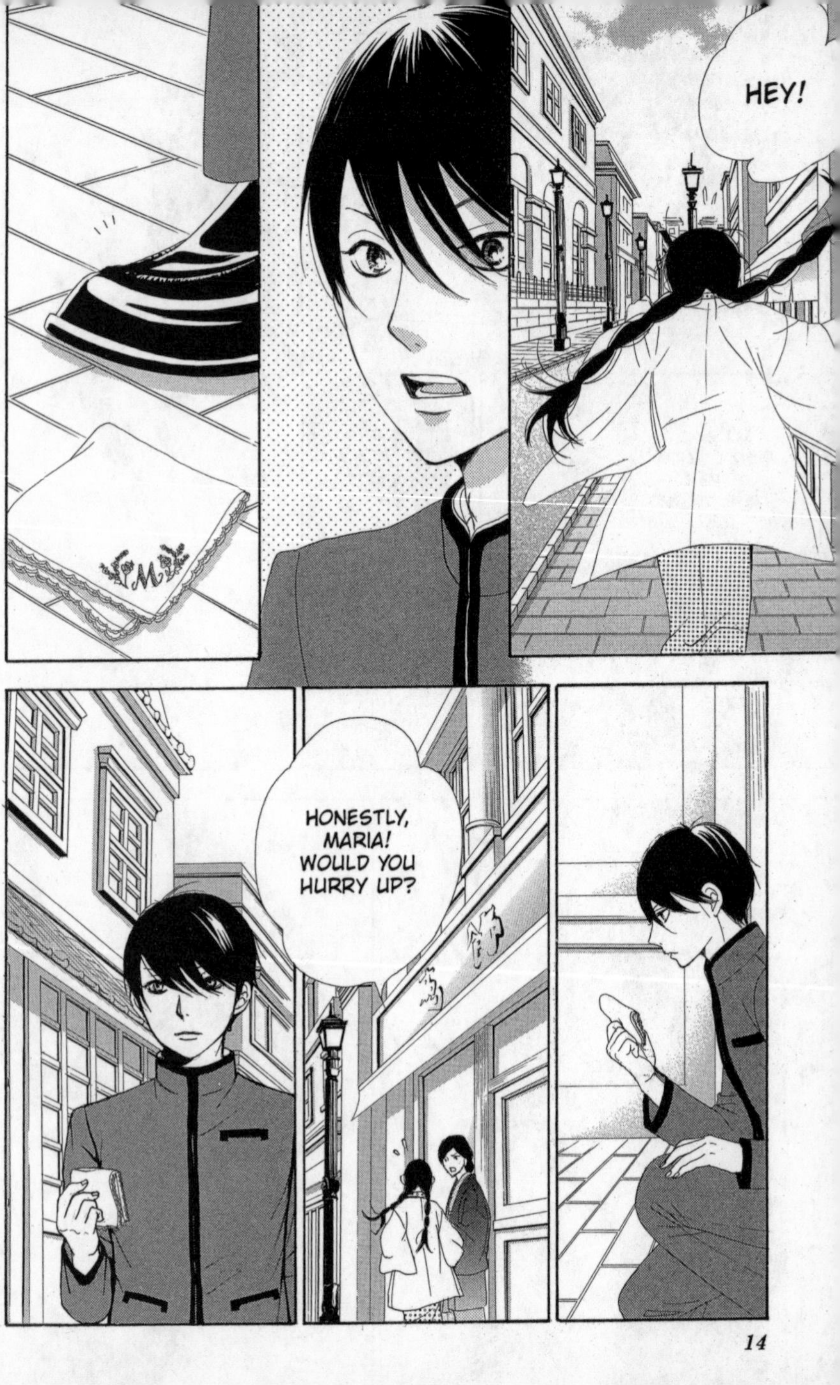
HEY!
HONESTLY, MARIA! WOULD YOU HURRY UP?

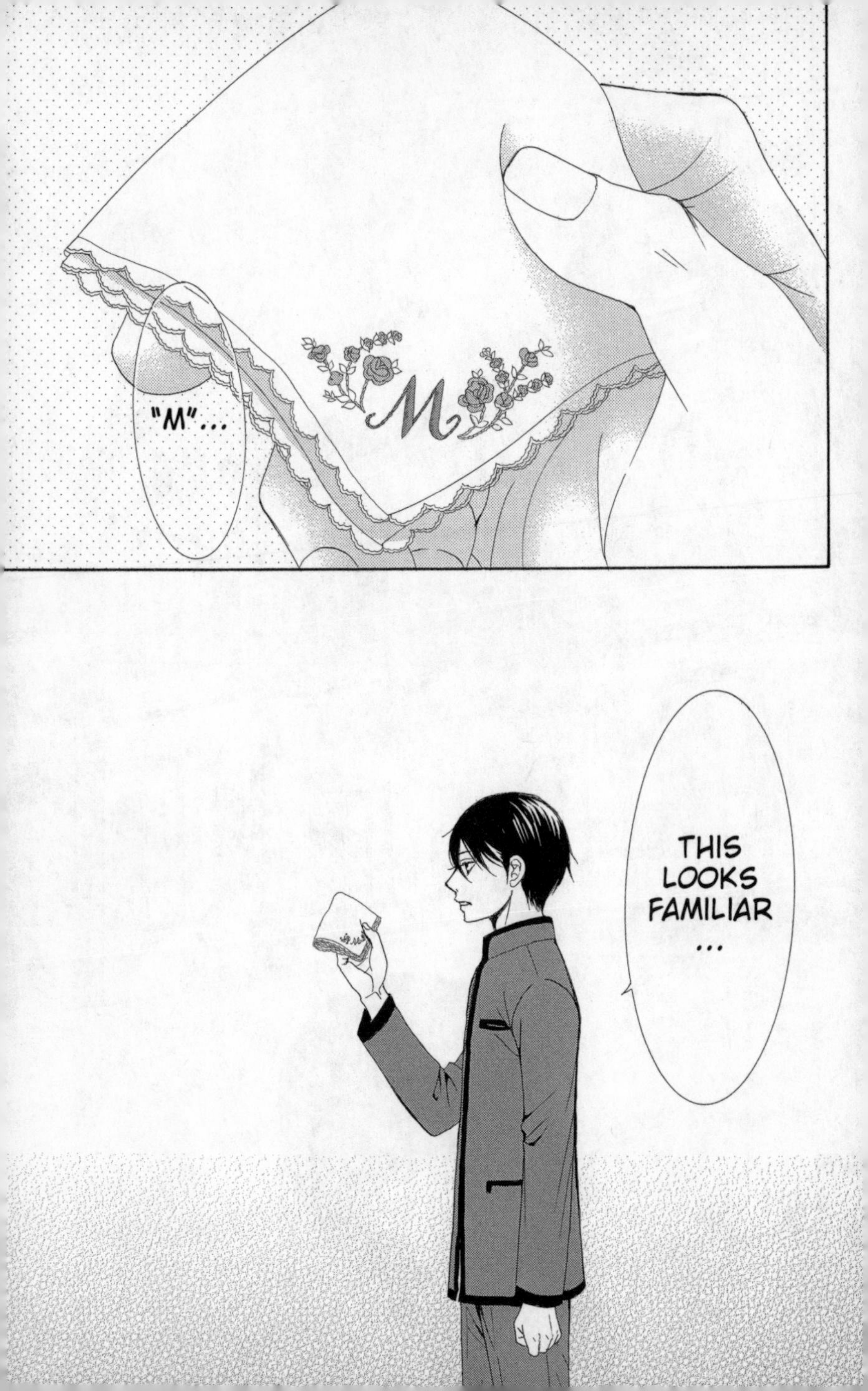
"M"...
THIS LOOKS FAMILIAR ...

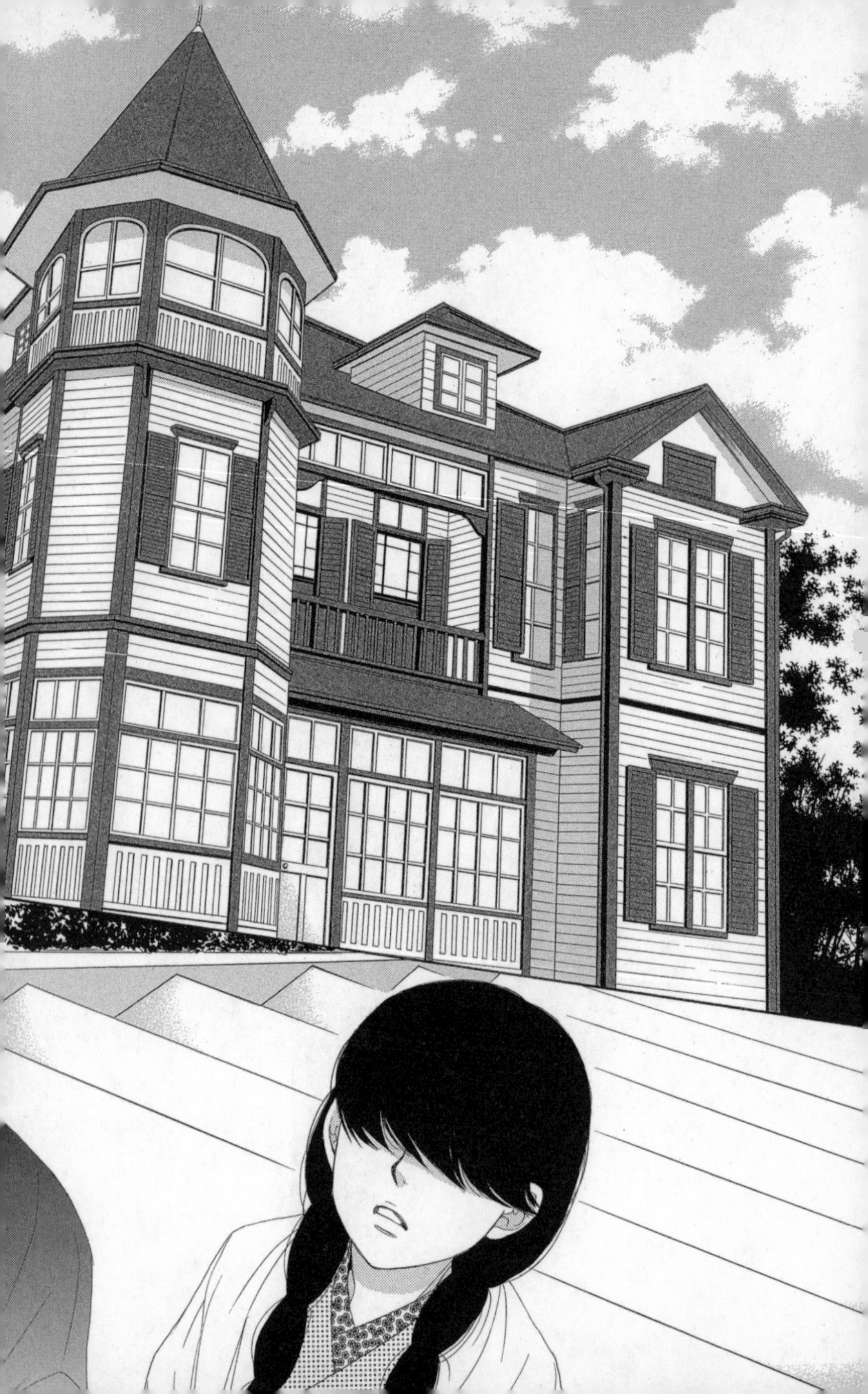

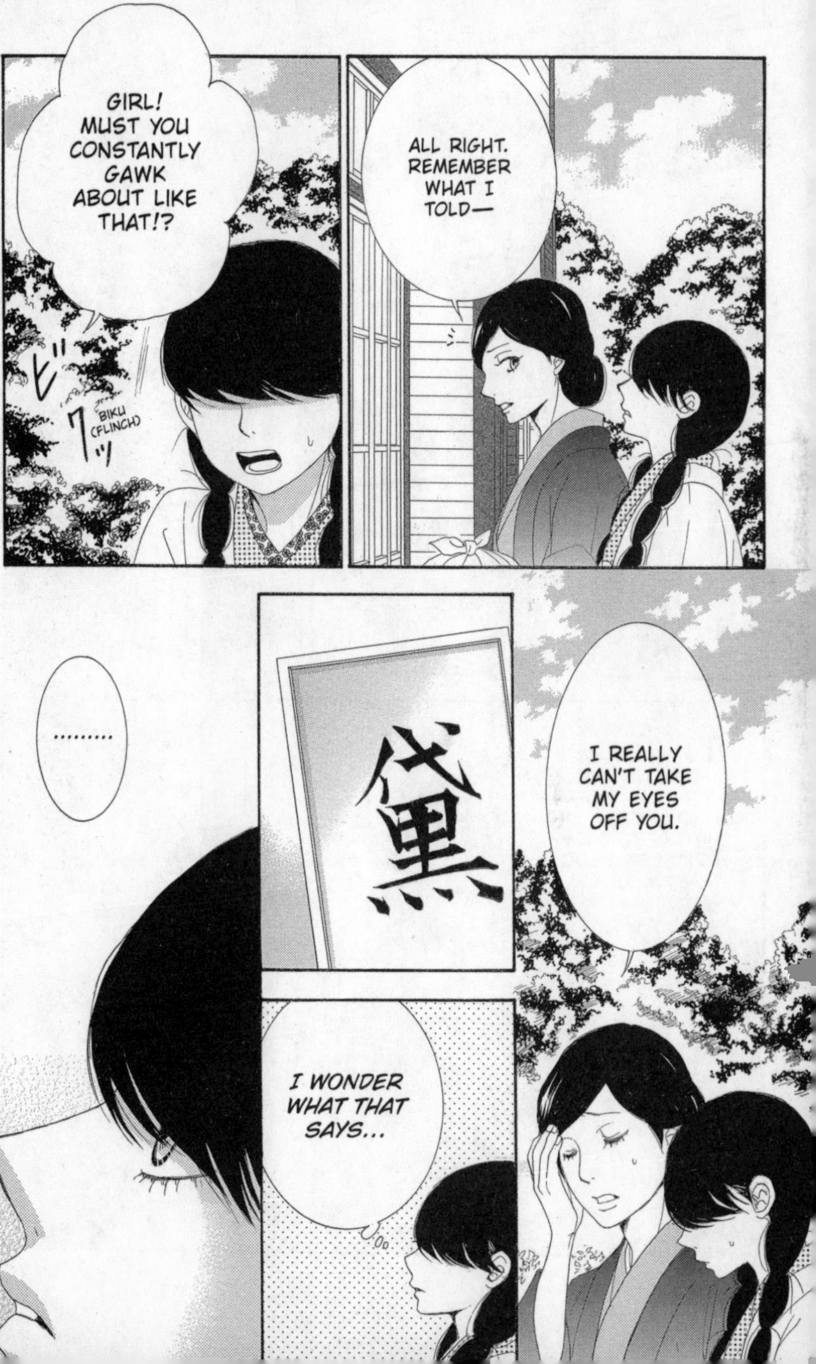
ALL RIGHT. REMEMBER WHAT I TOLD—
GIRL! MUST YOU CONSTANTLY GAWK ABOUT LIKE THAT!?
ビクッ
BIKU (FLINCH)
I REALLY CAN'T TAKE MY EYES OFF YOU.
黛
I WONDER WHAT THAT SAYS...
....

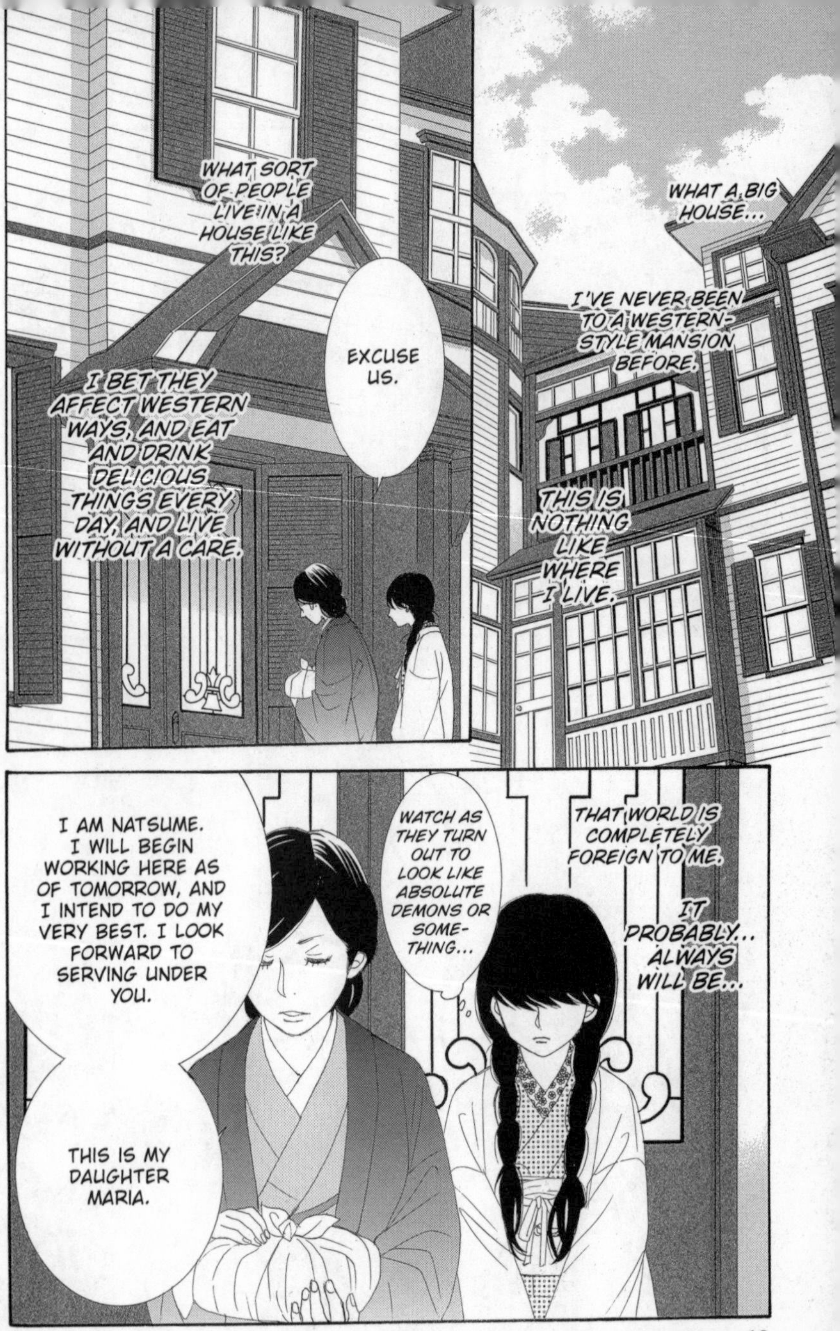
WHAT A BIG HOUSE...
I'VE NEVER BEEN TO A WESTERN-STYLE MANSION BEFORE.
THIS IS NOTHING LIKE WHERE I LIVE.
WHAT SORT OF PEOPLE LIVE IN A HOUSE LIKE THIS?
EXCUSE US.
I BET THEY AFFECT WESTERN WAYS, AND EAT AND DRINK DELICIOUS THINGS EVERY DAY, AND LIVE WITHOUT A CARE.
THAT WORLD IS COMPLETELY FOREIGN TO ME.
IT PROBABLY... ALWAYS WILL BE...
WATCH AS THEY TURN OUT TO LOOK LIKE ABSOLUTE DEMONS OR SOME-THING...
I AM NATSUME. I WILL BEGIN WORKING HERE AS OF TOMORROW, AND I INTEND TO DO MY VERY BEST. I LOOK FORWARD TO SERVING UNDER YOU.
THIS IS MY DAUGHTER MARIA.

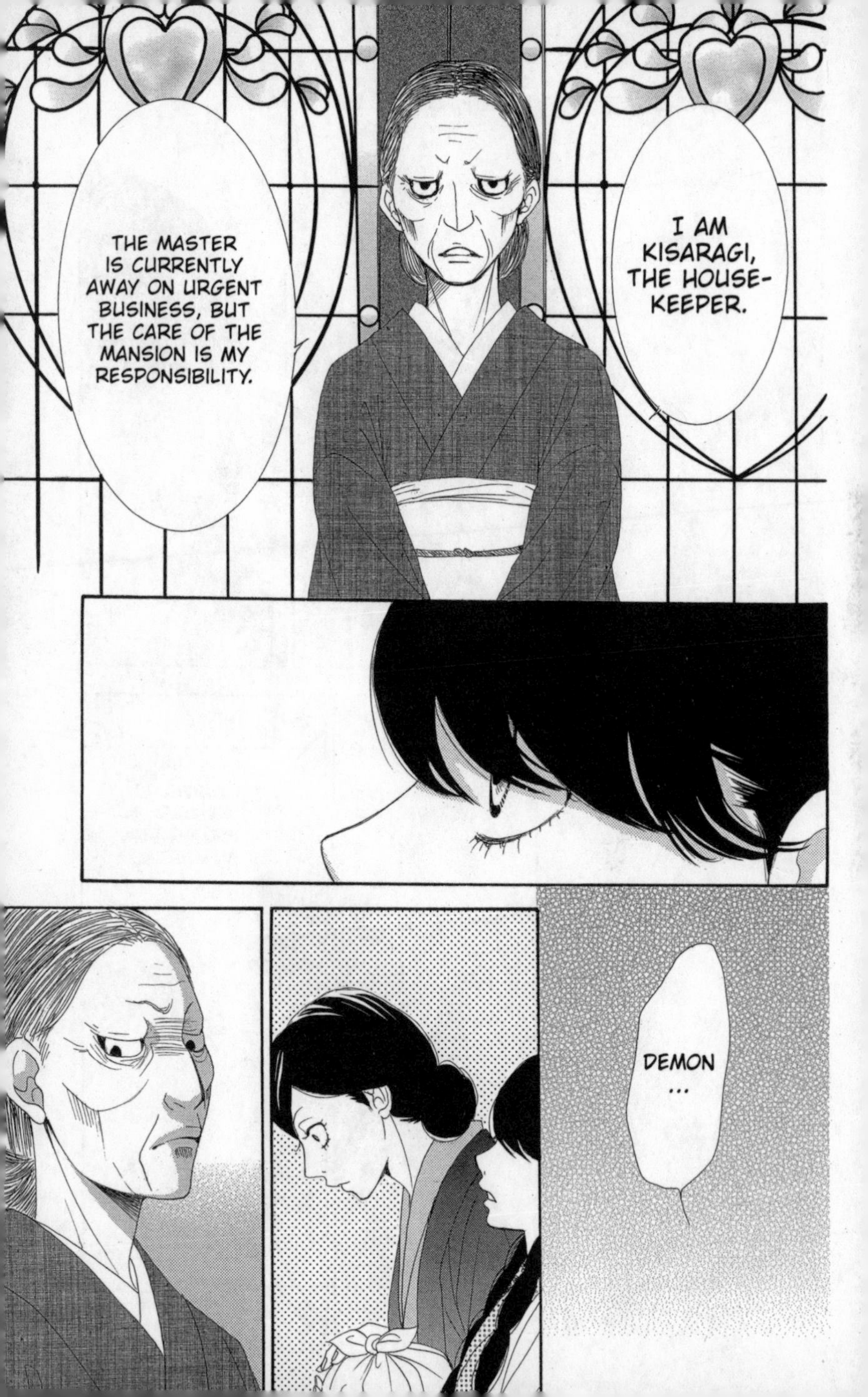
I AM KISARAGI, THE HOUSE-KEEPER.
THE MASTER IS CURRENTLY AWAY ON URGENT BUSINESS, BUT THE CARE OF THE MANSION IS MY RESPONSIBILITY.
DEMON ...

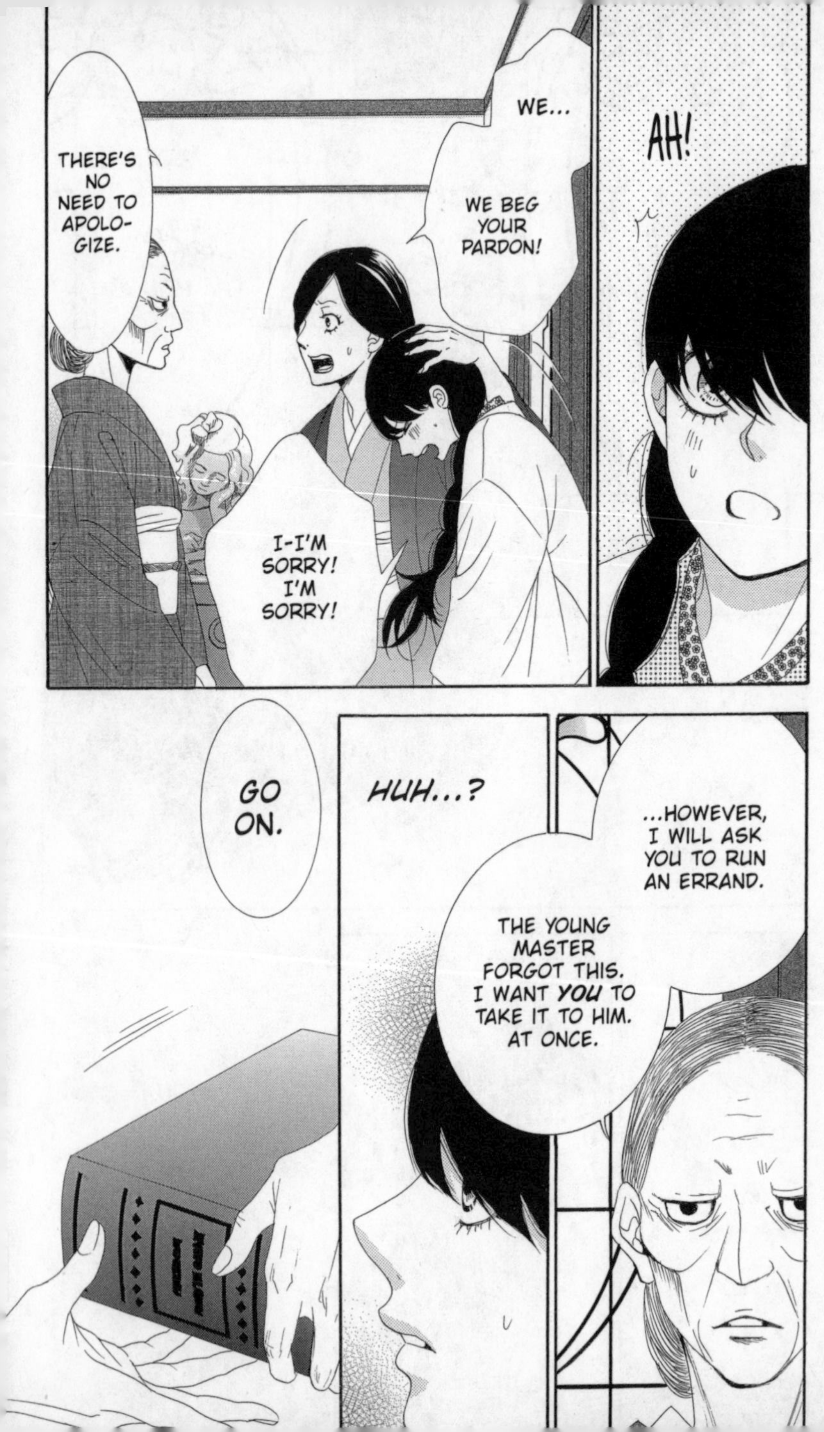
AH!
WE...
WE BEG YOUR PARDON!
THERE'S NO NEED TO APOLOGIZE.
I-I'M SORRY! I'M SORRY!
...HOWEVER, I WILL ASK YOU TO RUN AN ERRAND.
THE YOUNG MASTER FORGOT THIS. I WANT YOU TO TAKE IT TO HIM. AT ONCE.
HUH...?
GO ON.

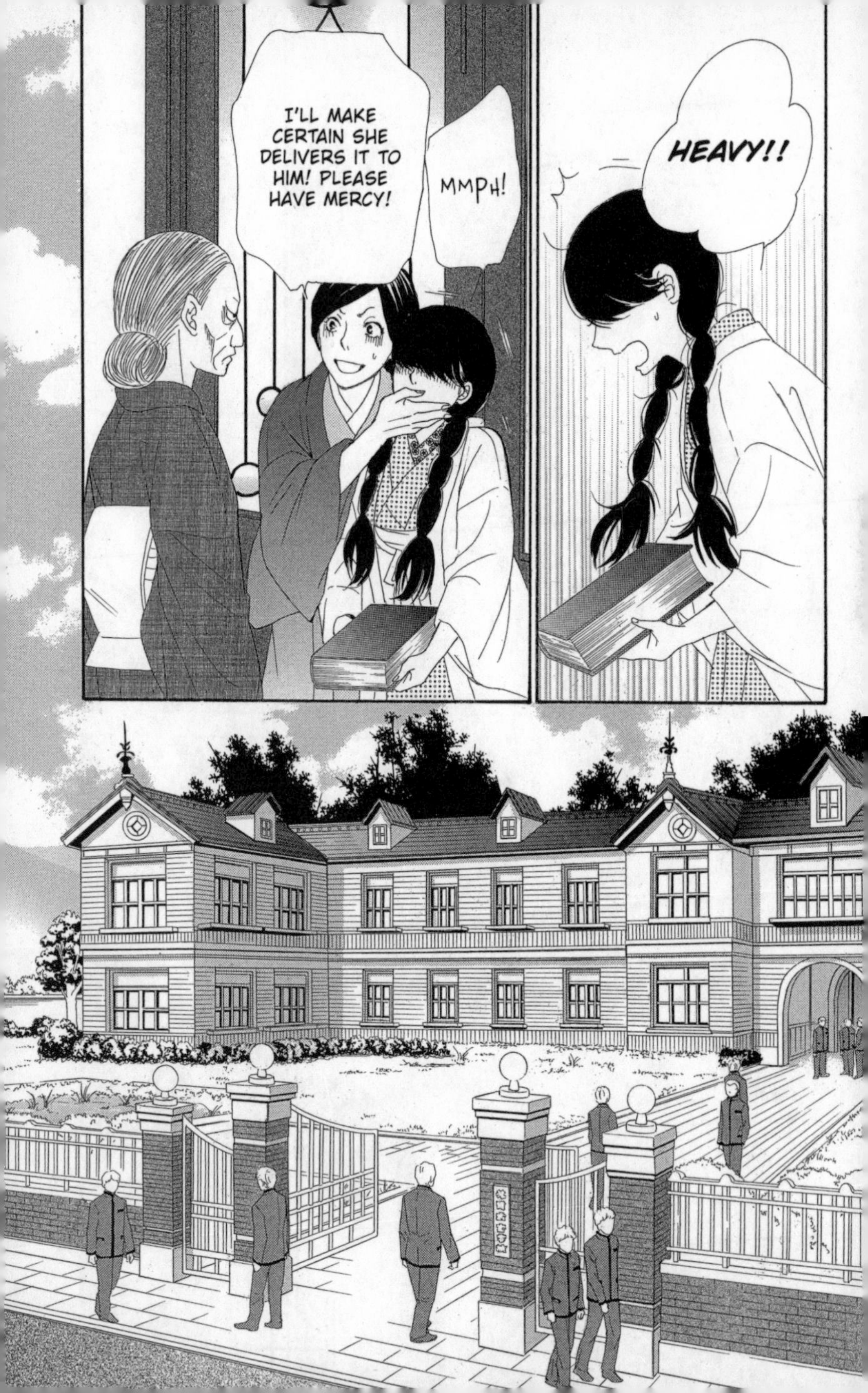
HEAVY!!
I'LL MAKE CERTAIN SHE DELIVERS IT TO HIM! PLEASE HAVE MERCY!
MMPH!

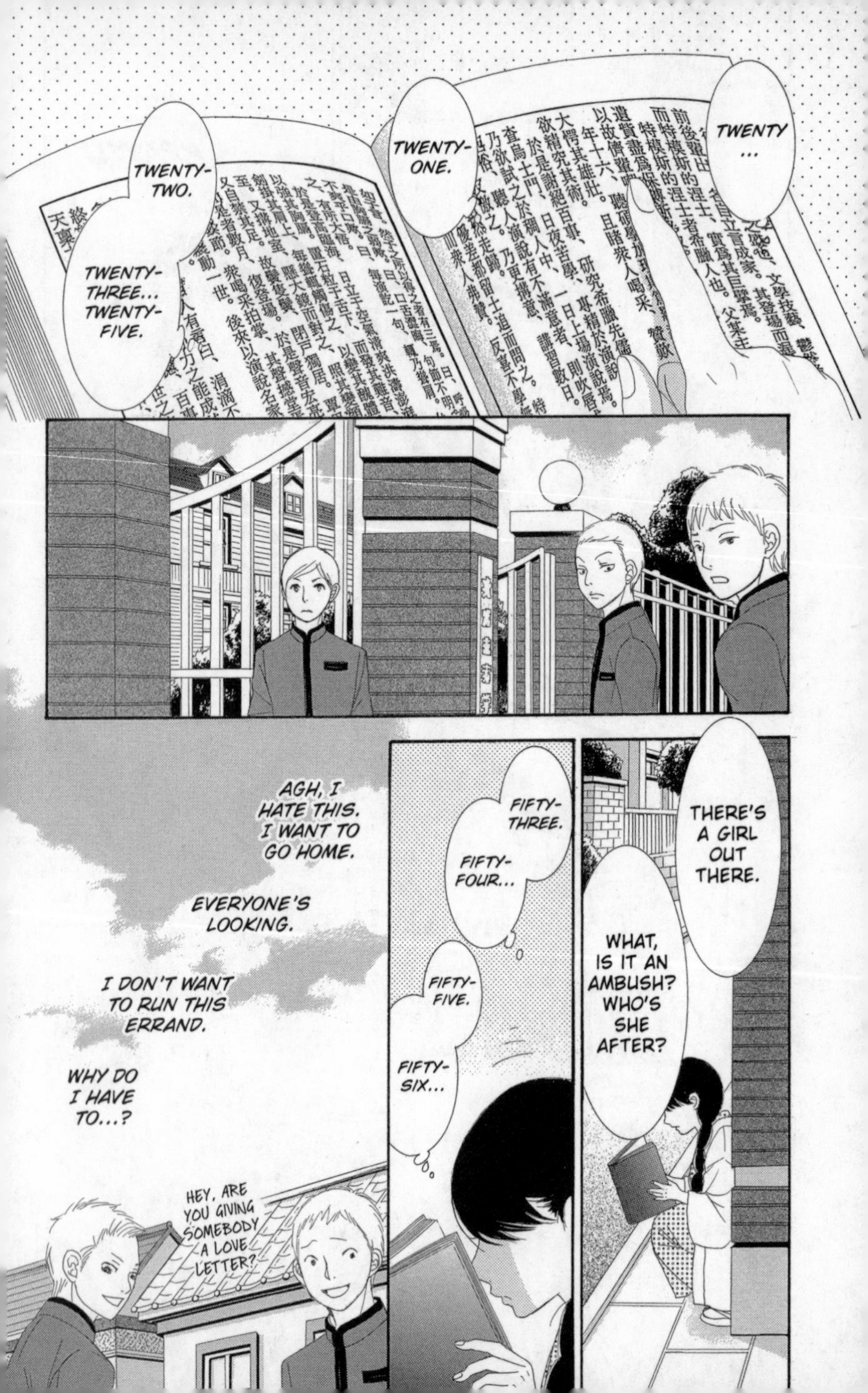
TWENTY...
TWENTY-ONE.
TWENTY-TWO.
TWENTY-THREE... TWENTY-FIVE.
THERE'S A GIRL OUT THERE.
WHAT, IS IT AN AMBUSH? WHO'S SHE AFTER?
FIFTY-THREE.
FIFTY-FOUR...
FIFTY-FIVE.
FIFTY-SIX...
AGH, I HATE THIS. I WANT TO GO HOME.
EVERYONE'S LOOKING.
I DON'T WANT TO RUN THIS ERRAND.
WHY DO I HAVE TO...?
HEY, ARE YOU GIVING SOMEBODY A LOVE LETTER?

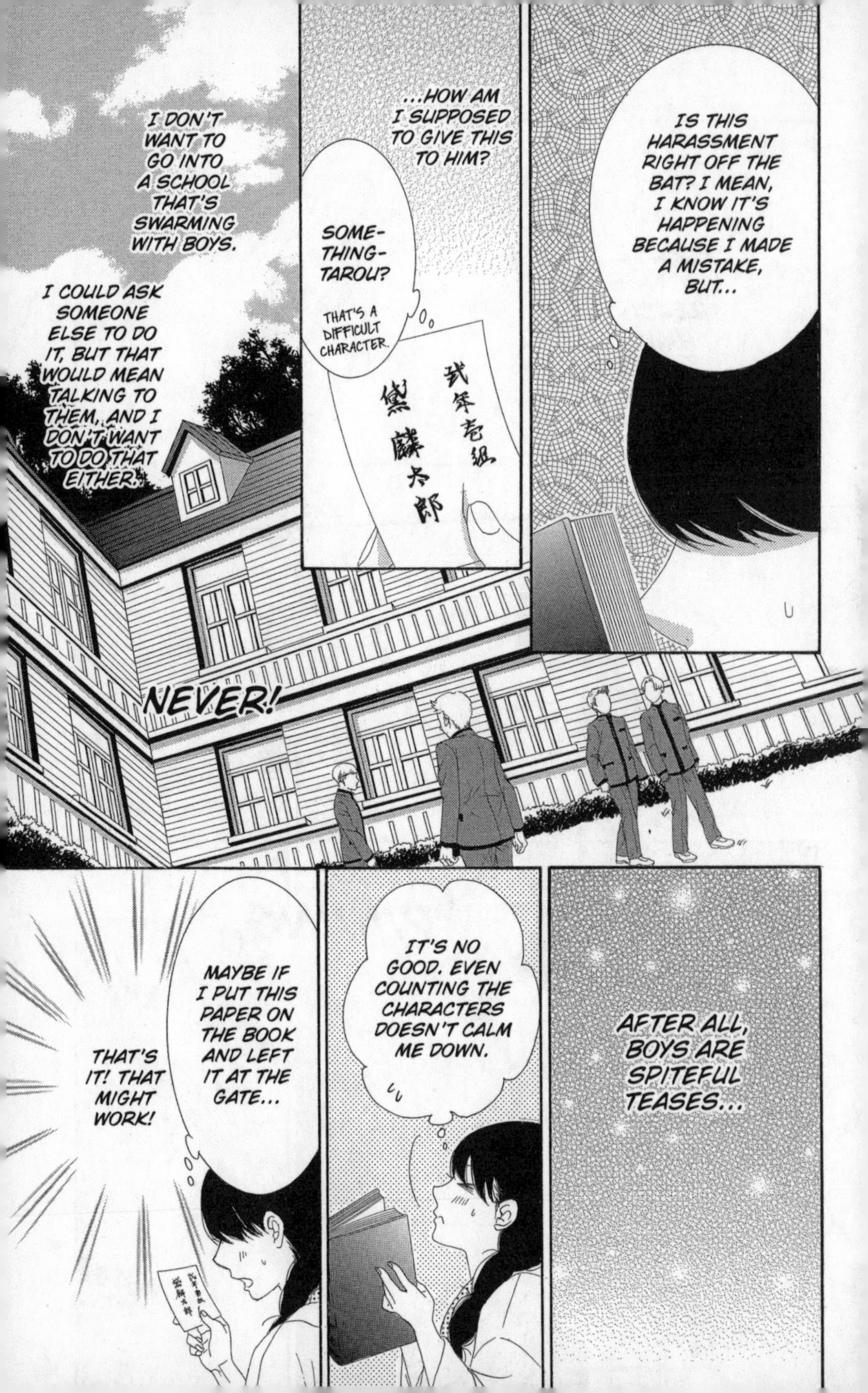
IS THIS HARASSMENT RIGHT OFF THE BAT? I MEAN, I KNOW IT'S HAPPENING BECAUSE I MADE A MISTAKE, BUT...
...HOW AM I SUPPOSED TO GIVE THIS TO HIM?
SOME-THING-TAROU?
THAT'S A DIFFICULT CHARACTER.
I DON'T WANT TO GO INTO A SCHOOL THAT'S SWARMING WITH BOYS.
I COULD ASK SOMEONE ELSE TO DO IT, BUT THAT WOULD MEAN TALKING TO THEM, AND I DON'T WANT TO DO THAT EITHER.
NEVER!
AFTER ALL, BOYS ARE SPITEFUL TEASES...
IT'S NO GOOD. EVEN COUNTING THE CHARACTERS DOESN'T CALM ME DOWN.
MAYBE IF I PUT THIS PAPER ON THE BOOK AND LEFT IT AT THE GATE...
THAT'S IT! THAT MIGHT WORK!

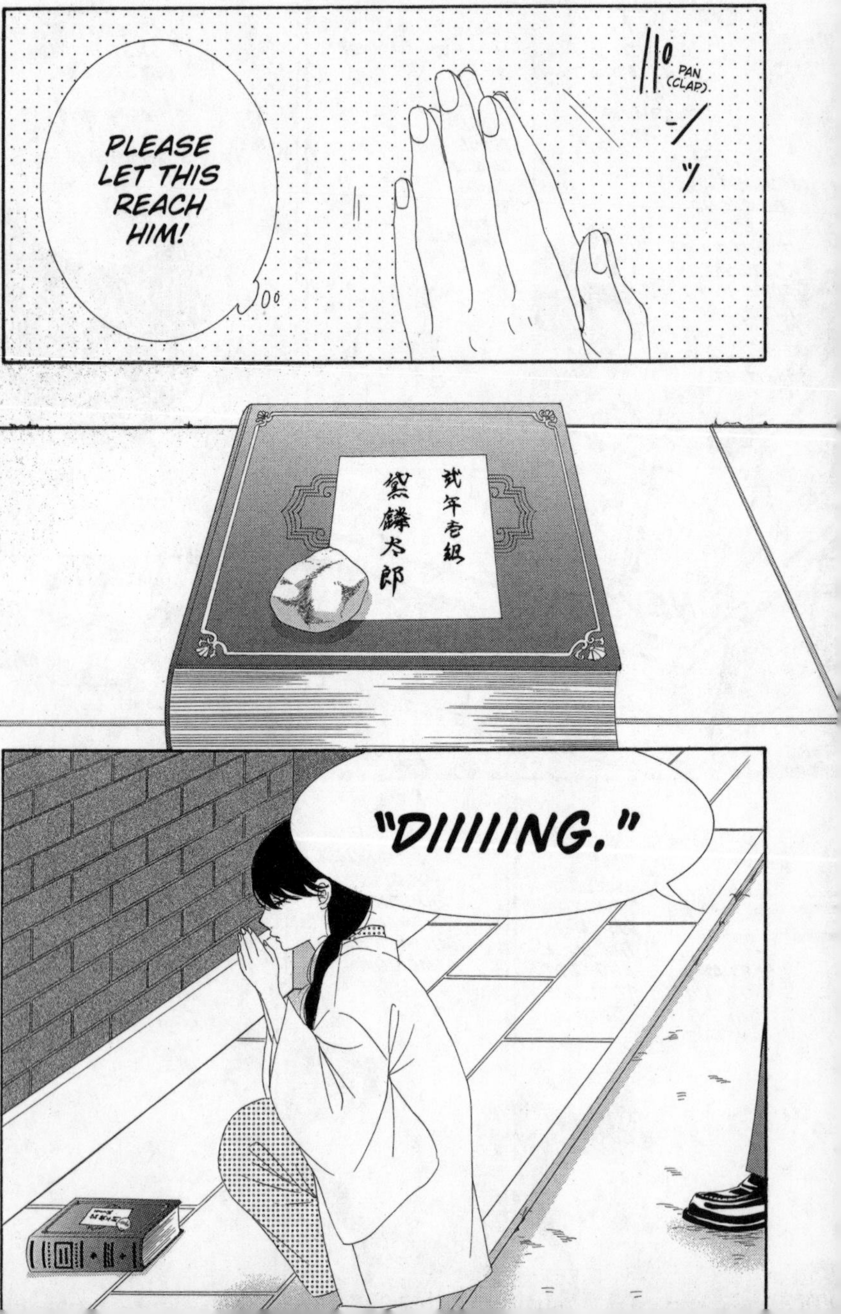
PAN (CLAP)
PLEASE LET THIS REACH HIM!
弐年壱組
黛麟太郎
"DIIIIING."

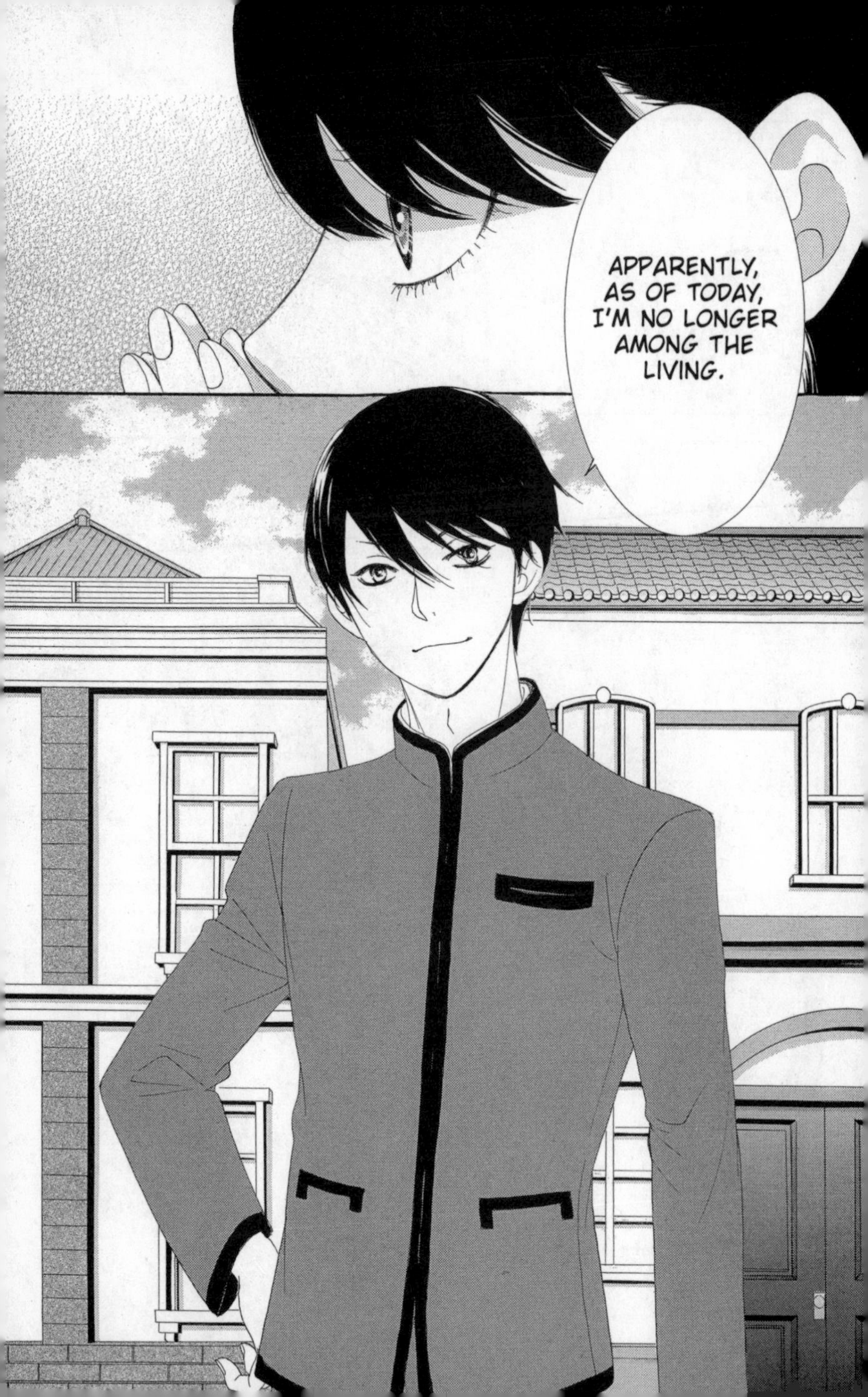
APPARENTLY, AS OF TODAY, I'M NO LONGER AMONG THE LIVING.

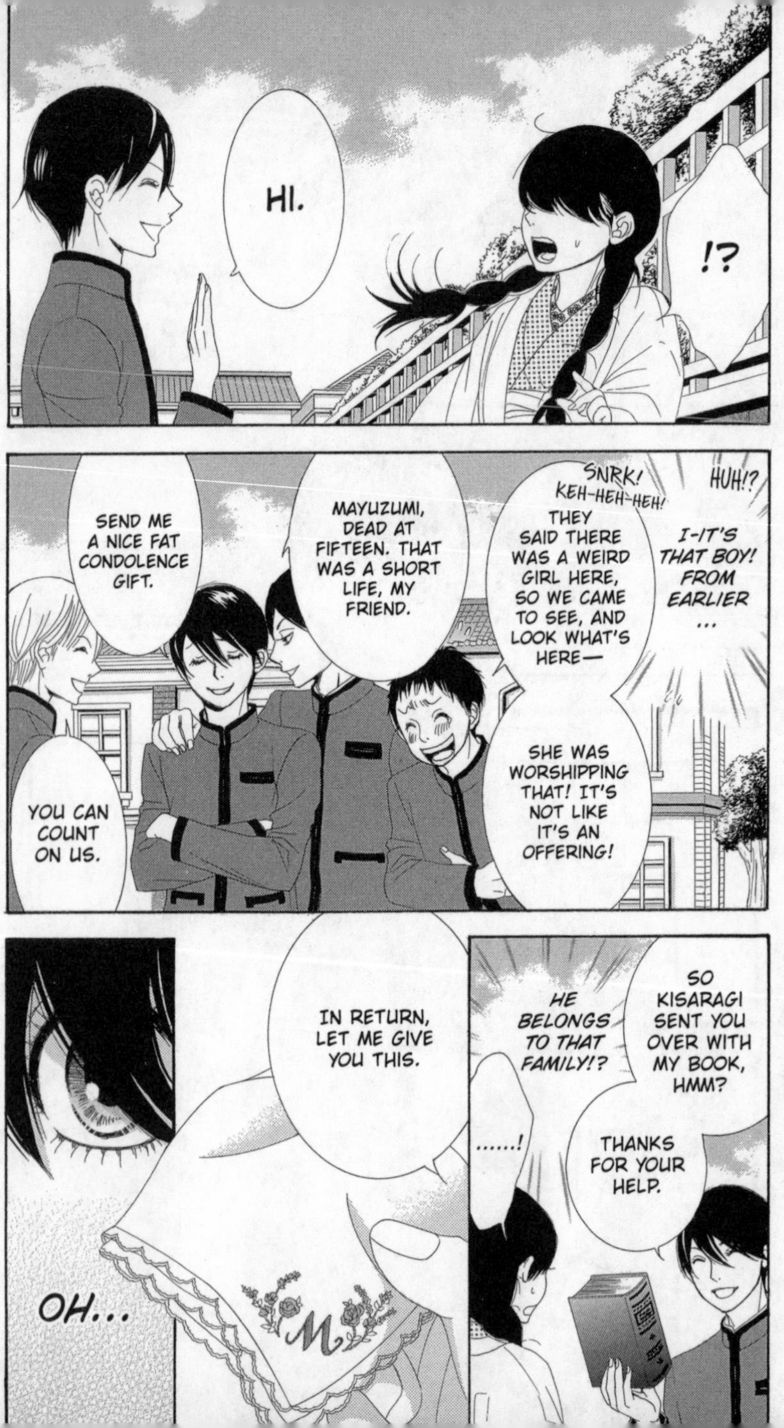
!?
HI.
HUH!?
I-IT'S THAT BOY! FROM EARLIER ...
SNRK! KEH-HEH-HEH!
THEY SAID THERE WAS A WEIRD GIRL HERE, SO WE CAME TO SEE, AND LOOK WHAT'S HERE—
SHE WAS WORSHIPPING THAT! IT'S NOT LIKE IT'S AN OFFERING!
MAYUZUMI, DEAD AT FIFTEEN. THAT WAS A SHORT LIFE, MY FRIEND.
SEND ME A NICE FAT CONDOLENCE GIFT.
YOU CAN COUNT ON US.
SO KISARAGI SENT YOU OVER WITH MY BOOK, HMM?
HE BELONGS TO THAT FAMILY!?
THANKS FOR YOUR HELP.
......!
IN RETURN, LET ME GIVE YOU THIS.
OH...

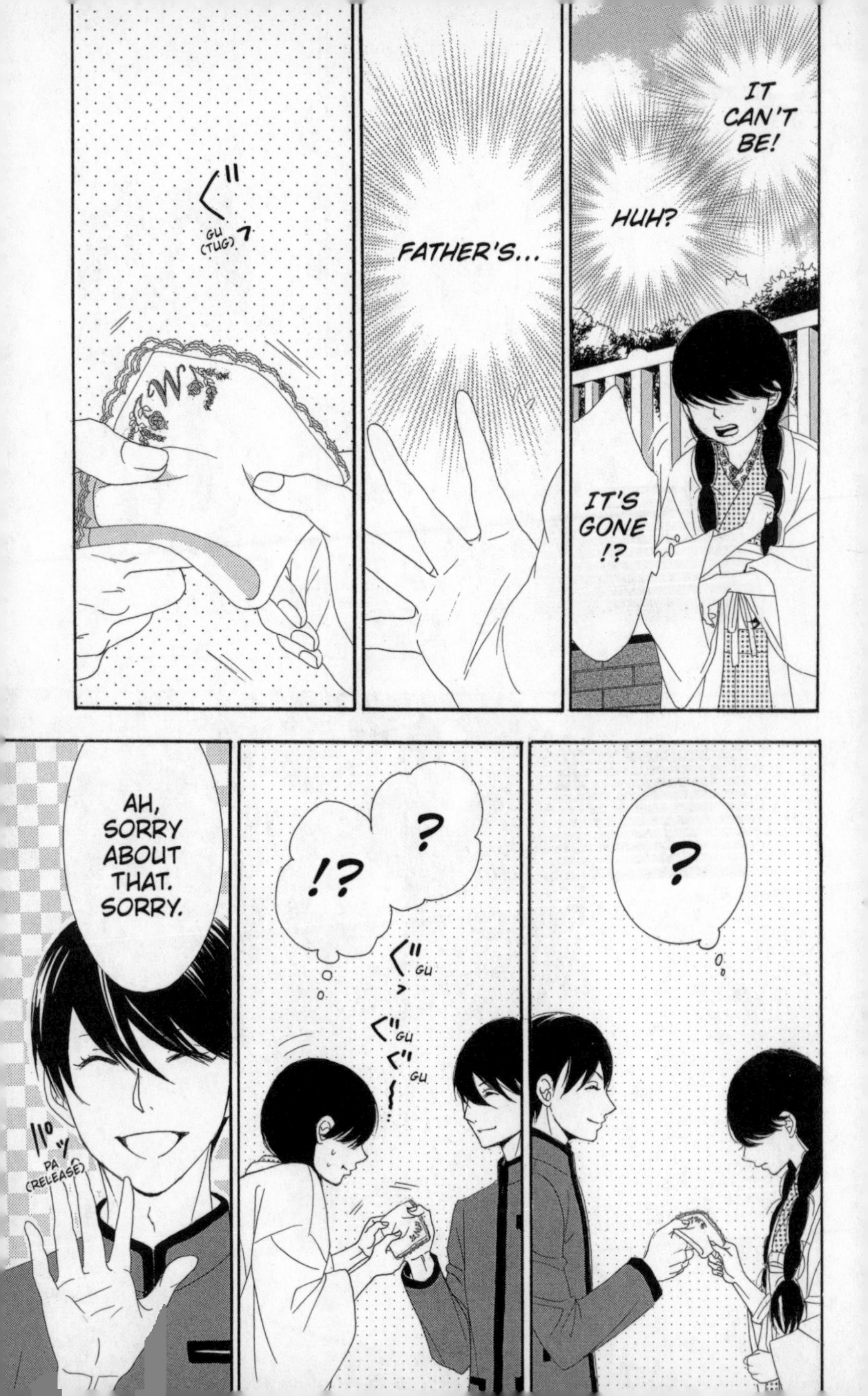
IT CAN'T BE!
HUH?
IT'S GONE!?
FATHER'S...
GU (TUG)
?
?
!?
GU
GU
GU
AH, SORRY ABOUT THAT. SORRY.
PA (RELEASE)

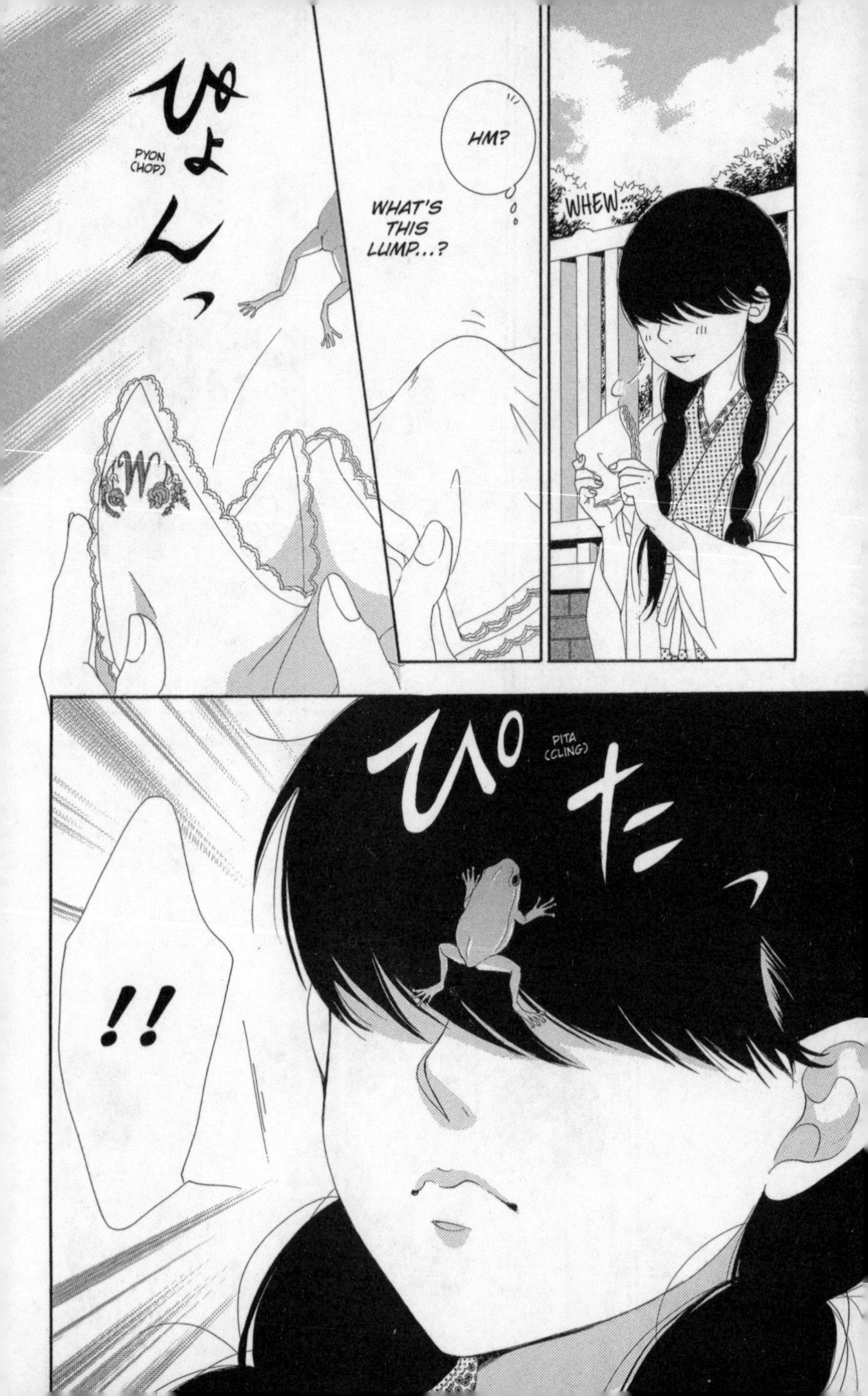
WHEW...
HM?
WHAT'S THIS LUMP...?
ぴょんっ
PYON (HOP)
ぴたっ
PITA (CLING)
!!

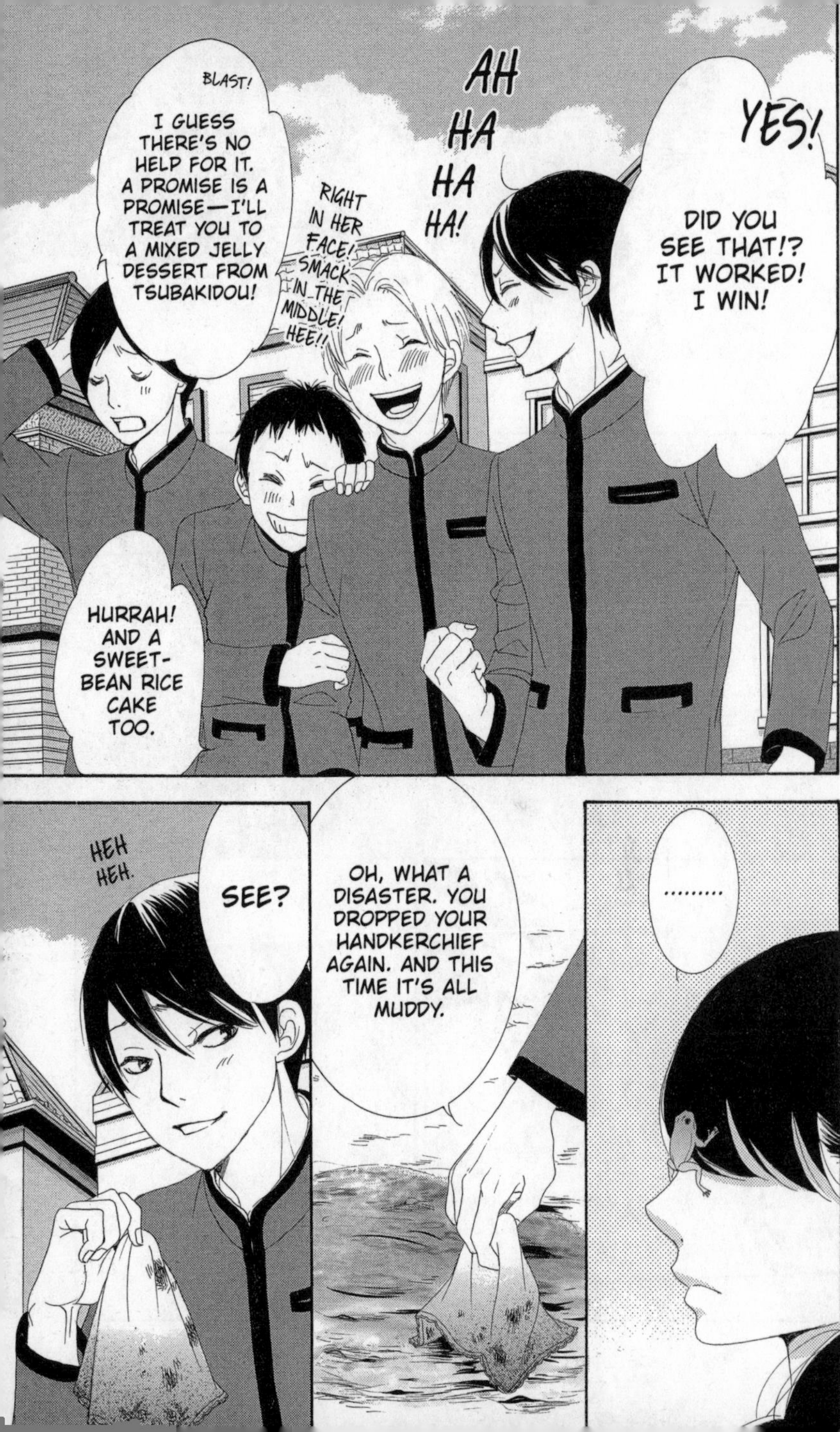
YES!
DID YOU SEE THAT!? IT WORKED! I WIN!
AH HA HA HA!
RIGHT IN HER FACE! SMACK IN THE MIDDLE! HEE!!
BLAST!
I GUESS THERE'S NO HELP FOR IT. A PROMISE IS A PROMISE—I'LL TREAT YOU TO A MIXED JELLY DESSERT FROM TSUBAKIDOU!
HURRAH! AND A SWEET-BEAN RICE CAKE TOO.
....
OH, WHAT A DISASTER. YOU DROPPED YOUR HANDKERCHIEF AGAIN. AND THIS TIME IT'S ALL MUDDY.
SEE?
HEH HEH.

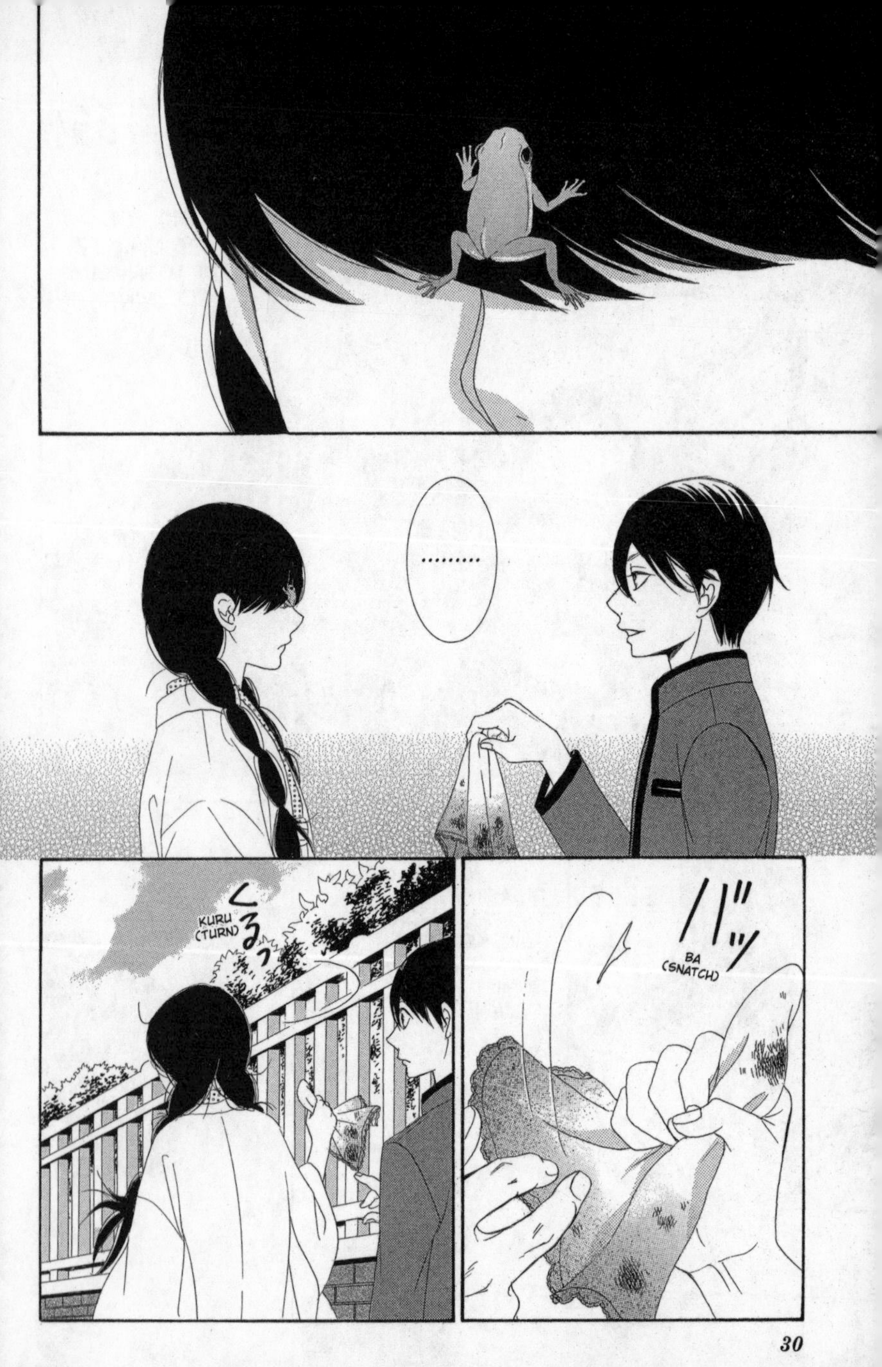
....
バッ
BA (SNATCH)
くるっ
KURU (TURN)

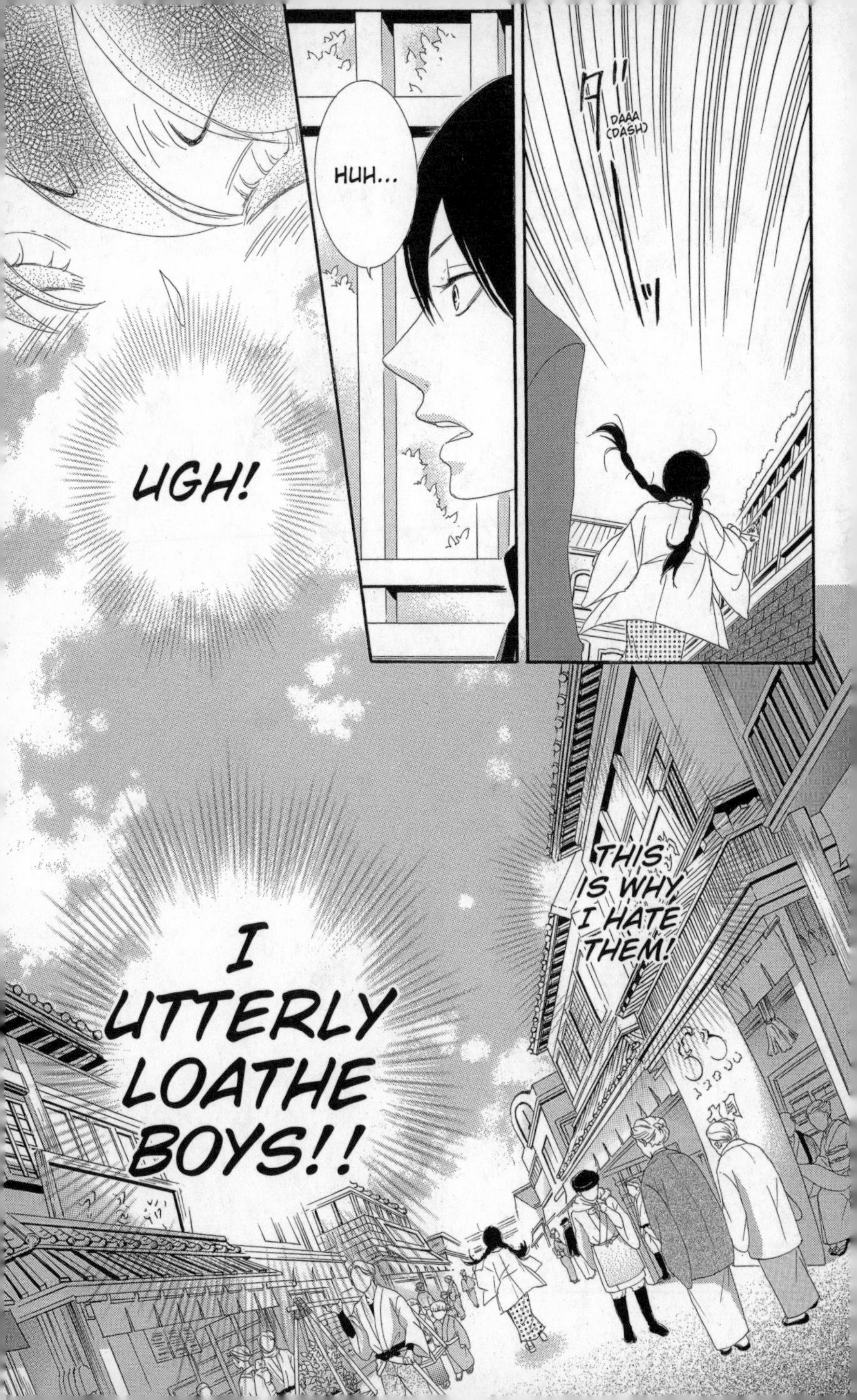
DAAA (DASH)
HUH...
UGH!
THIS IS WHY I HATE THEM!
I UTTERLY LOATHE BOYS!!

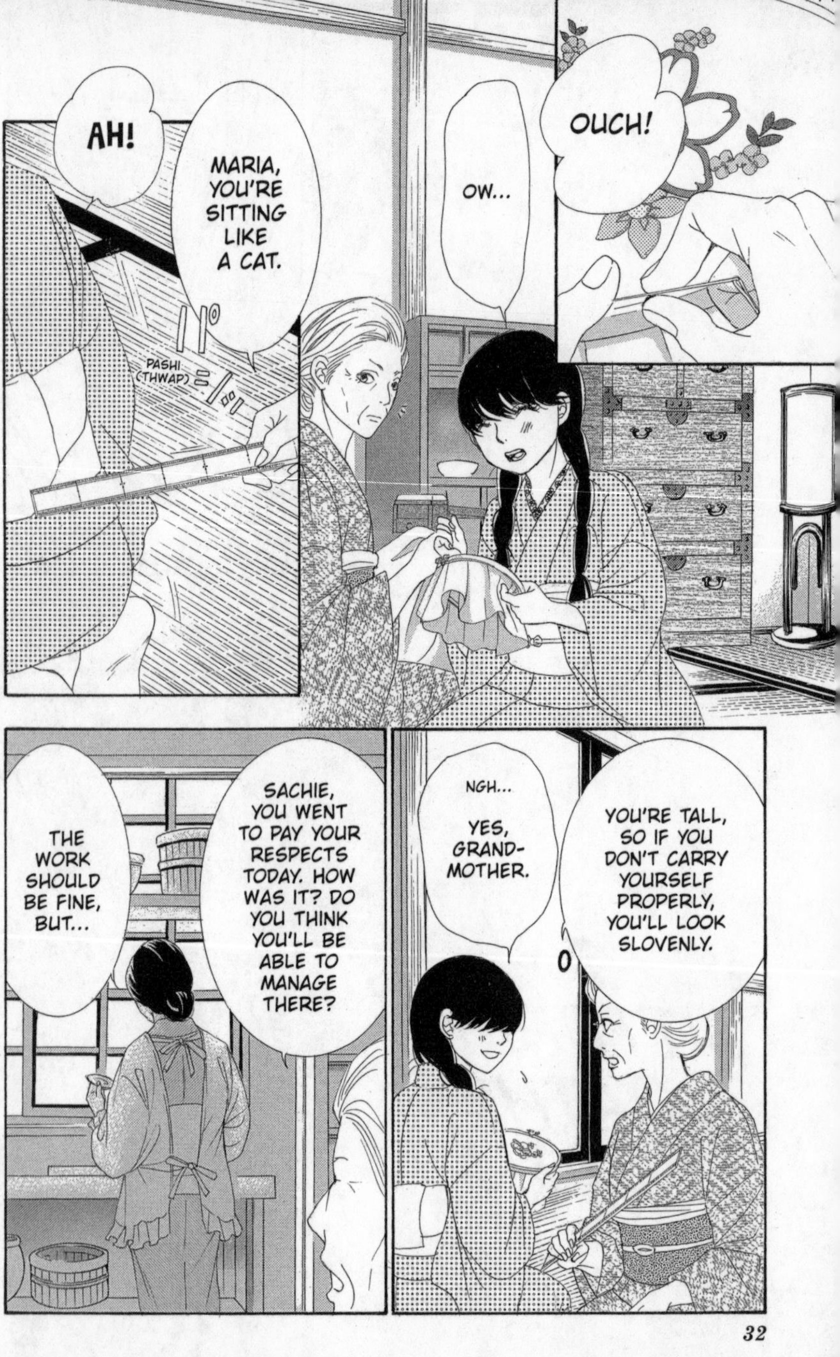
OUCH!
OW...
AH!
MARIA, YOU'RE SITTING LIKE A CAT.
PASHI (THWAP)
YOU'RE TALL, SO IF YOU DON'T CARRY YOURSELF PROPERLY, YOU'LL LOOK SLOVENLY.
NGH...
YES, GRANDMOTHER.
SACHIE, YOU WENT TO PAY YOUR RESPECTS TODAY. HOW WAS IT? DO YOU THINK YOU'LL BE ABLE TO MANAGE THERE?
THE WORK SHOULD BE FINE, BUT...

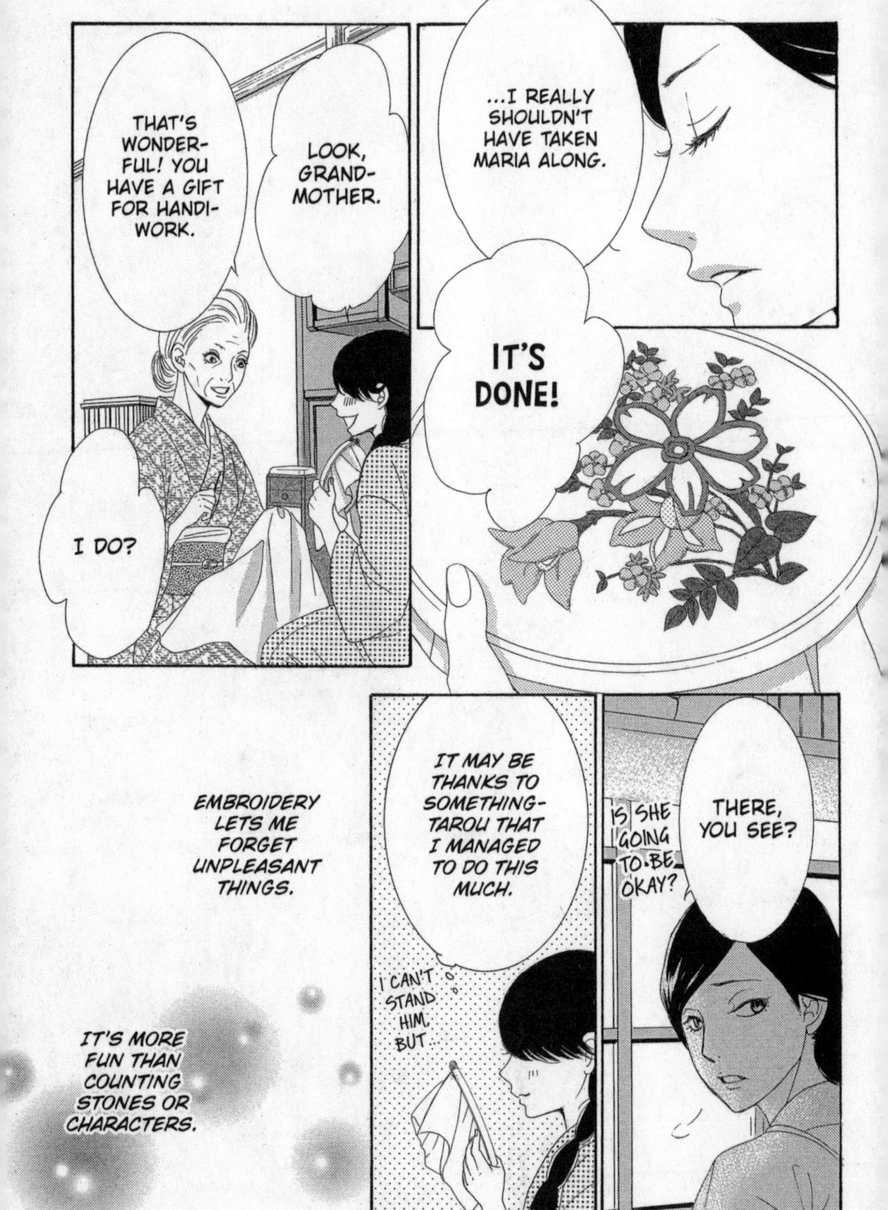
...I REALLY SHOULDN'T HAVE TAKEN MARIA ALONG.
IT'S DONE!
LOOK, GRANDMOTHER.
THAT'S WONDERFUL! YOU HAVE A GIFT FOR HANDIWORK.
I DO?
THERE, YOU SEE?
IS SHE GOING TO BE OKAY?
IT MAY BE THANKS TO SOMETHING-TAROU THAT I MANAGED TO DO THIS MUCH.
I CAN'T STAND HIM, BUT...
EMBROIDERY LETS ME FORGET UNPLEASANT THINGS.
IT'S MORE FUN THAN COUNTING STONES OR CHARACTERS.

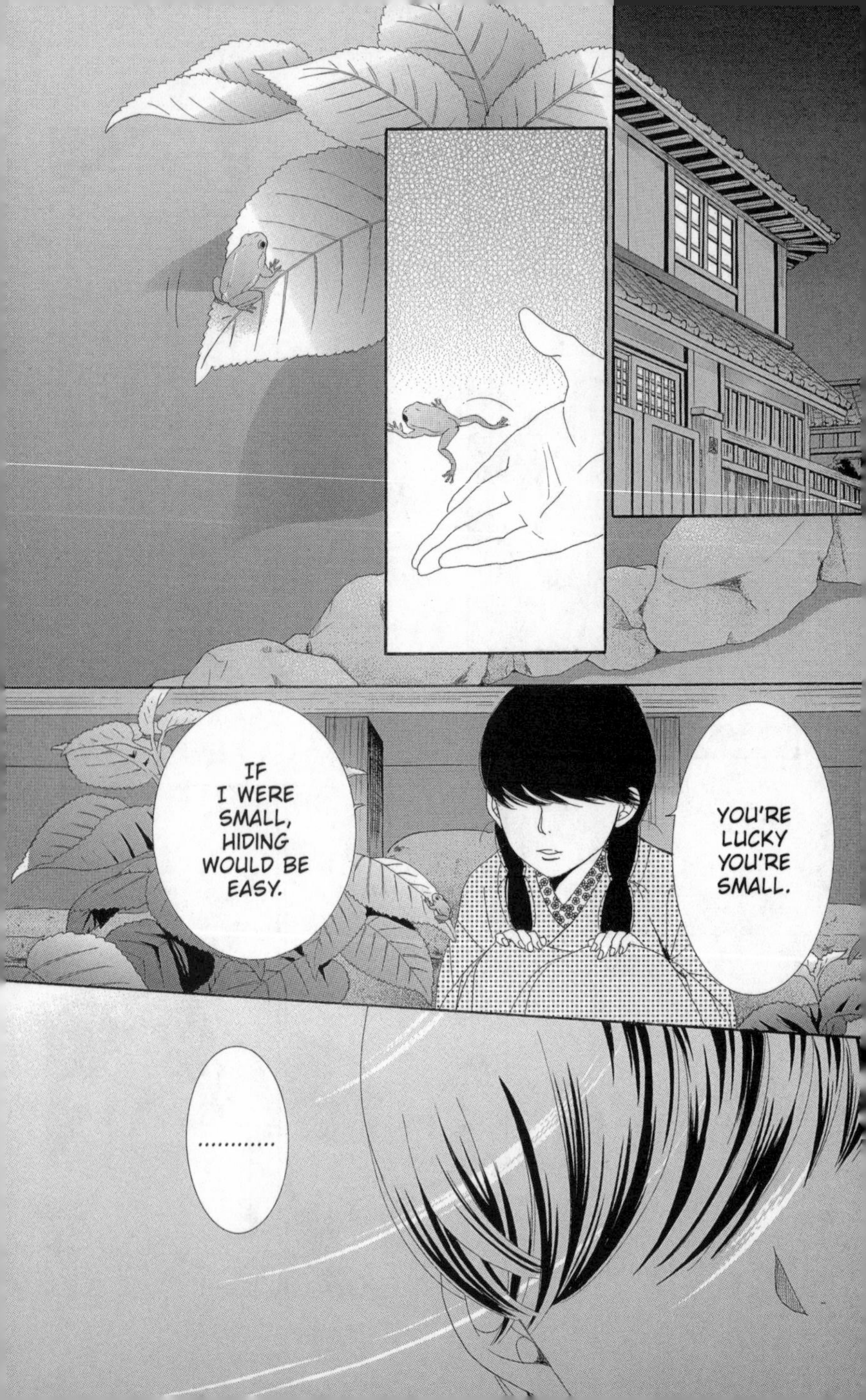
YOU'RE LUCKY YOU'RE SMALL.
IF I WERE SMALL, HIDING WOULD BE EASY.
....

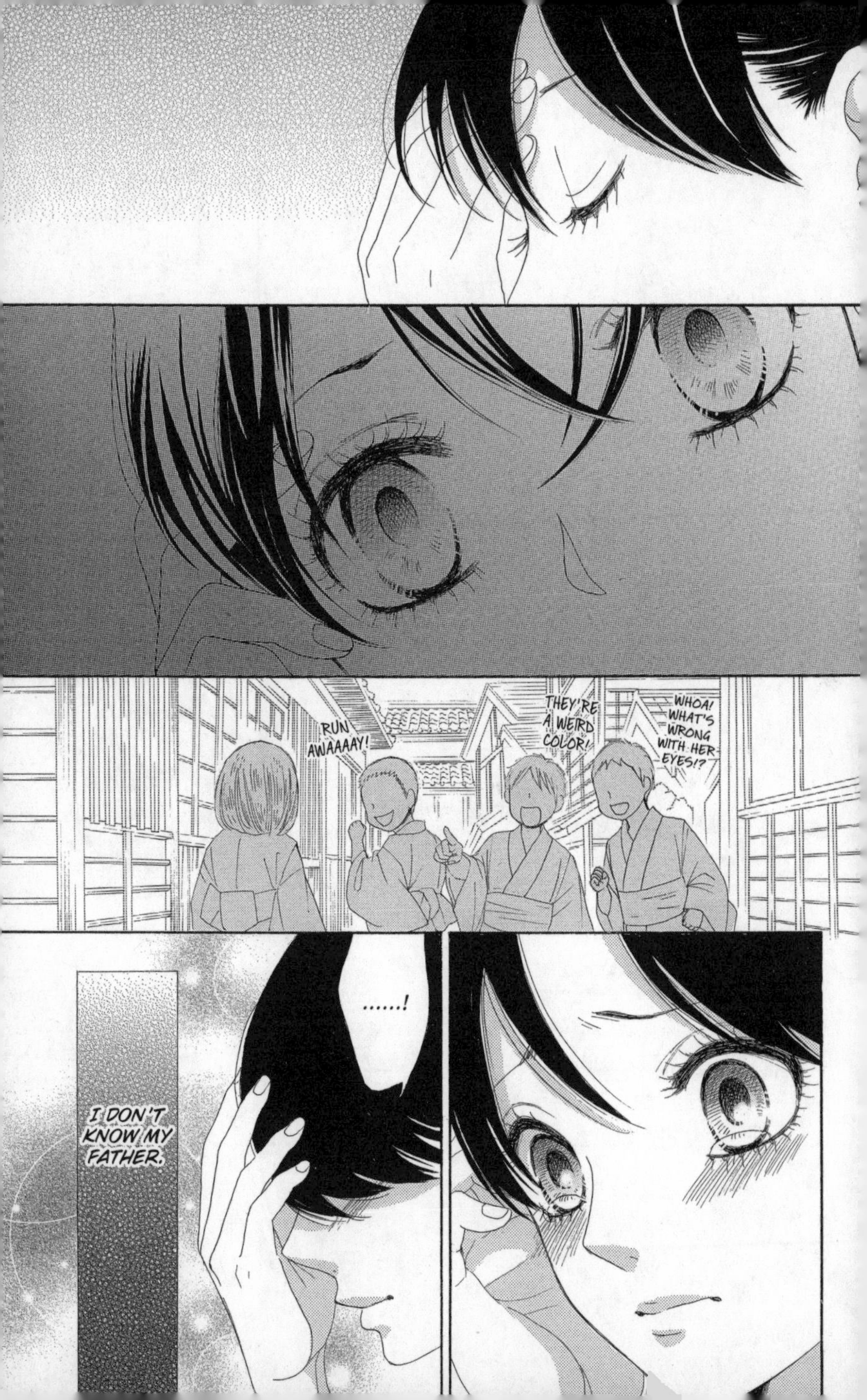
WHOA! WHAT'S WRONG WITH HER EYES!?
THEY'RE A WEIRD COLOR!
RUN AWAAAAY!
......!
I DON'T KNOW MY FATHER.

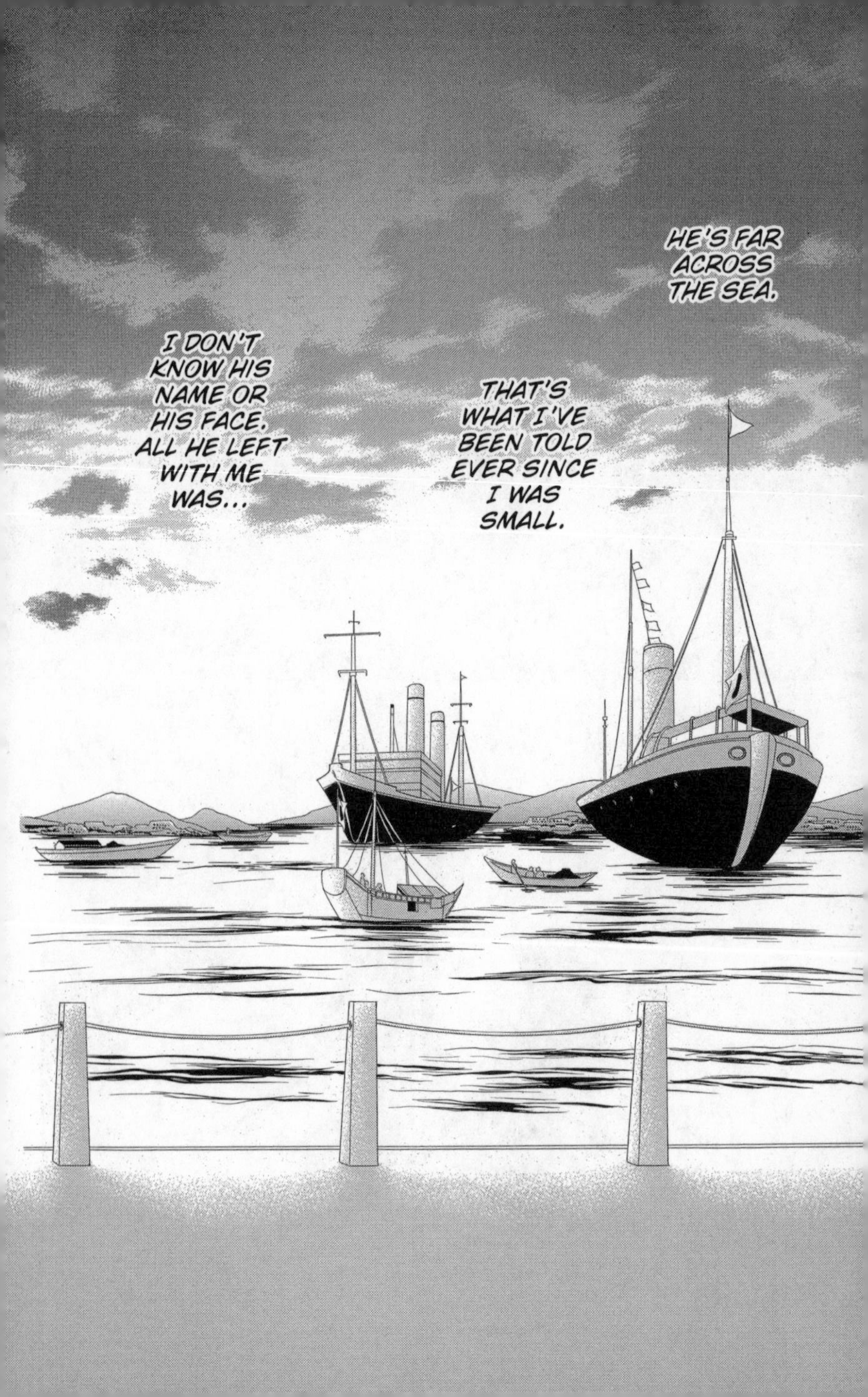
HE'S FAR ACROSS THE SEA.
THAT'S WHAT I'VE BEEN TOLD EVER SINCE I WAS SMALL.
I DON'T KNOW HIS NAME OR HIS FACE. ALL HE LEFT WITH ME WAS...

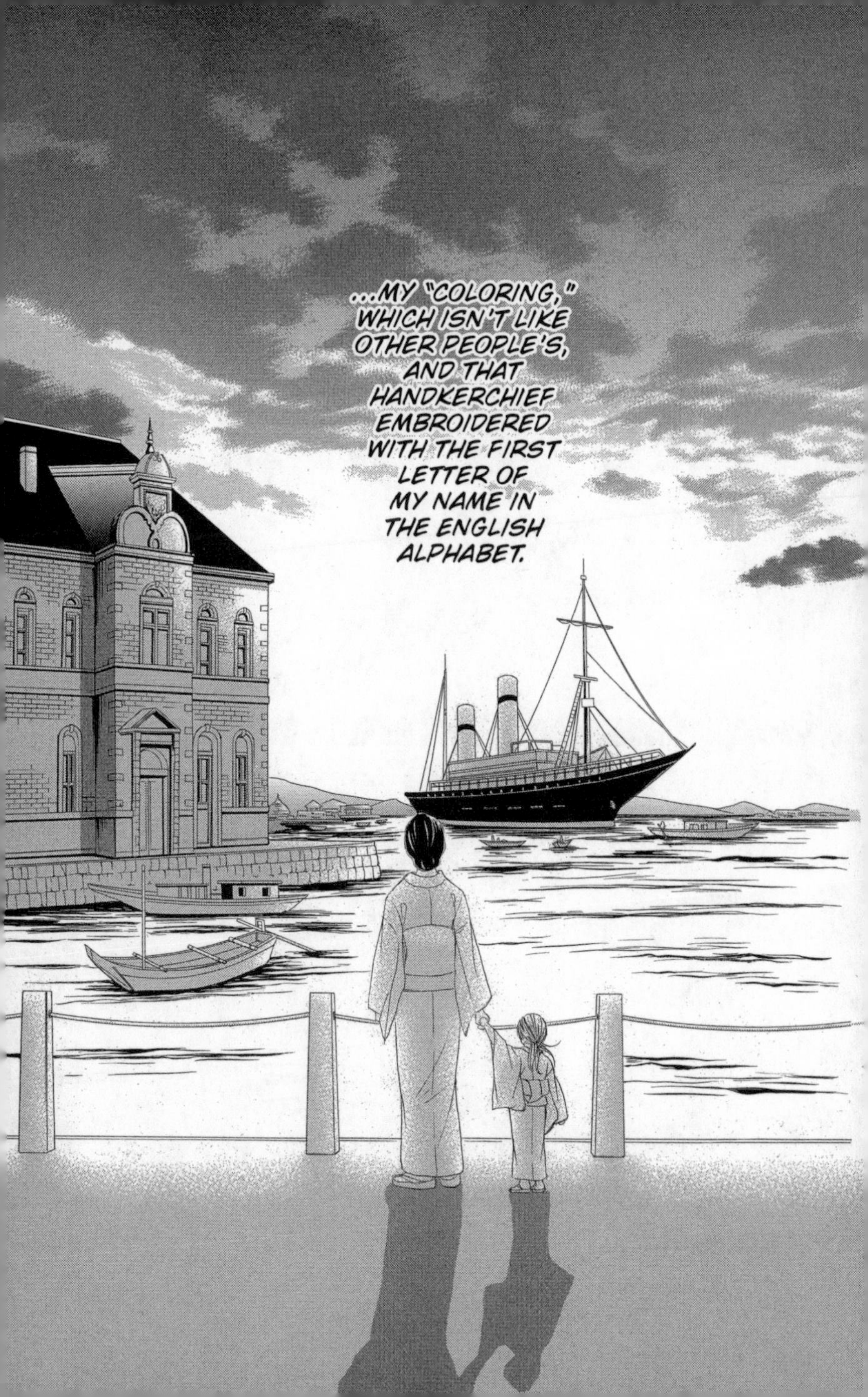
...MY "COLORING," WHICH ISN'T LIKE OTHER PEOPLE'S, AND THAT HANDKERCHIEF EMBROIDERED WITH THE FIRST LETTER OF MY NAME IN THE ENGLISH ALPHABET.

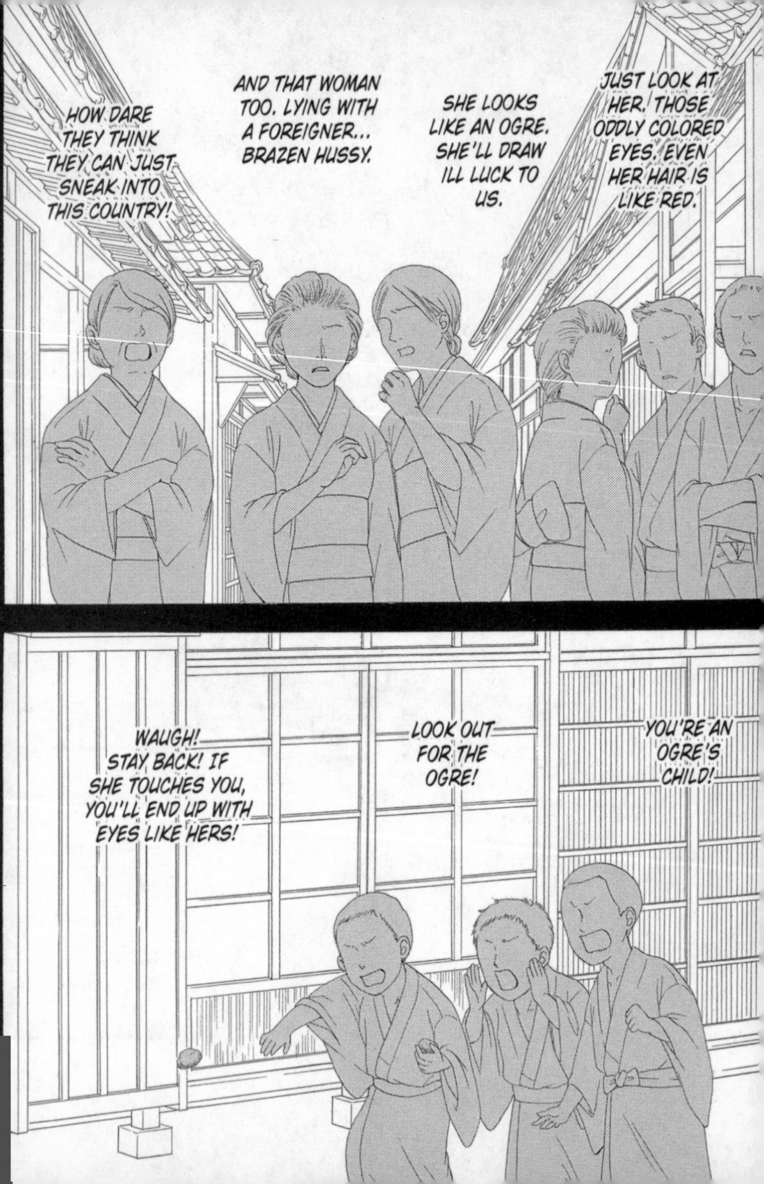
JUST LOOK AT HER. THOSE ODDLY COLORED EYES. EVEN HER HAIR IS LIKE RED.
SHE LOOKS LIKE AN OGRE. SHE'LL DRAW ILL LUCK TO US.
AND THAT WOMAN TOO. LYING WITH A FOREIGNER... BRAZEN HUSSY.
HOW DARE THEY THINK THEY CAN JUST SNEAK INTO THIS COUNTRY!
YOU'RE AN OGRE'S CHILD!
LOOK OUT FOR THE OGRE!
WAUGH! STAY BACK! IF SHE TOUCHES YOU, YOU'LL END UP WITH EYES LIKE HERS!

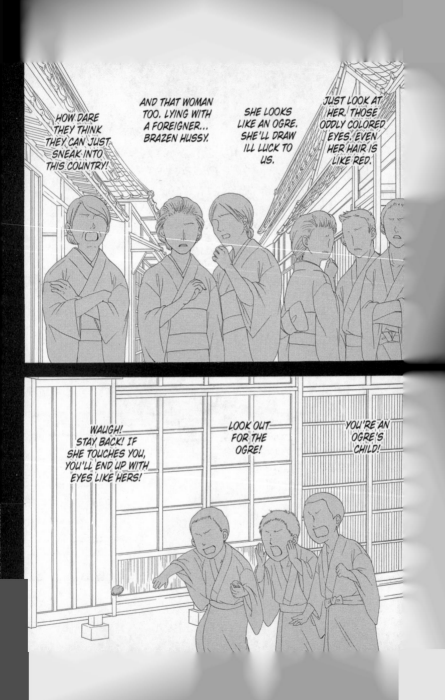

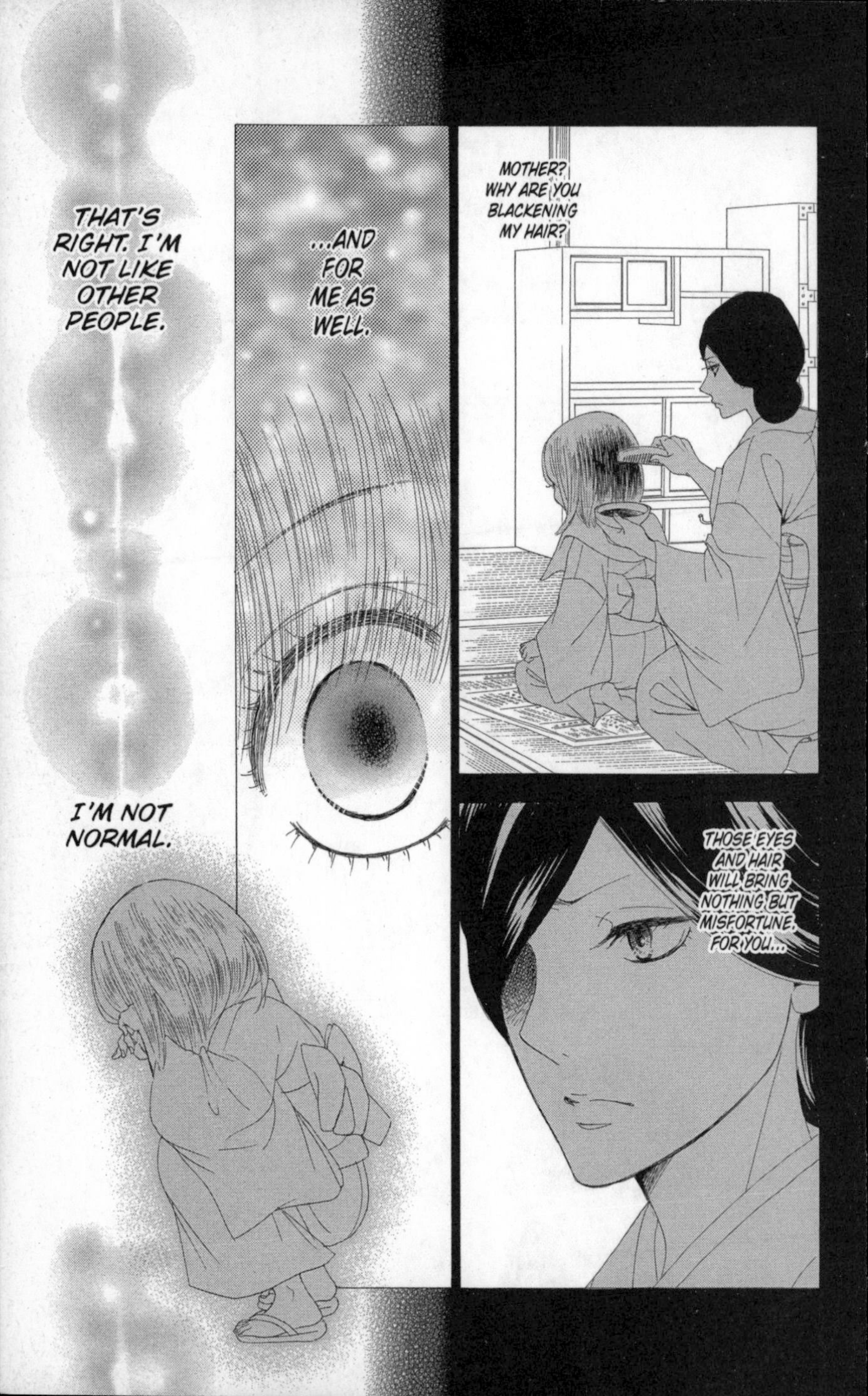
MOTHER? WHY ARE YOU BLACKENING MY HAIR?
THOSE EYES AND HAIR WILL BRING NOTHING BUT MISFORTUNE FOR YOU...
...AND FOR ME AS WELL.
THAT'S RIGHT. I'M NOT LIKE OTHER PEOPLE.
I'M NOT NORMAL.

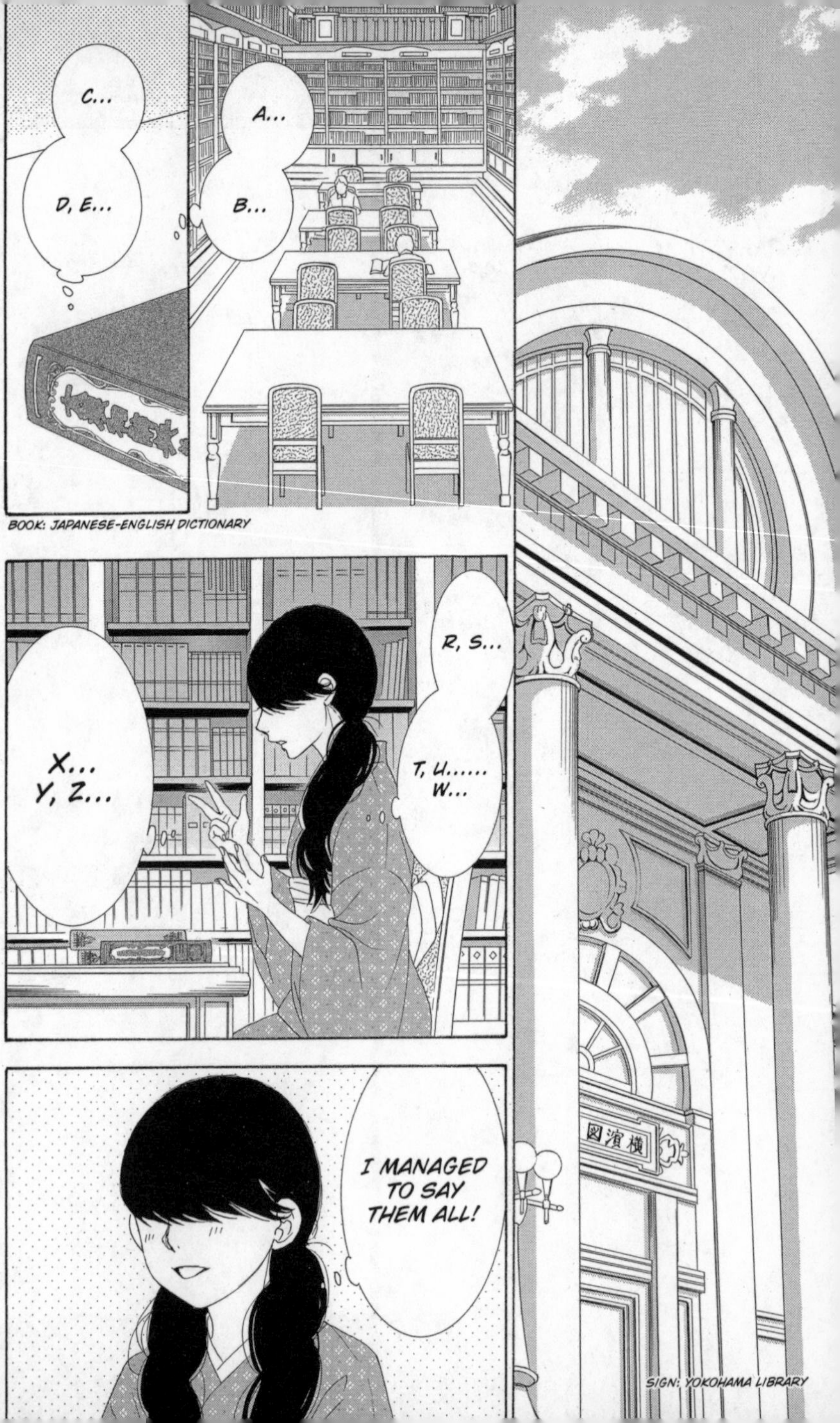
SIGN: YOKOHAMA LIBRARY
A...
B...
C...
D, E...
BOOK: JAPANESE-ENGLISH DICTIONARY
R, S...
T, U...... W...
X... Y, Z...
I MANAGED TO SAY THEM ALL!

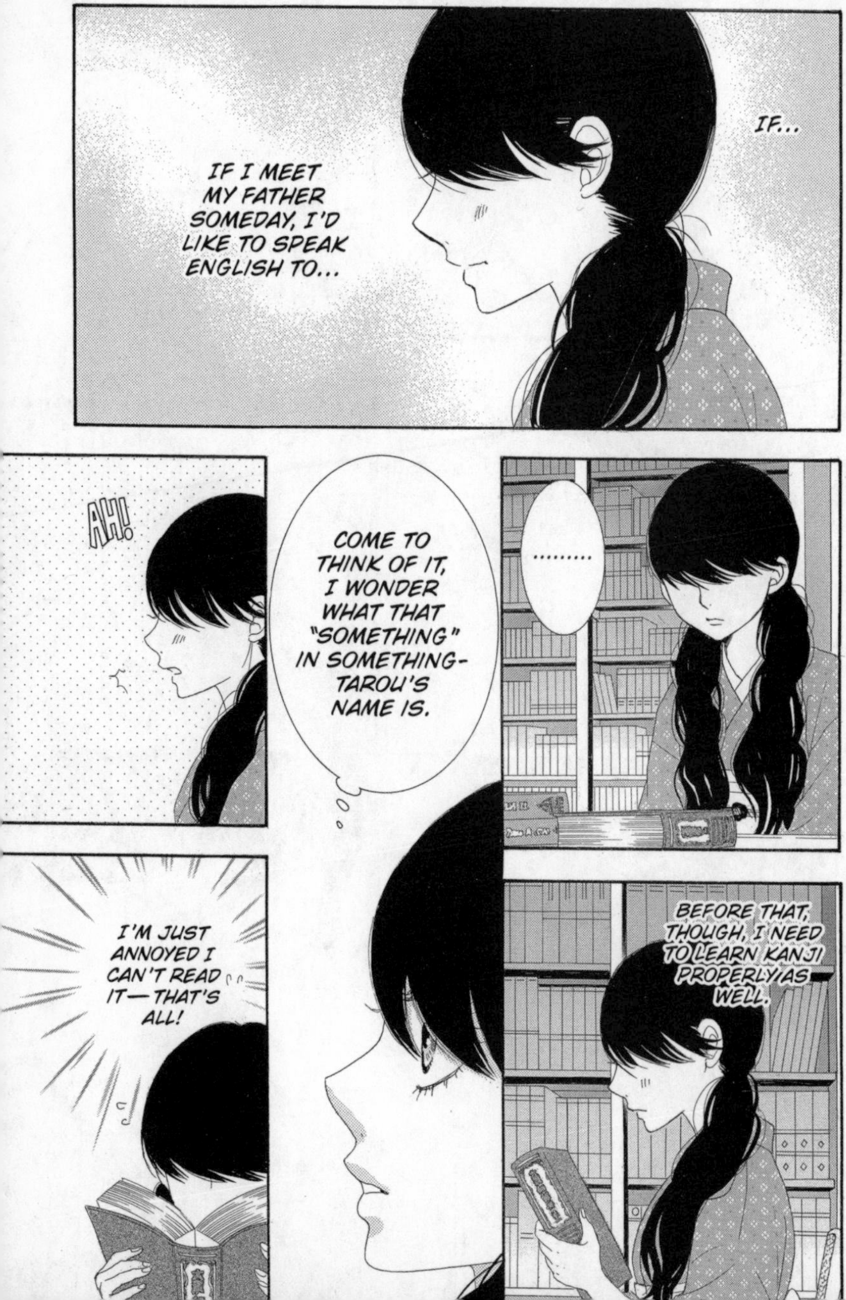
IF...
IF I MEET MY FATHER SOMEDAY, I'D LIKE TO SPEAK ENGLISH TO...
....
BEFORE THAT, THOUGH, I NEED TO LEARN KANJI PROPERLY AS WELL.
COME TO THINK OF IT, I WONDER WHAT THAT "SOMETHING" IN SOMETHING-TAROU'S NAME IS.
AH!
I'M JUST ANNOYED I CAN'T READ IT—THAT'S ALL!

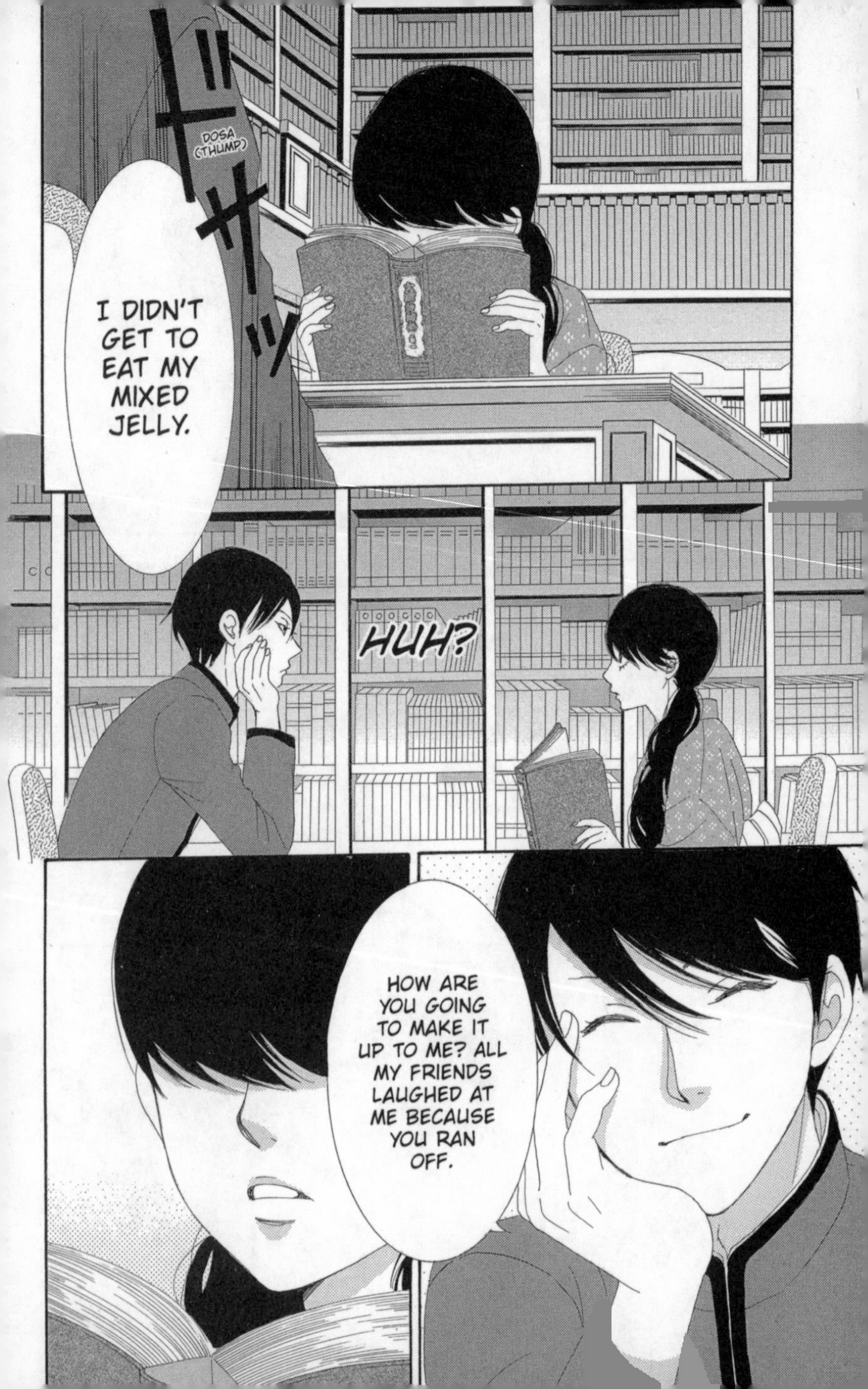
DOSA (THUMP)
I DIDN'T GET TO EAT MY MIXED JELLY.
HUH?
HOW ARE YOU GOING TO MAKE IT UP TO ME? ALL MY FRIENDS LAUGHED AT ME BECAUSE YOU RAN OFF.

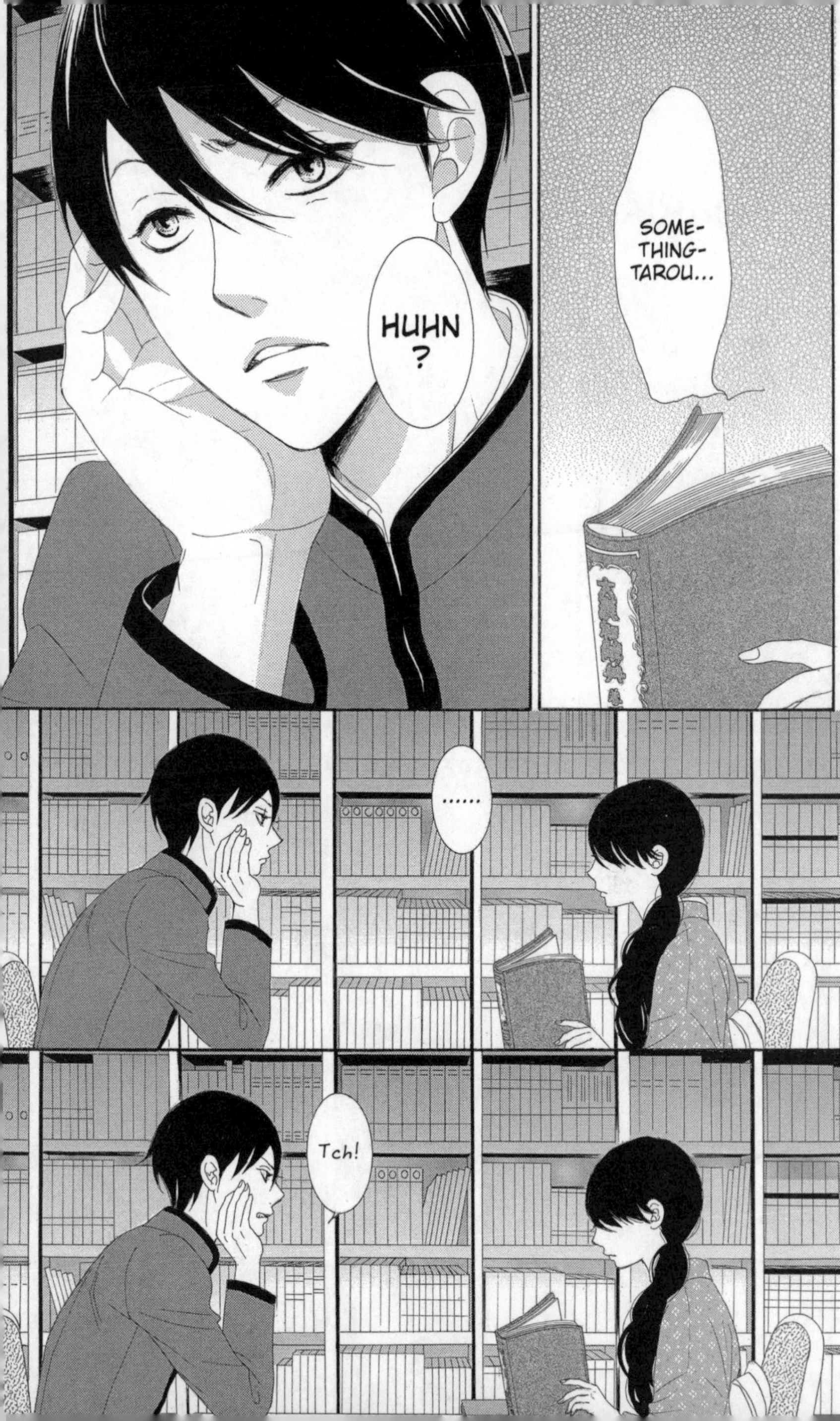
SOME-
THING-
TAROU...
HUHN
?
......
Tch!

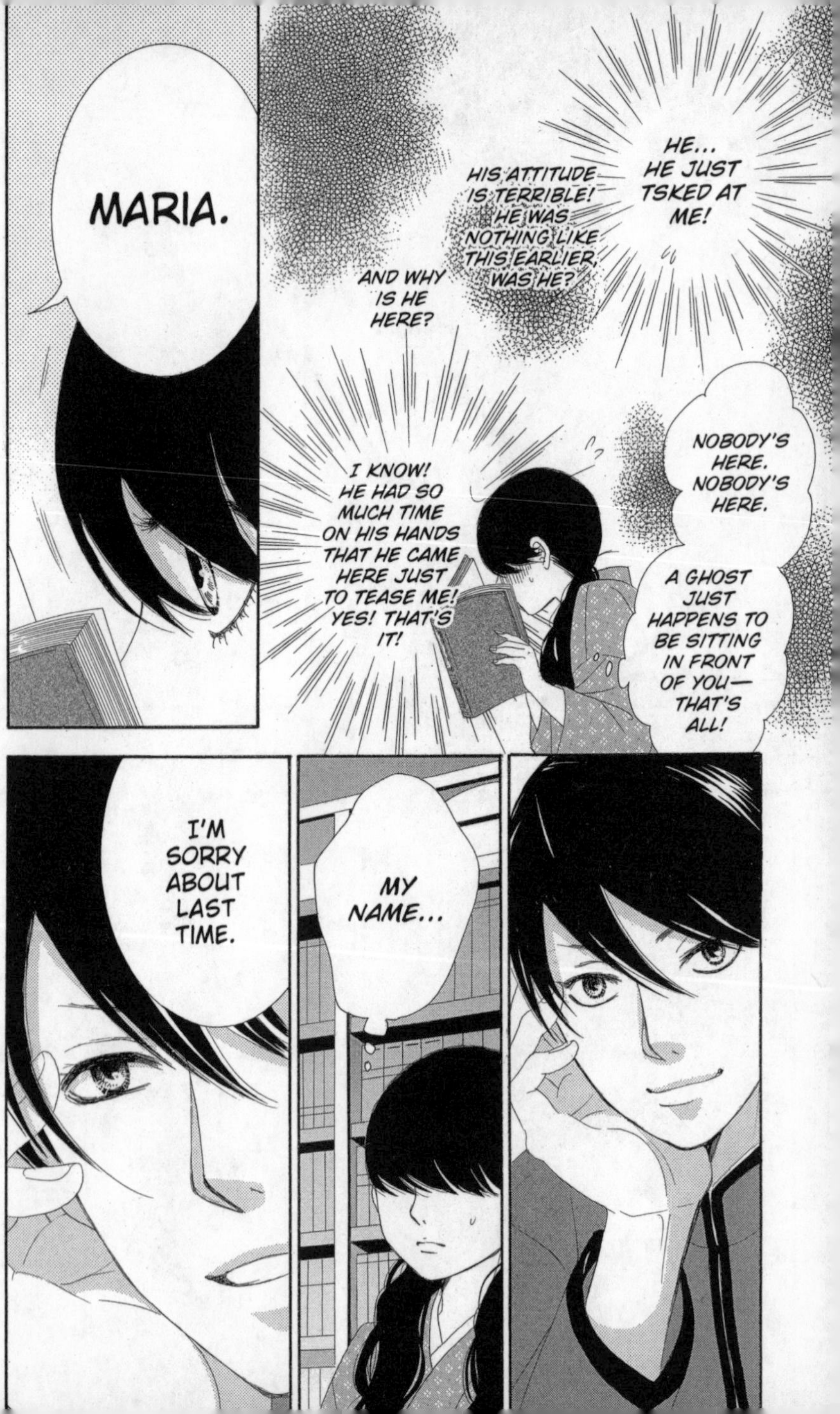
HE... HE JUST TSKED AT ME!
HIS ATTITUDE IS TERRIBLE! HE WAS NOTHING LIKE THIS EARLIER, WAS HE?
AND WHY IS HE HERE?
NOBODY'S HERE. NOBODY'S HERE.
A GHOST JUST HAPPENS TO BE SITTING IN FRONT OF YOU—THAT'S ALL!
I KNOW! HE HAD SO MUCH TIME ON HIS HANDS THAT HE CAME HERE JUST TO TEASE ME! YES! THAT'S IT!
MARIA.
MY NAME...
I'M SORRY ABOUT LAST TIME.

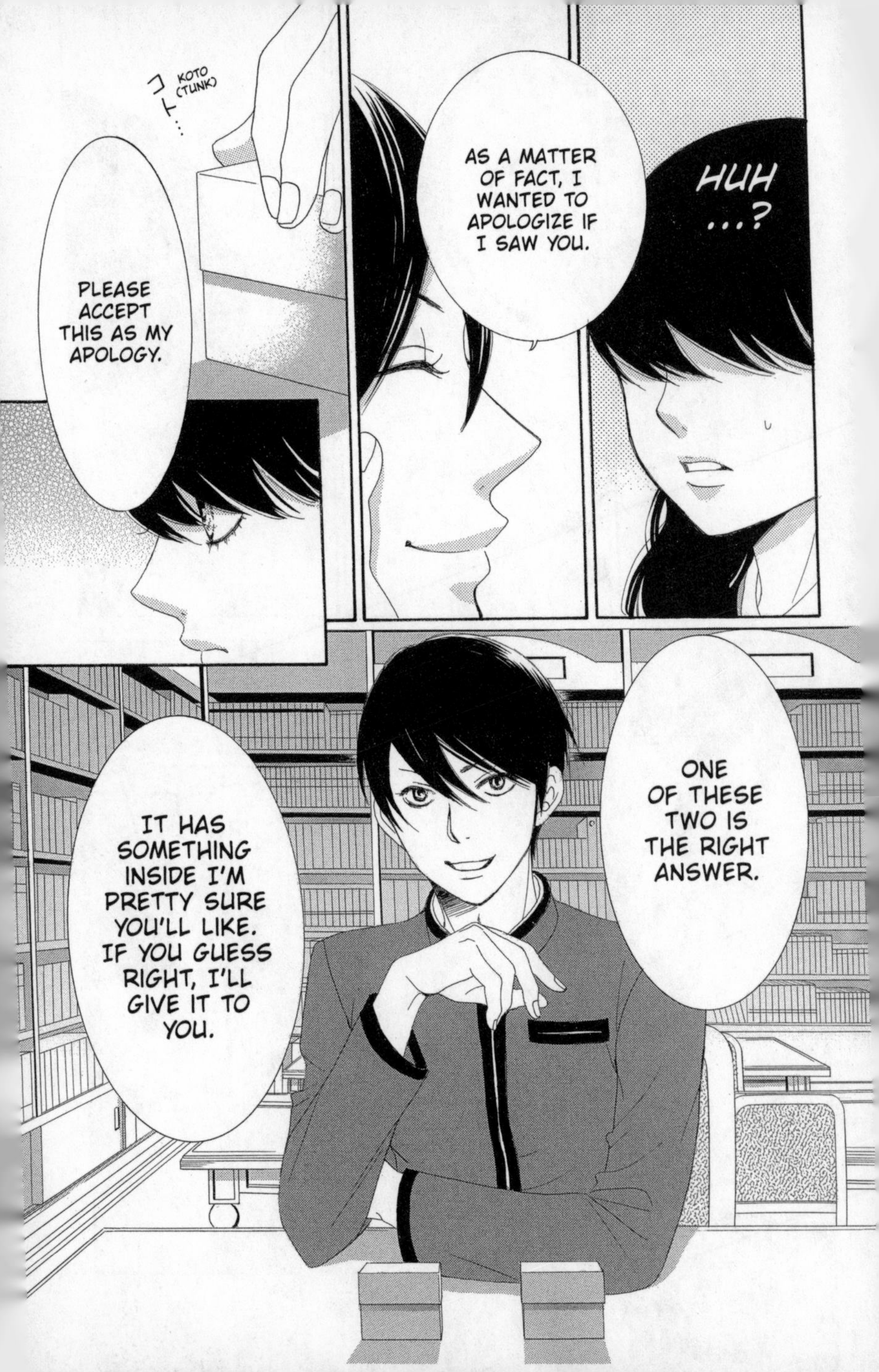
HUH ...?
AS A MATTER OF FACT, I WANTED TO APOLOGIZE IF I SAW YOU.
KOTO (TUNK)
PLEASE ACCEPT THIS AS MY APOLOGY.
ONE OF THESE TWO IS THE RIGHT ANSWER.
IT HAS SOMETHING INSIDE I'M PRETTY SURE YOU'LL LIKE. IF YOU GUESS RIGHT, I'LL GIVE IT TO YOU.

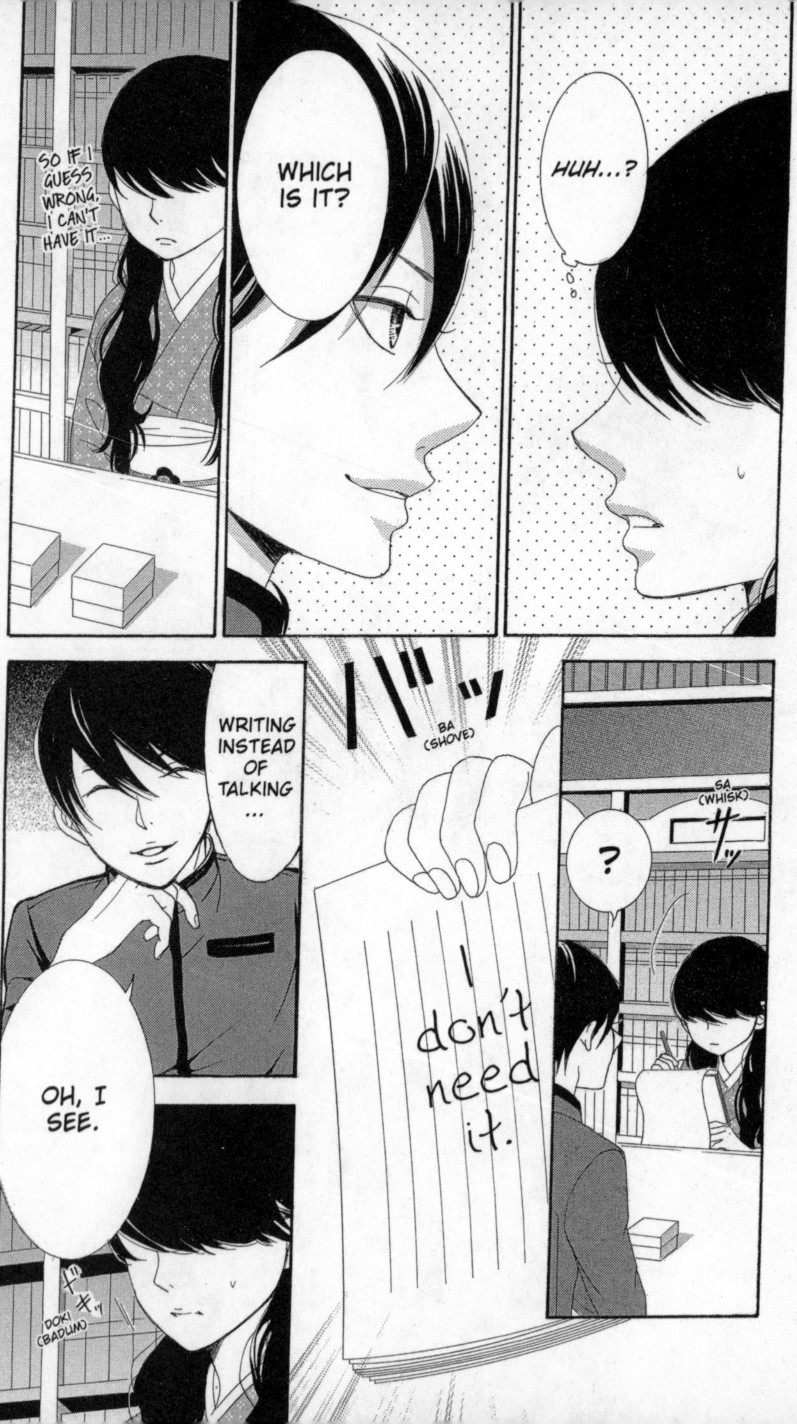
HUH...?
WHICH IS IT?
SO IF I GUESS WRONG, I CAN'T HAVE IT...
SA (WHISK)
?
BA (SHOVE)
I don't need it.
WRITING INSTEAD OF TALKING...
OH, I SEE.
DOKI (BADUM)

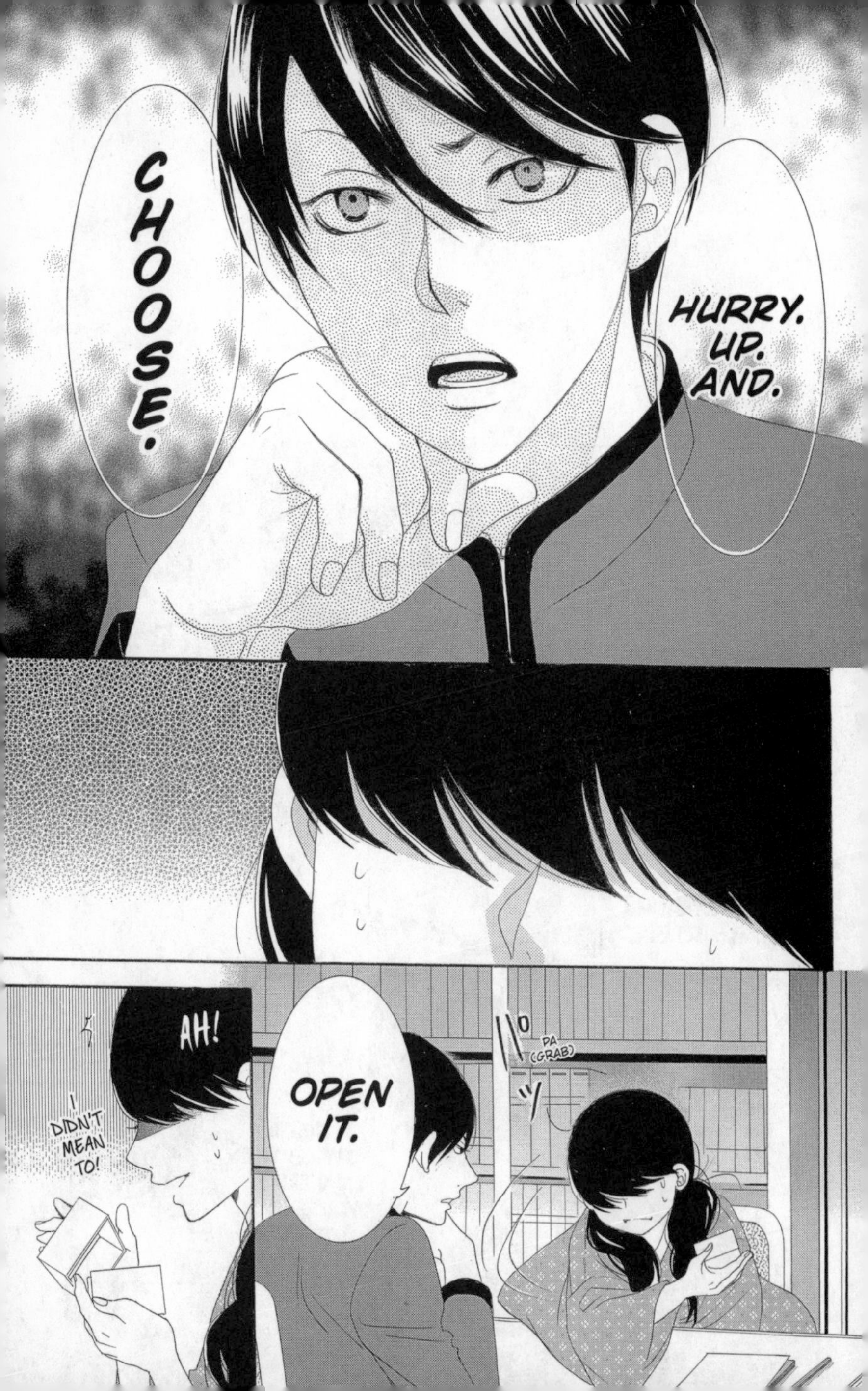
HURRY. UP. AND.
CHOOSE.
PA (GRAB)
OPEN IT.
AH!
I DIDN'T MEAN TO!

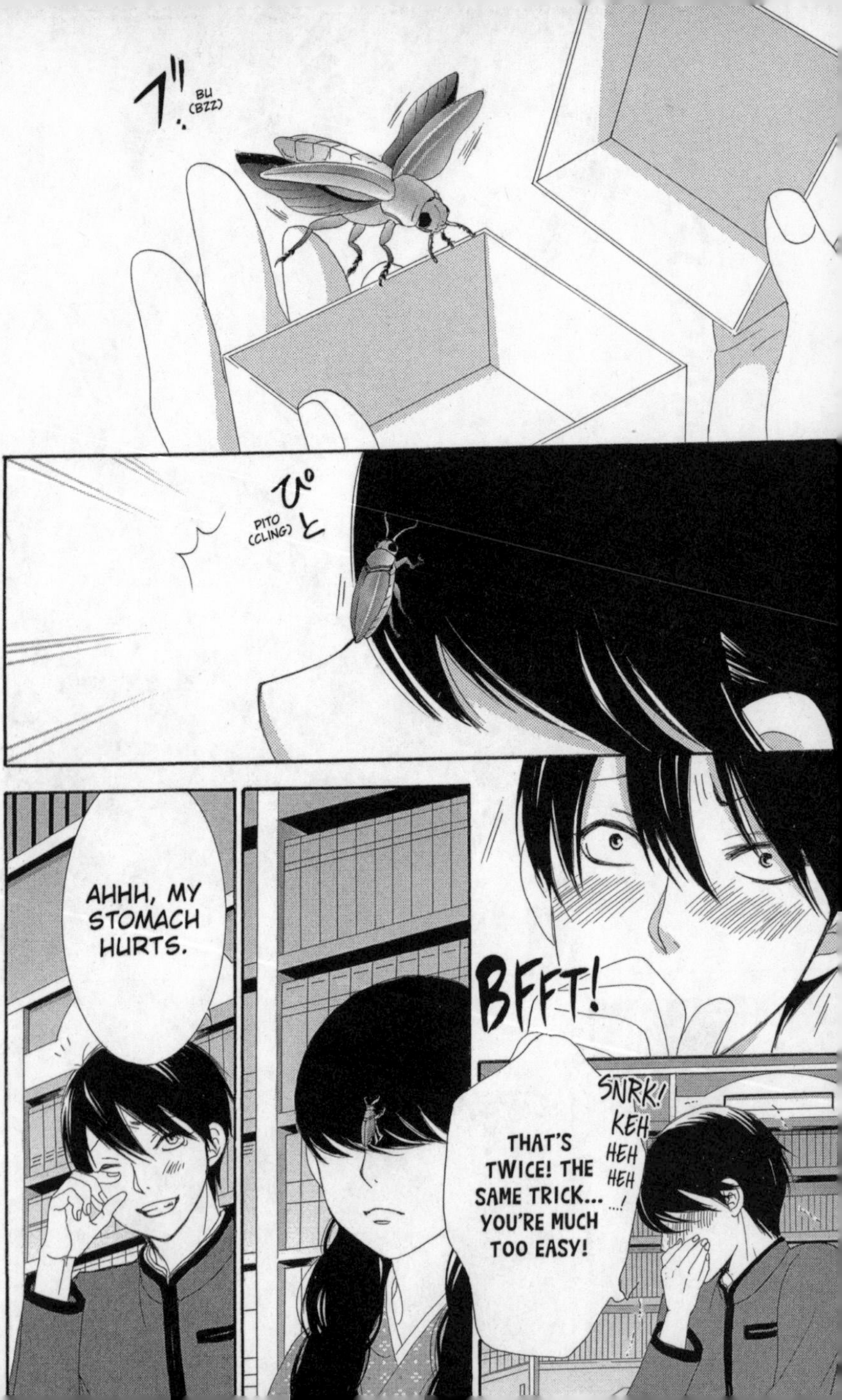
ブ
BU (BZZ)
ぴと
PITO (CLING)
BFFT!
SNRK! KEH HEH HEH...!
THAT'S TWICE! THE SAME TRICK... YOU'RE MUCH TOO EASY!
AHHH, MY STOMACH HURTS.

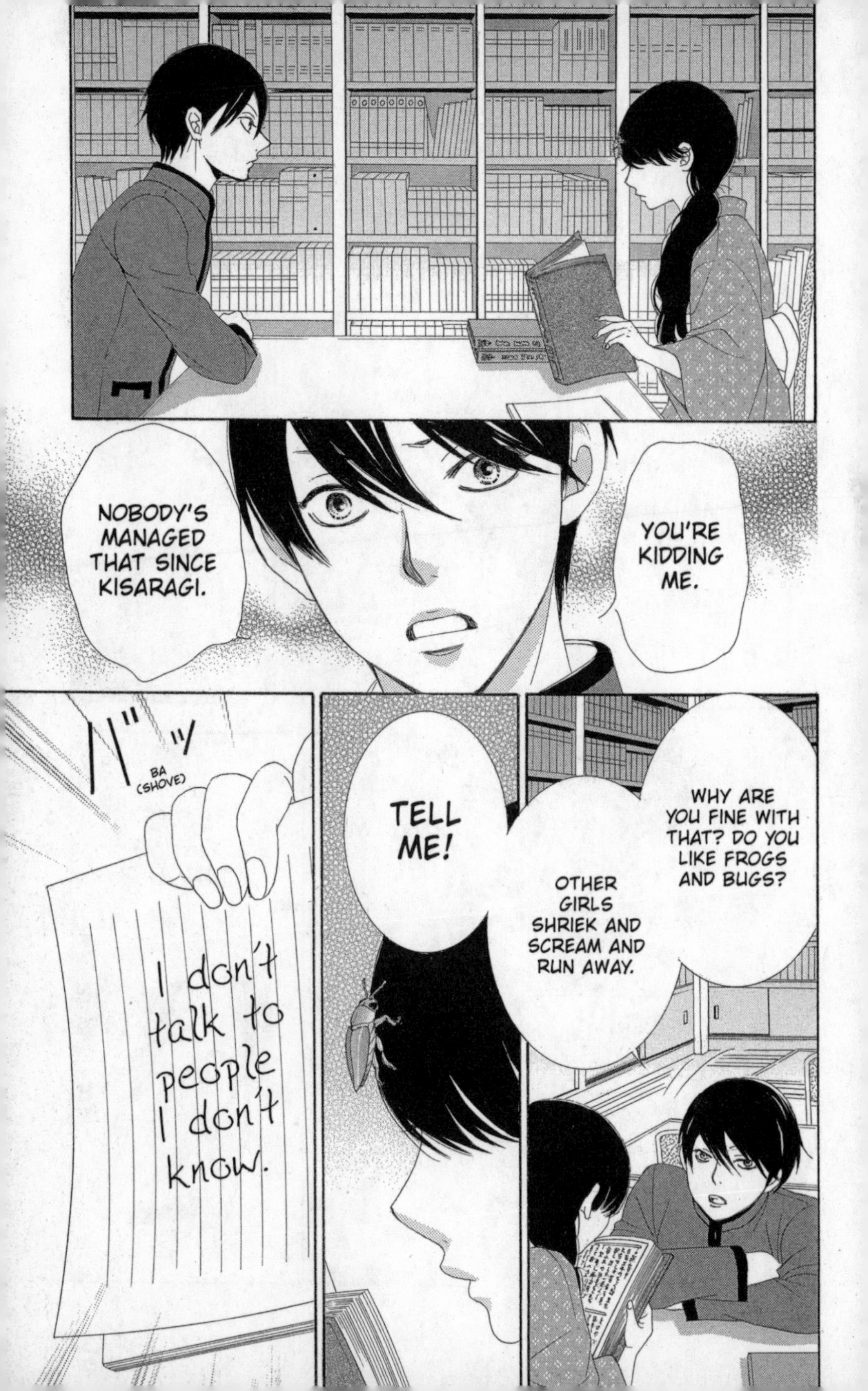
YOU'RE KIDDING ME.
NOBODY'S MANAGED THAT SINCE KISARAGI.
WHY ARE YOU FINE WITH THAT? DO YOU LIKE FROGS AND BUGS?
OTHER GIRLS SHRIEK AND SCREAM AND RUN AWAY.
TELL ME!
バッ
BA (SHOVE)
I don't talk to people I don't know.

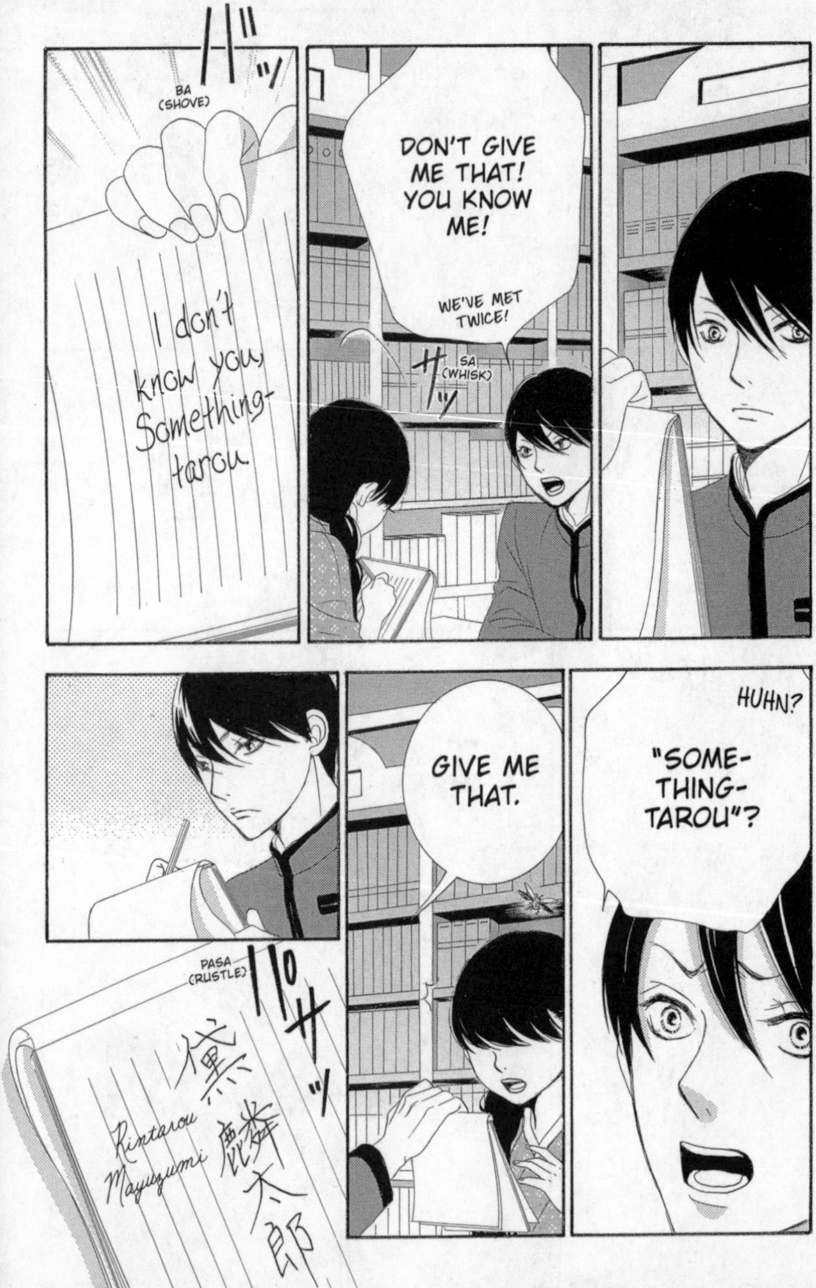
DON'T GIVE ME THAT! YOU KNOW ME!
WE'VE MET TWICE!
サッ
SA (WHISK)
バッ
BA (SHOVE)
I don't know you, Something-tarou.
HUHN?
"SOME-THING-TAROU"?
GIVE ME THAT.
パサッ
PASA (RUSTLE)
黛 麟太郎
Rintarou Mayuzumi

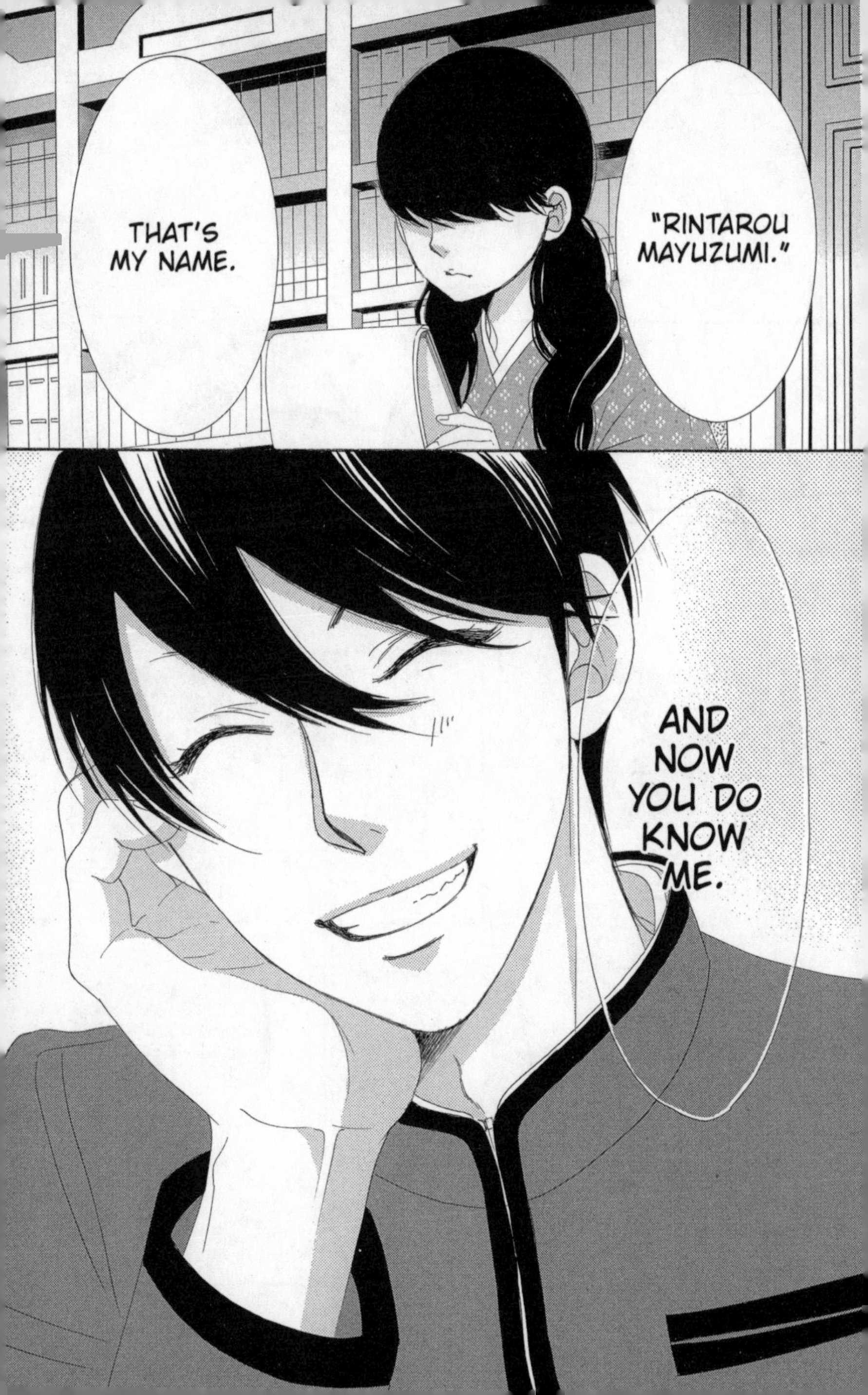
"RINTAROU MAYUZUMI."
THAT'S MY NAME.
AND NOW YOU DO KNOW ME.

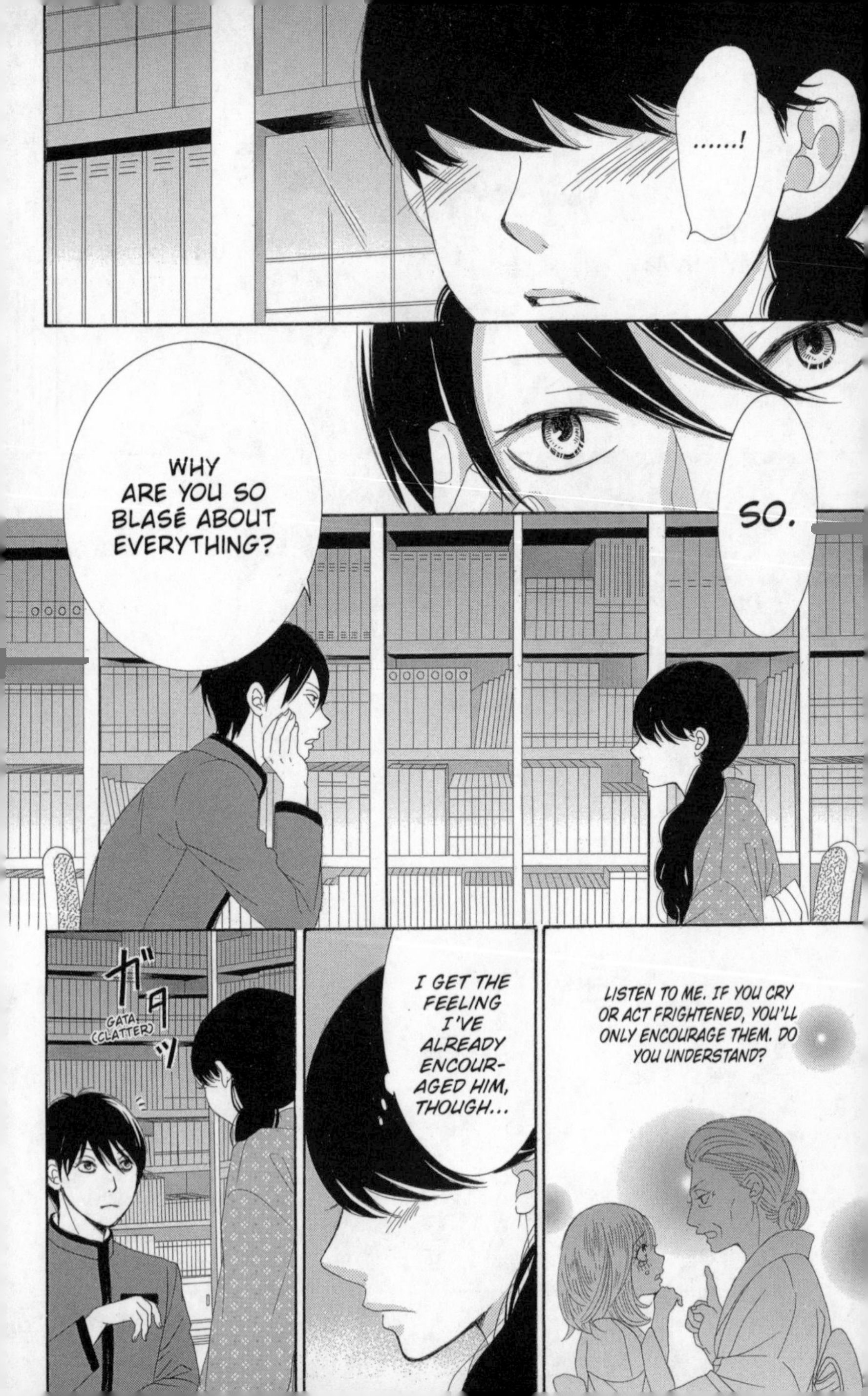
......!
SO.
WHY ARE YOU SO BLASÉ ABOUT EVERYTHING?
LISTEN TO ME. IF YOU CRY OR ACT FRIGHTENED, YOU'LL ONLY ENCOURAGE THEM. DO YOU UNDERSTAND?
I GET THE FEELING I'VE ALREADY ENCOUR-AGED HIM, THOUGH...
ガタッ
GATA (CLATTER)

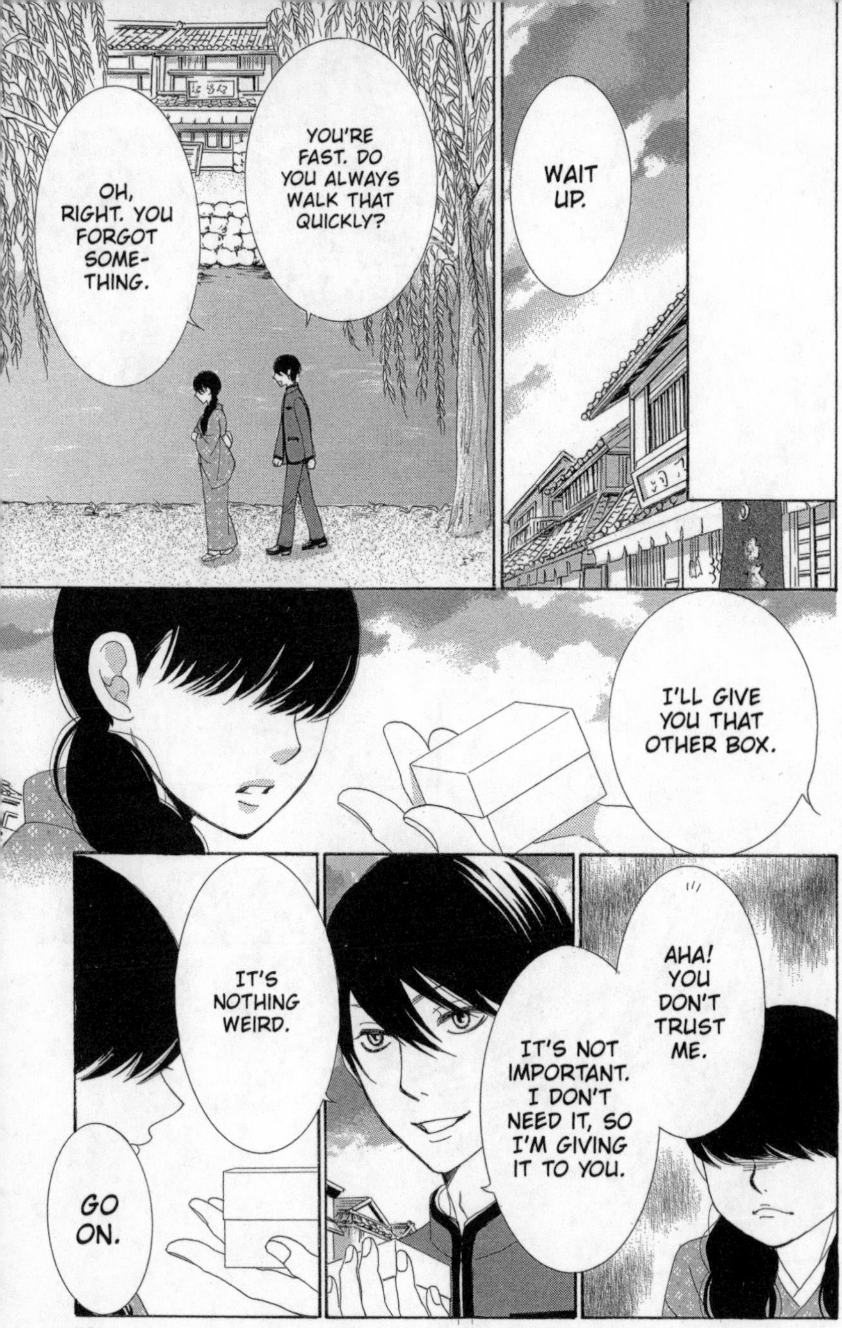
WAIT UP.
YOU'RE FAST. DO YOU ALWAYS WALK THAT QUICKLY?
OH, RIGHT. YOU FORGOT SOME-THING.
I'LL GIVE YOU THAT OTHER BOX.
AHA! YOU DON'T TRUST ME.
IT'S NOT IMPORTANT. I DON'T NEED IT, SO I'M GIVING IT TO YOU.
IT'S NOTHING WEIRD.
GO ON.

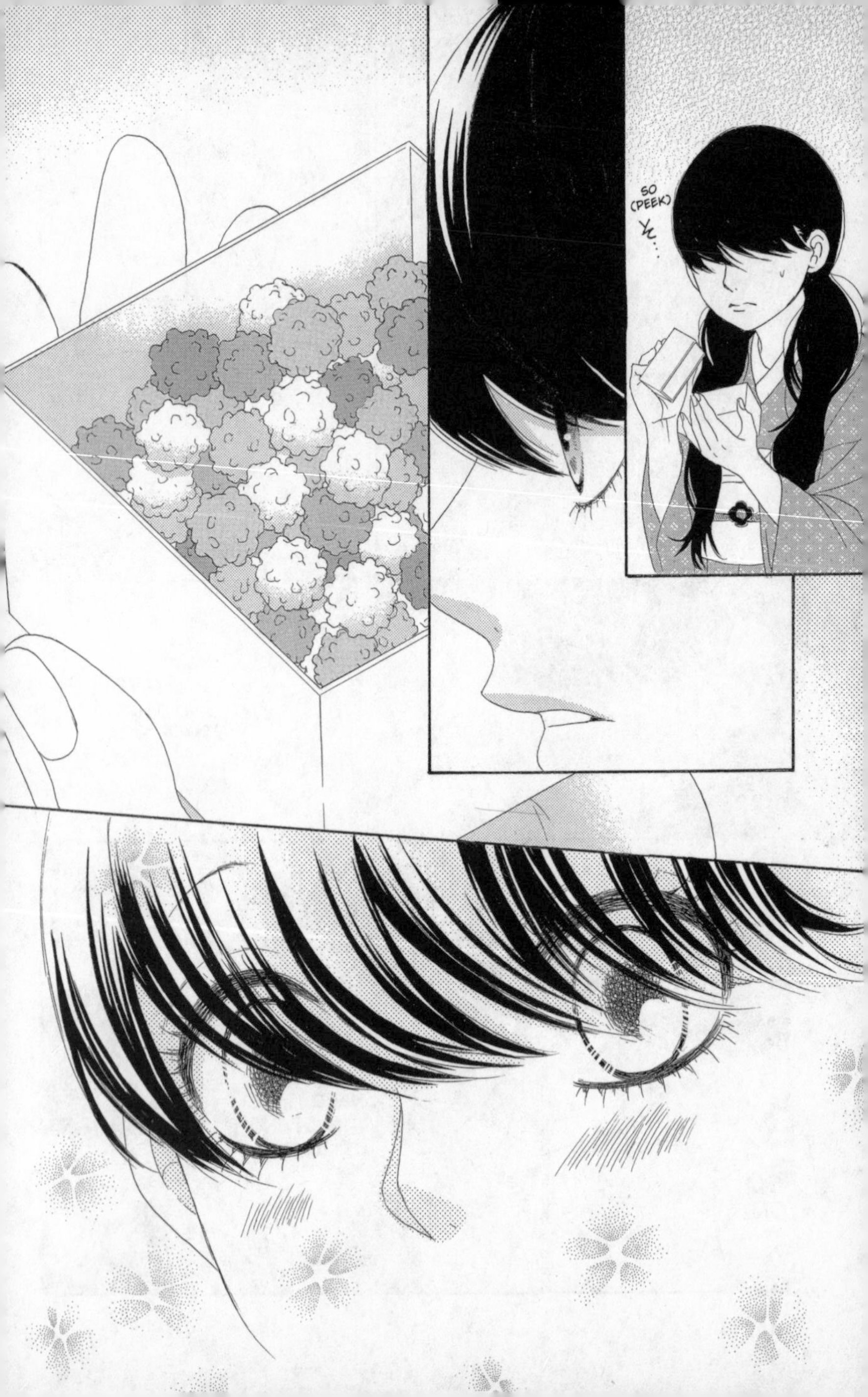
SO (PEEK)

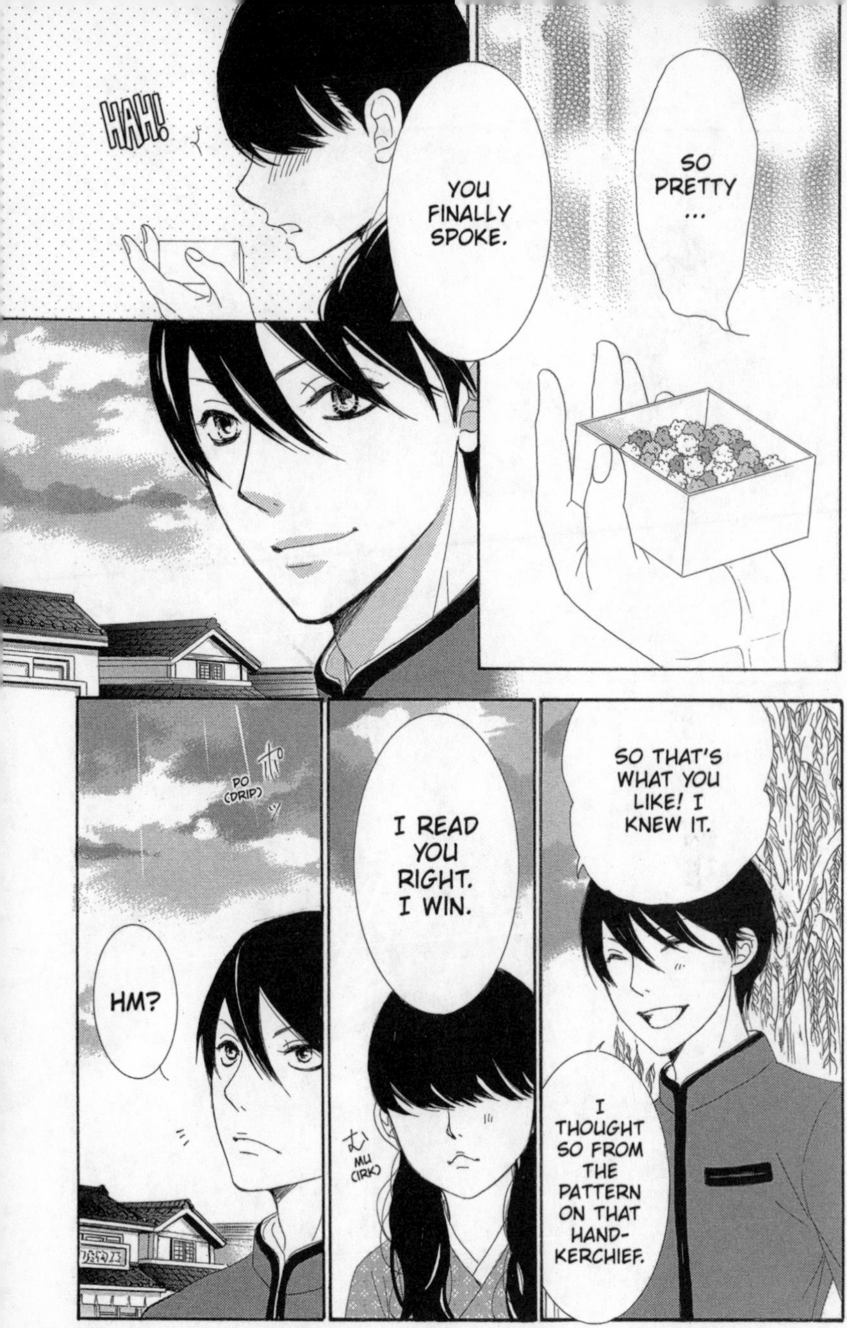
SO PRETTY...
YOU FINALLY SPOKE.
HAH!
SO THAT'S WHAT YOU LIKE! I KNEW IT.
I THOUGHT SO FROM THE PATTERN ON THAT HAND-KERCHIEF.
I READ YOU RIGHT. I WIN.
MU (IRK)
PO (DRIP)
HM?

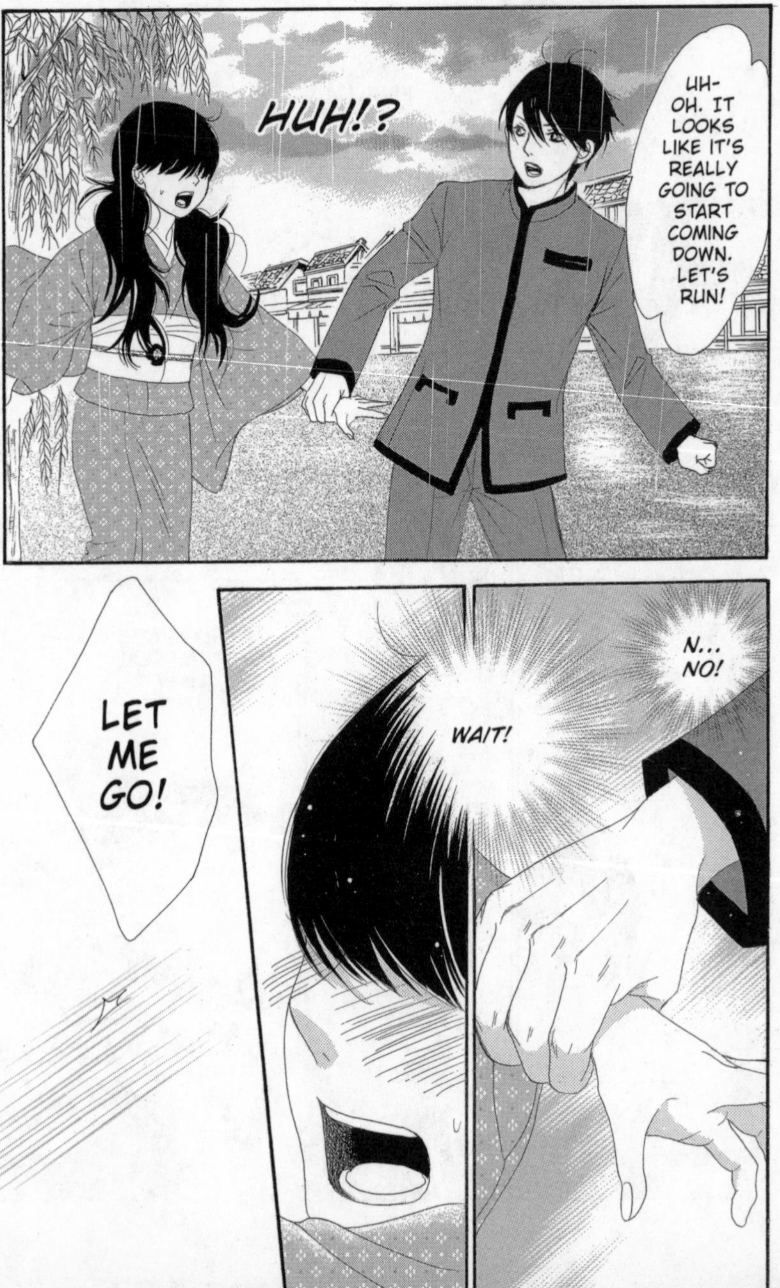
UH-OH. IT LOOKS LIKE IT'S REALLY GOING TO START COMING DOWN. LET'S RUN!
HUH!?
N... NO!
WAIT!
LET ME GO!

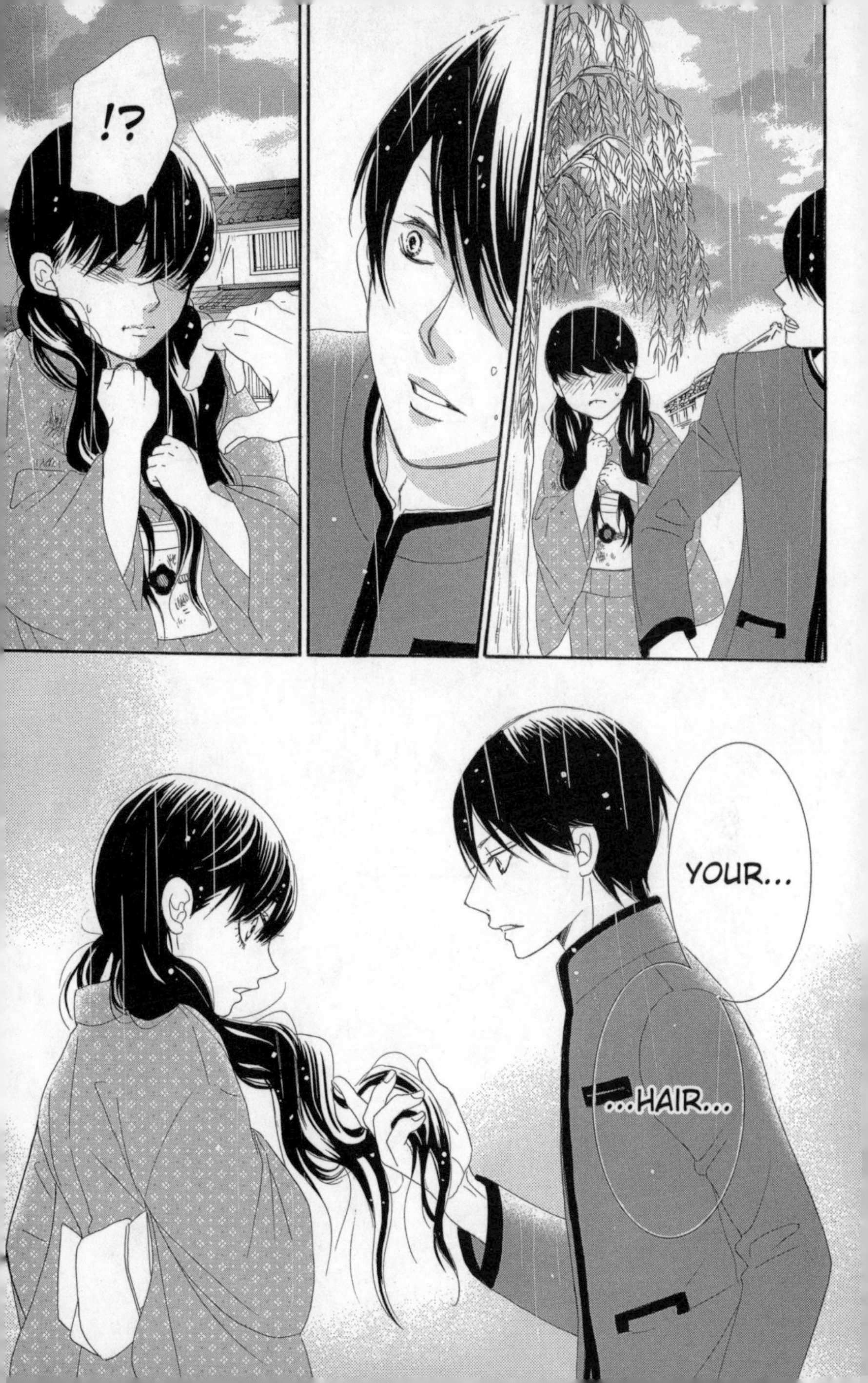
!?
YOUR...
...HAIR...

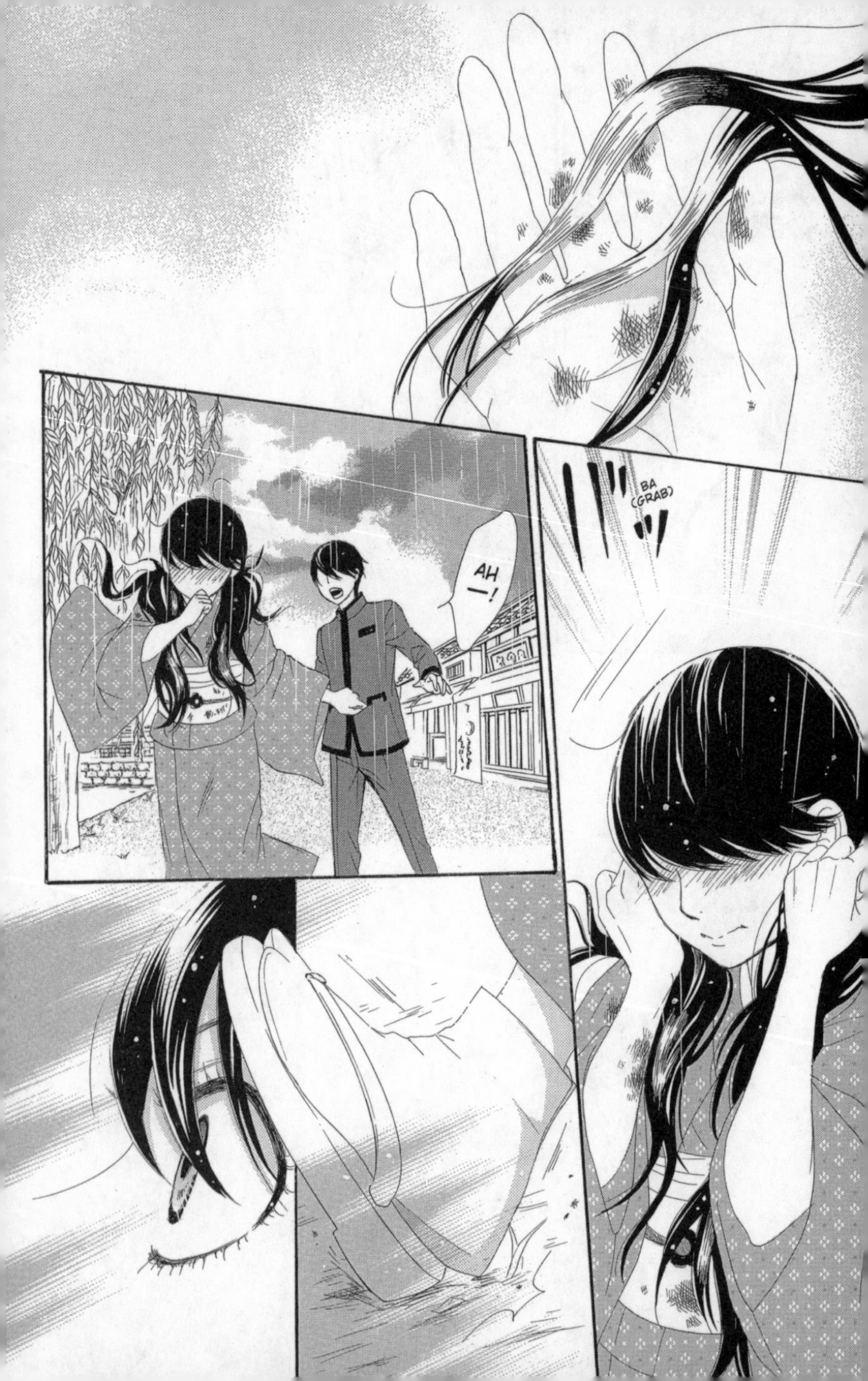
BA
(GRAB)
AH—!

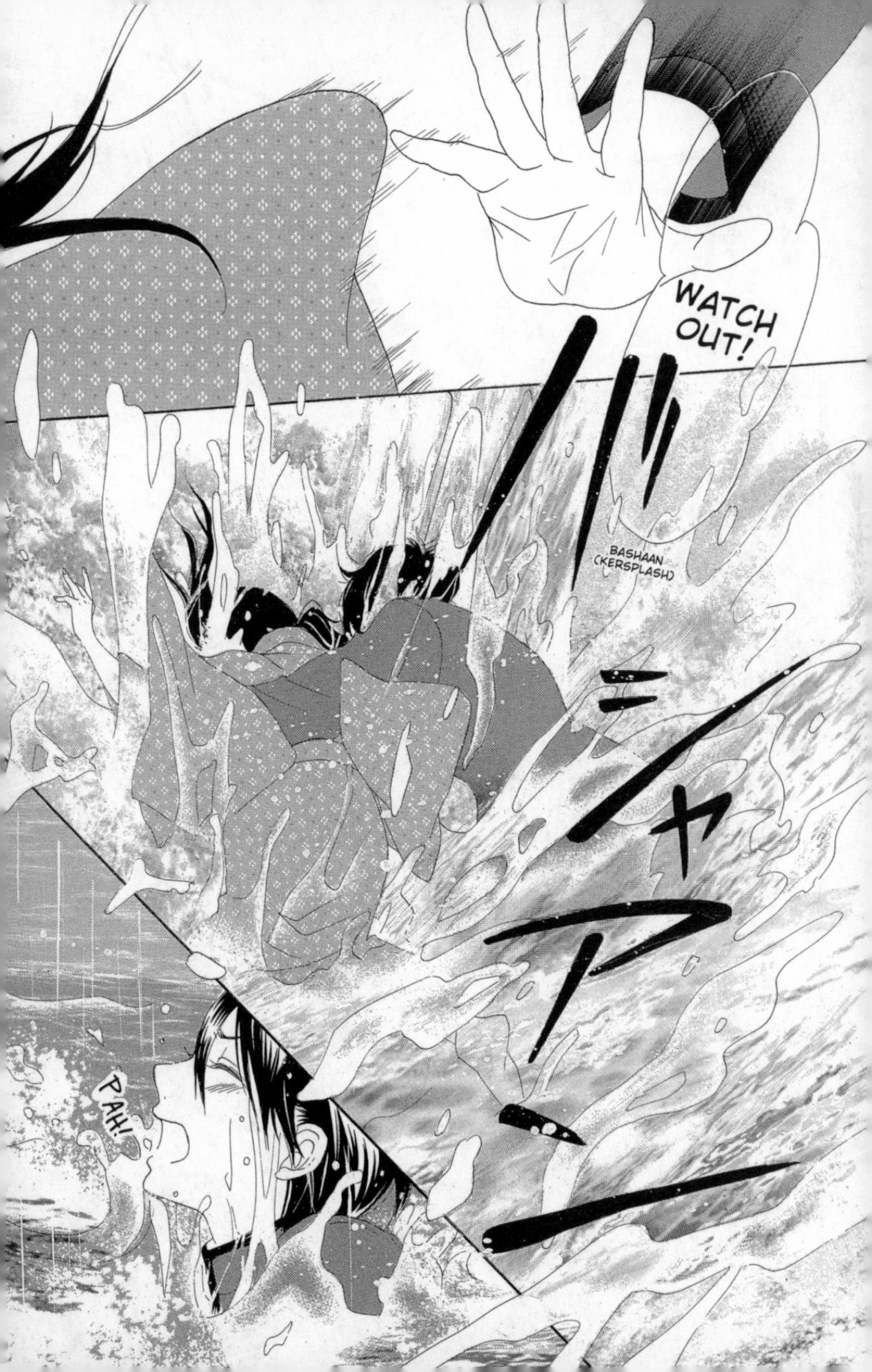
WATCH OUT!
BASHAAN (KERSPLASH)
PAH!

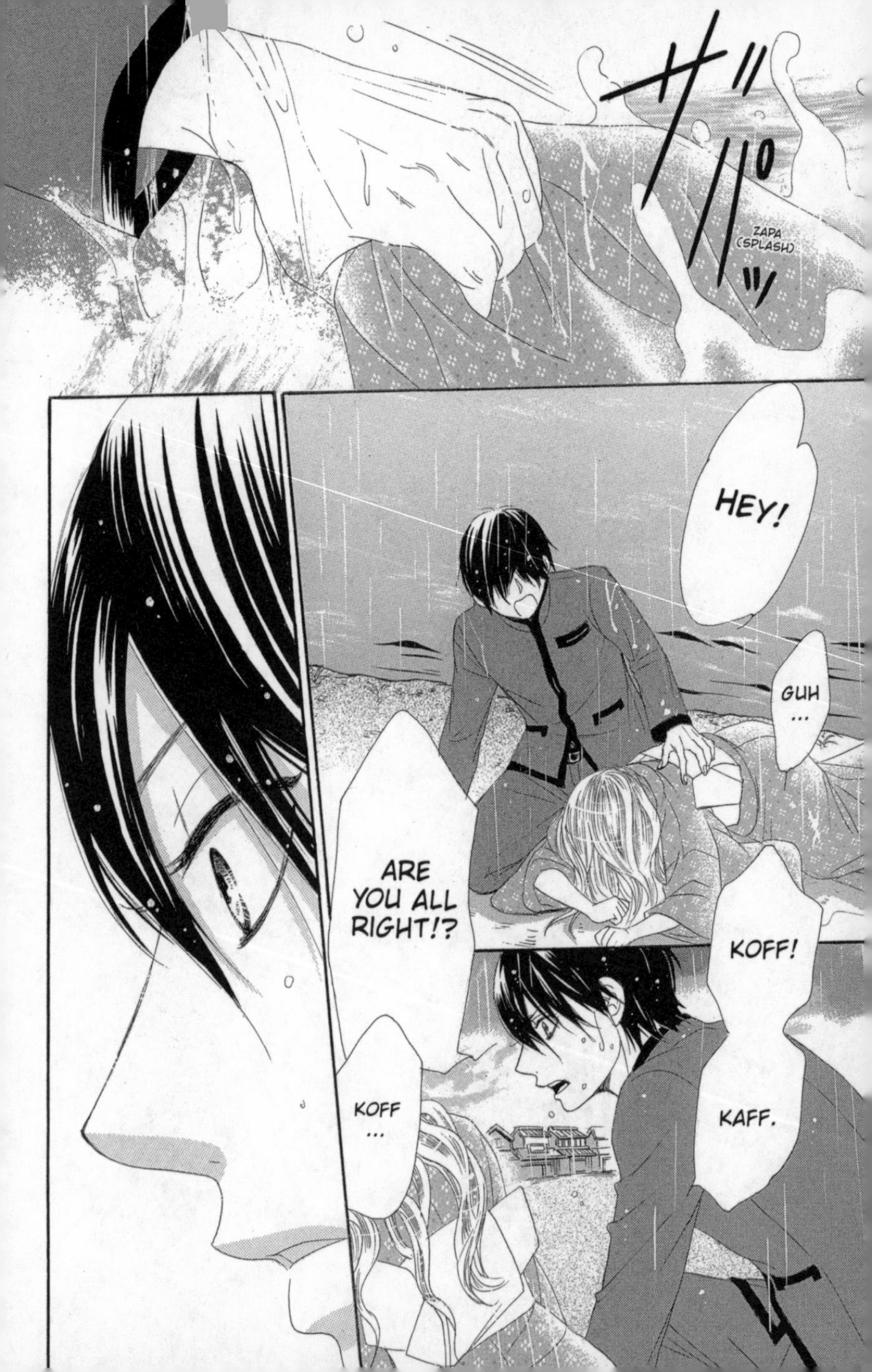
ザパッ
ZAPA (SPLASH)
HEY!
GUH ...
ARE YOU ALL RIGHT!?
KOFF!
KAFF.
KOFF ...

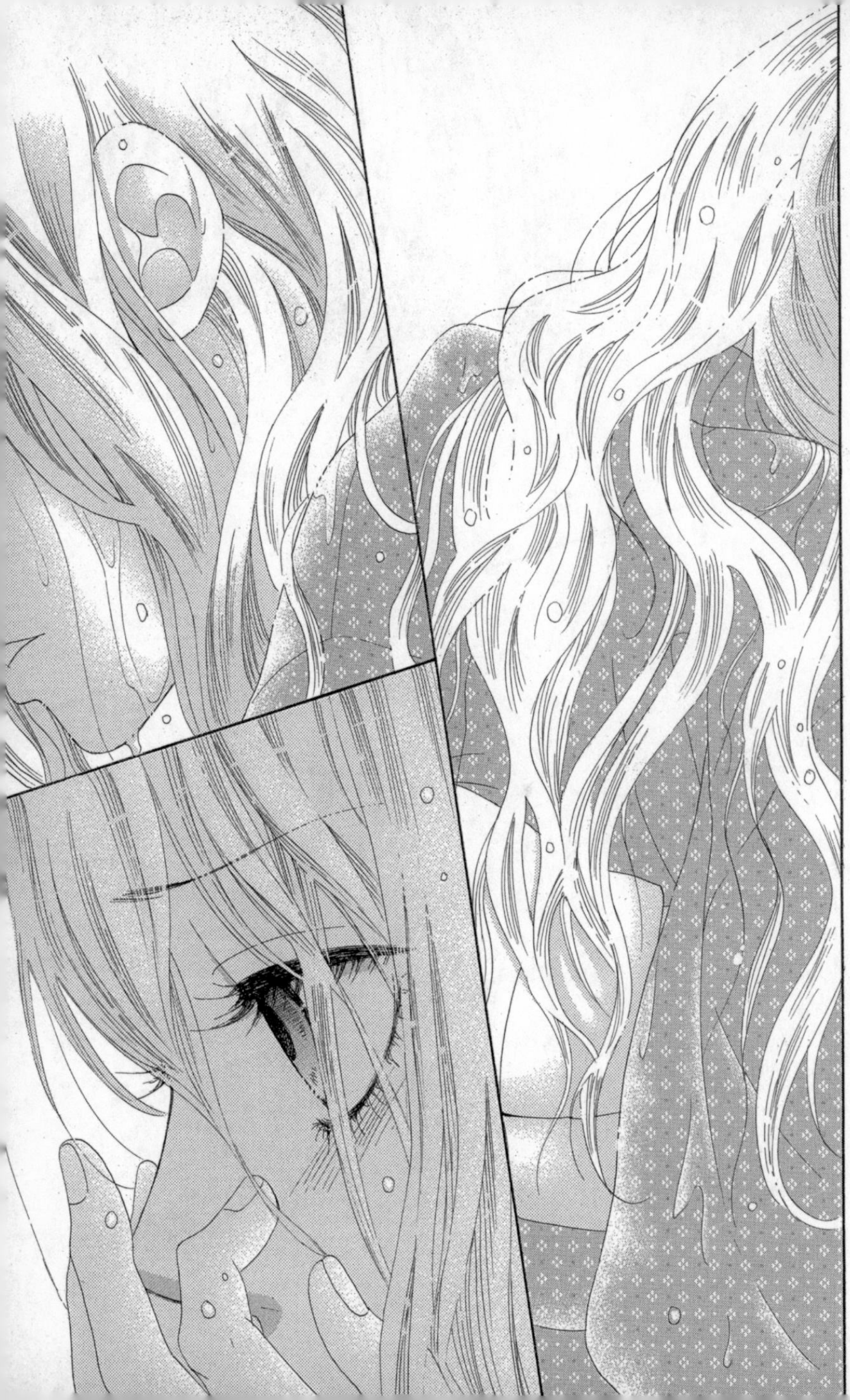

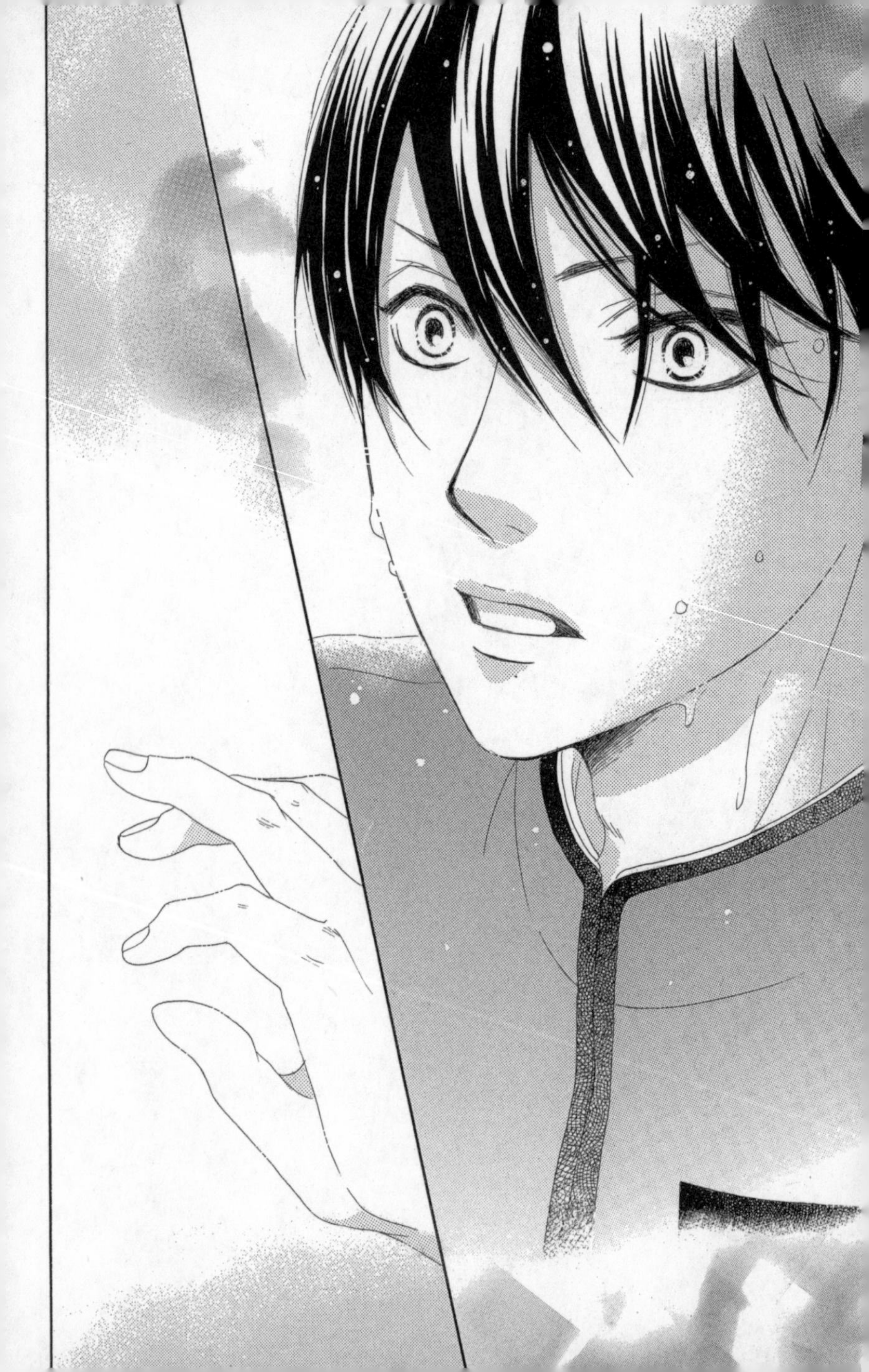

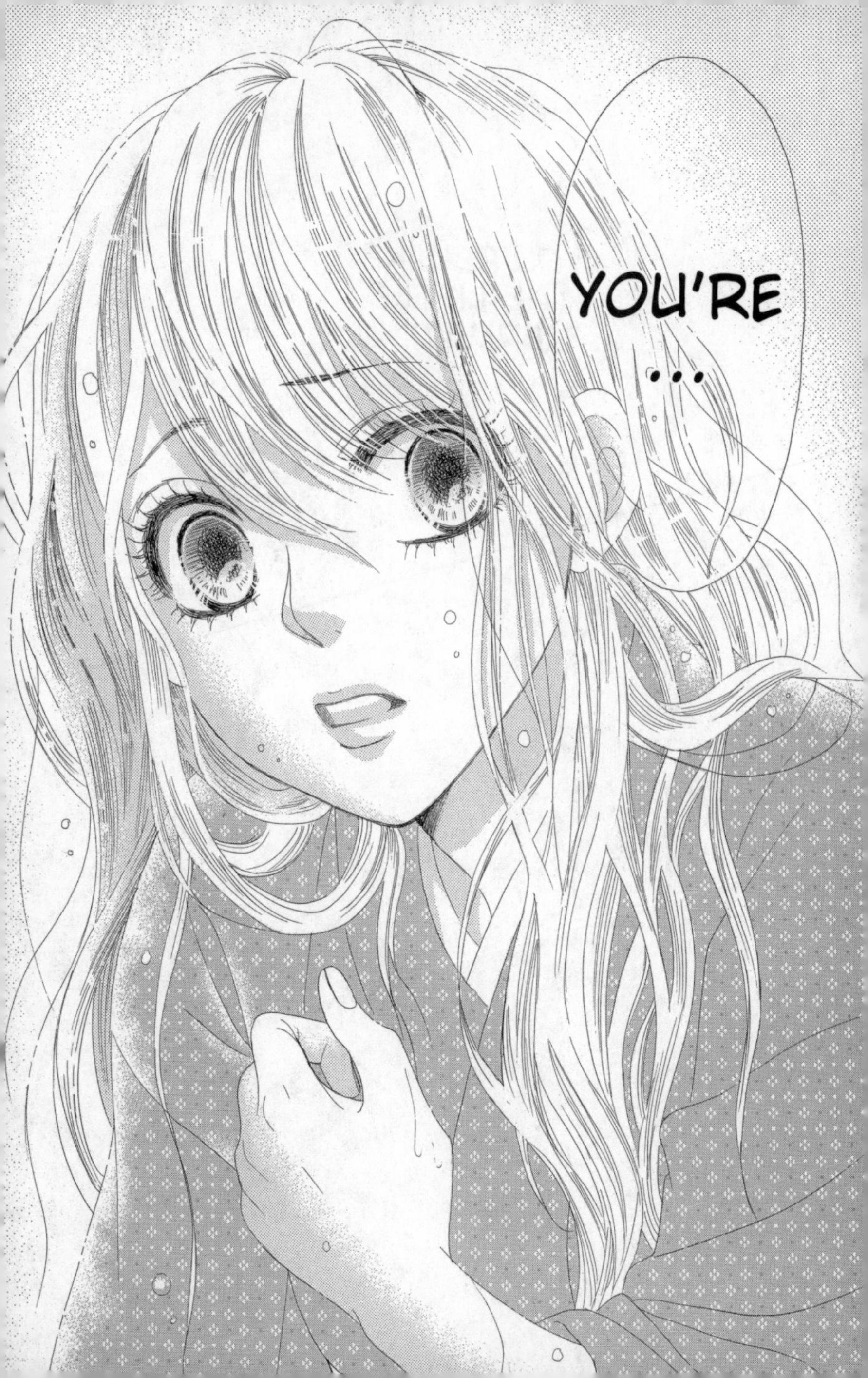
YOU'RE
...

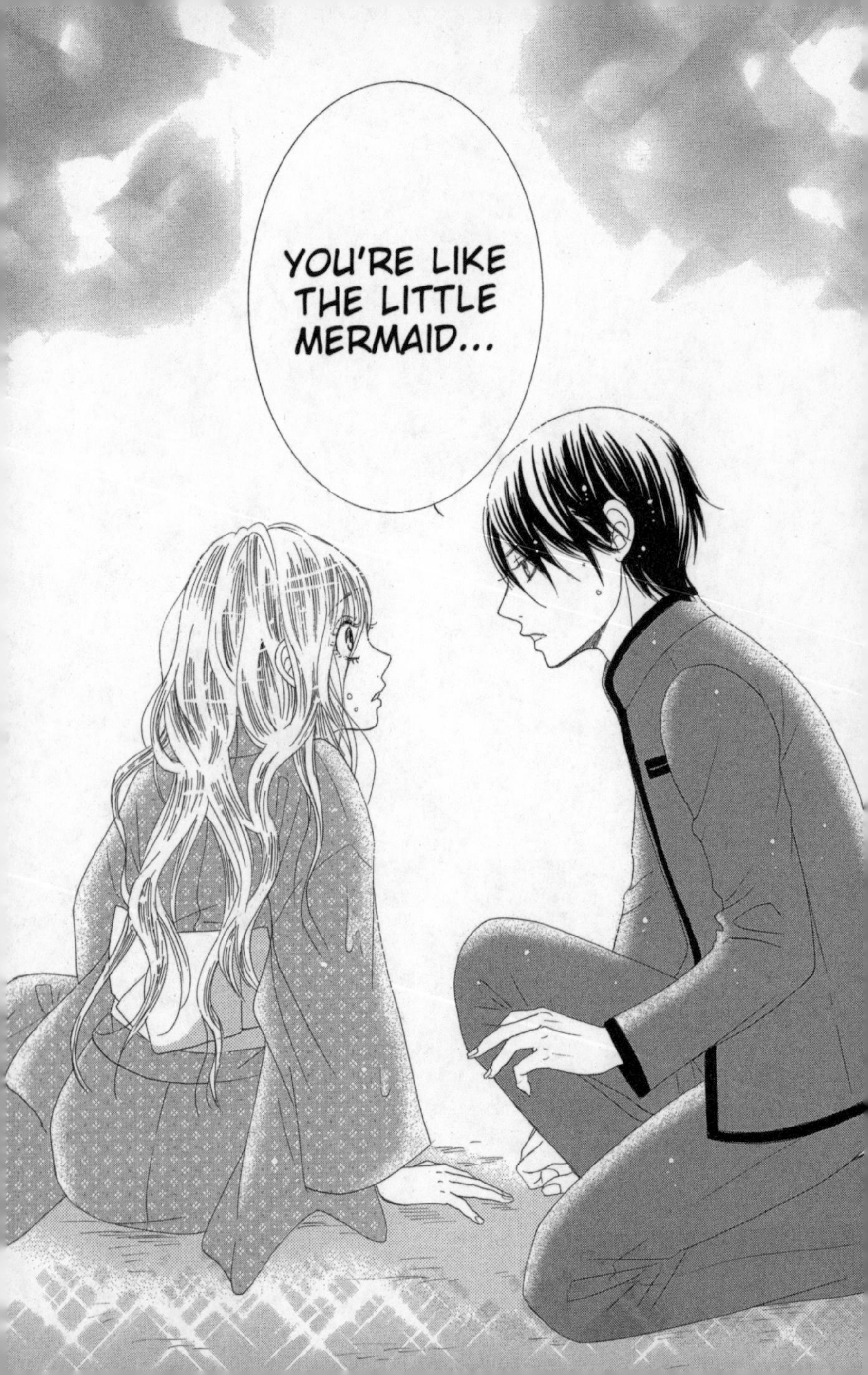
YOU'RE LIKE THE LITTLE MERMAID...

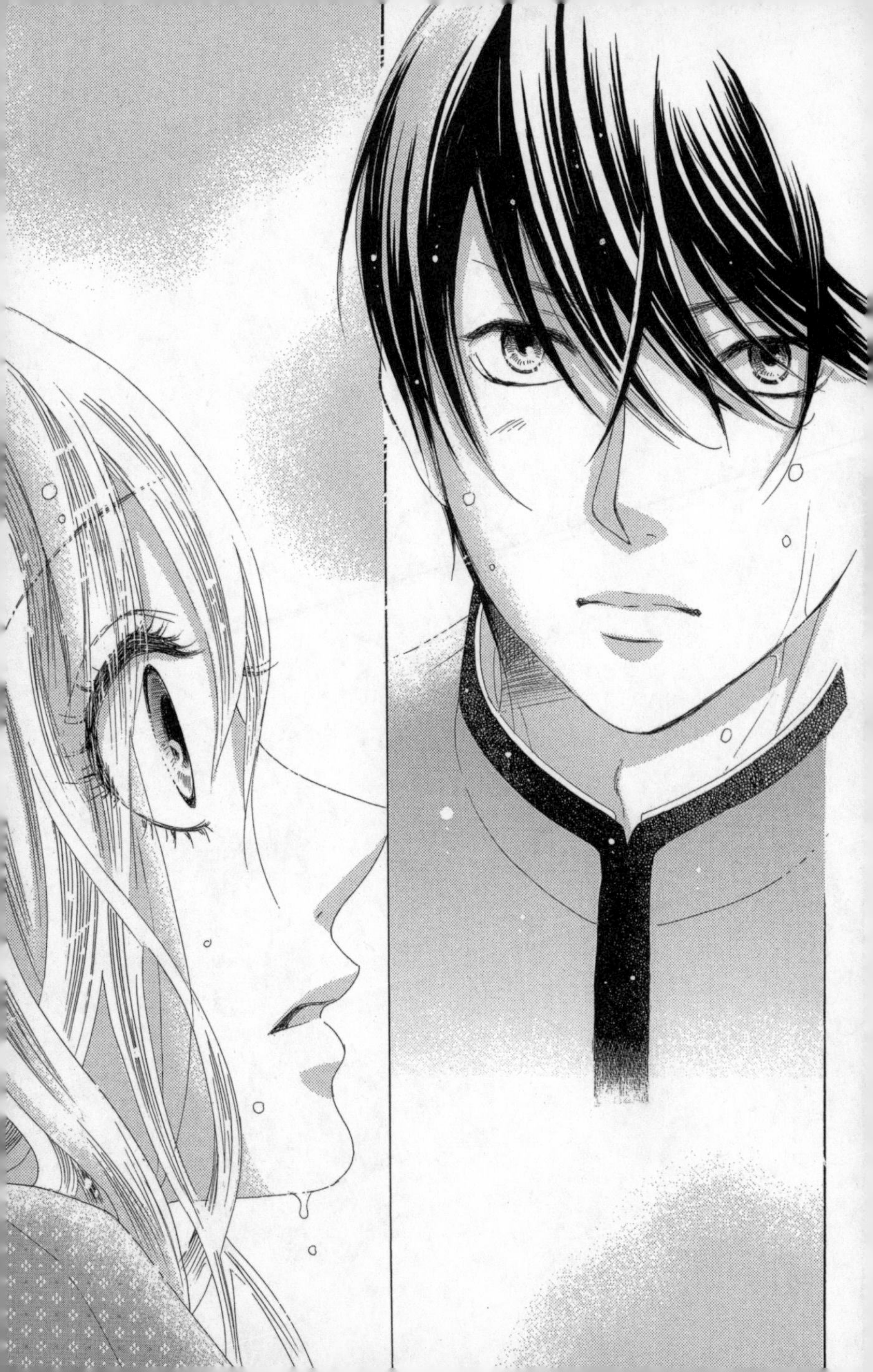

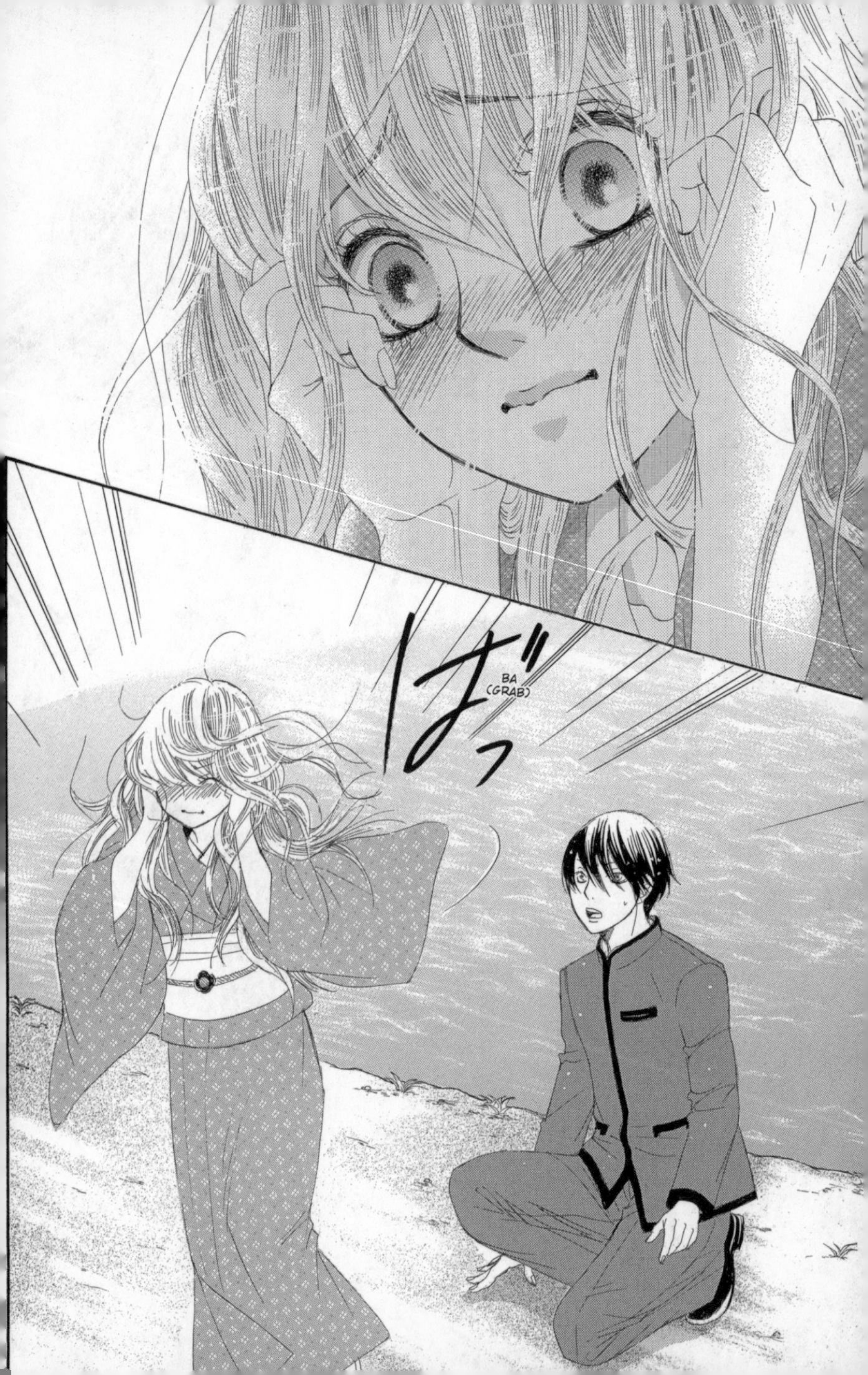
ばっ
BA
(GRAB)

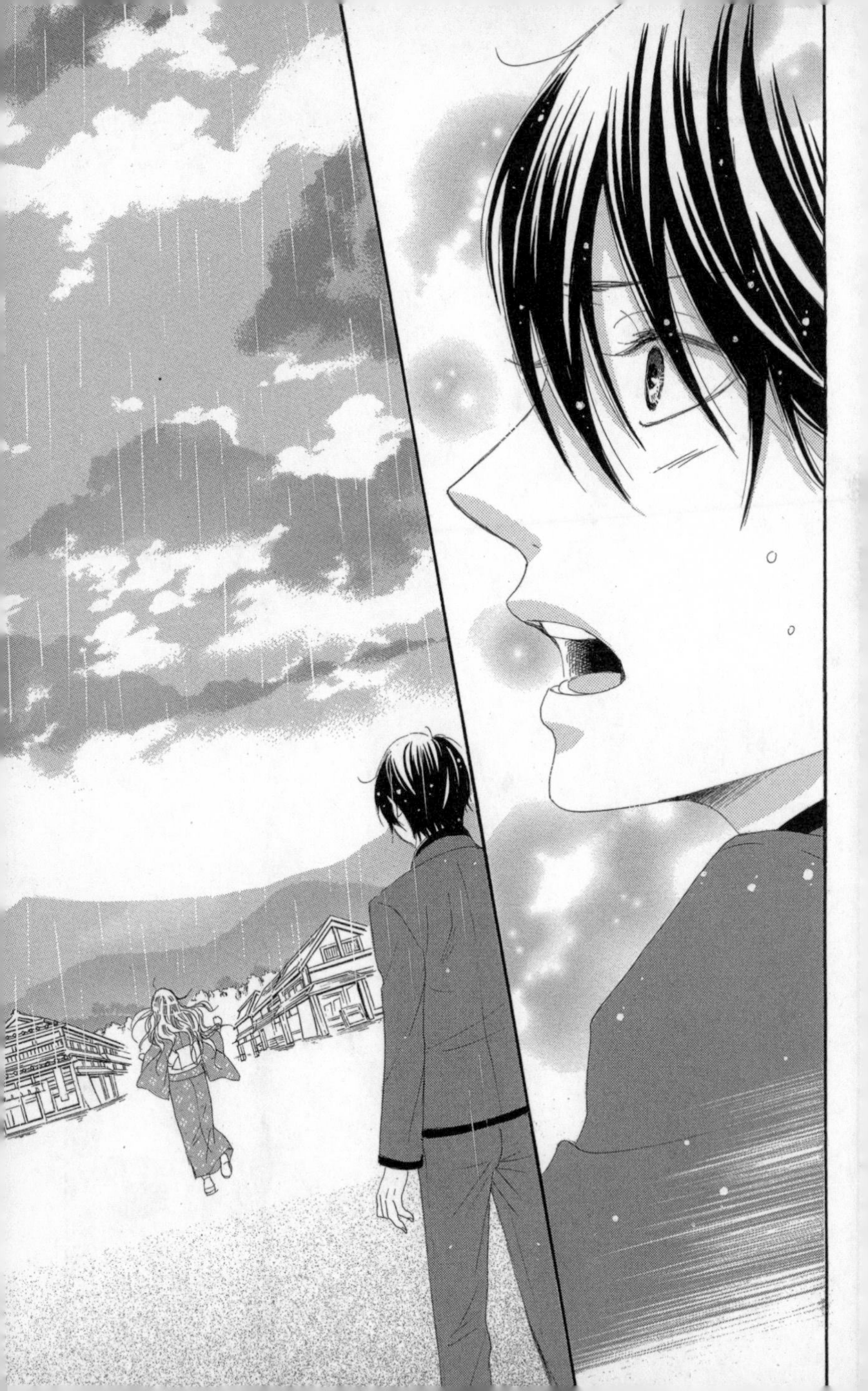

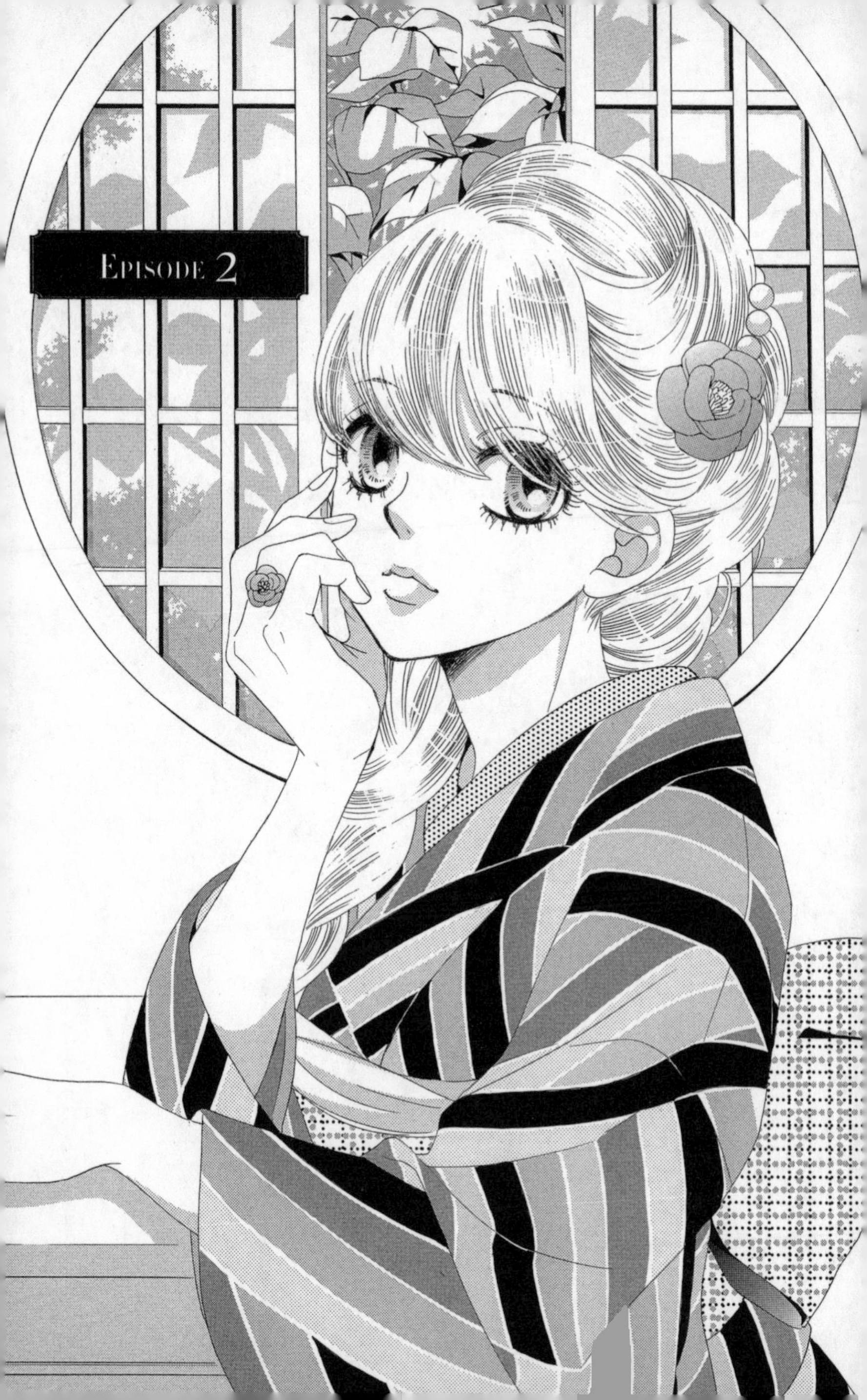
Episode 2

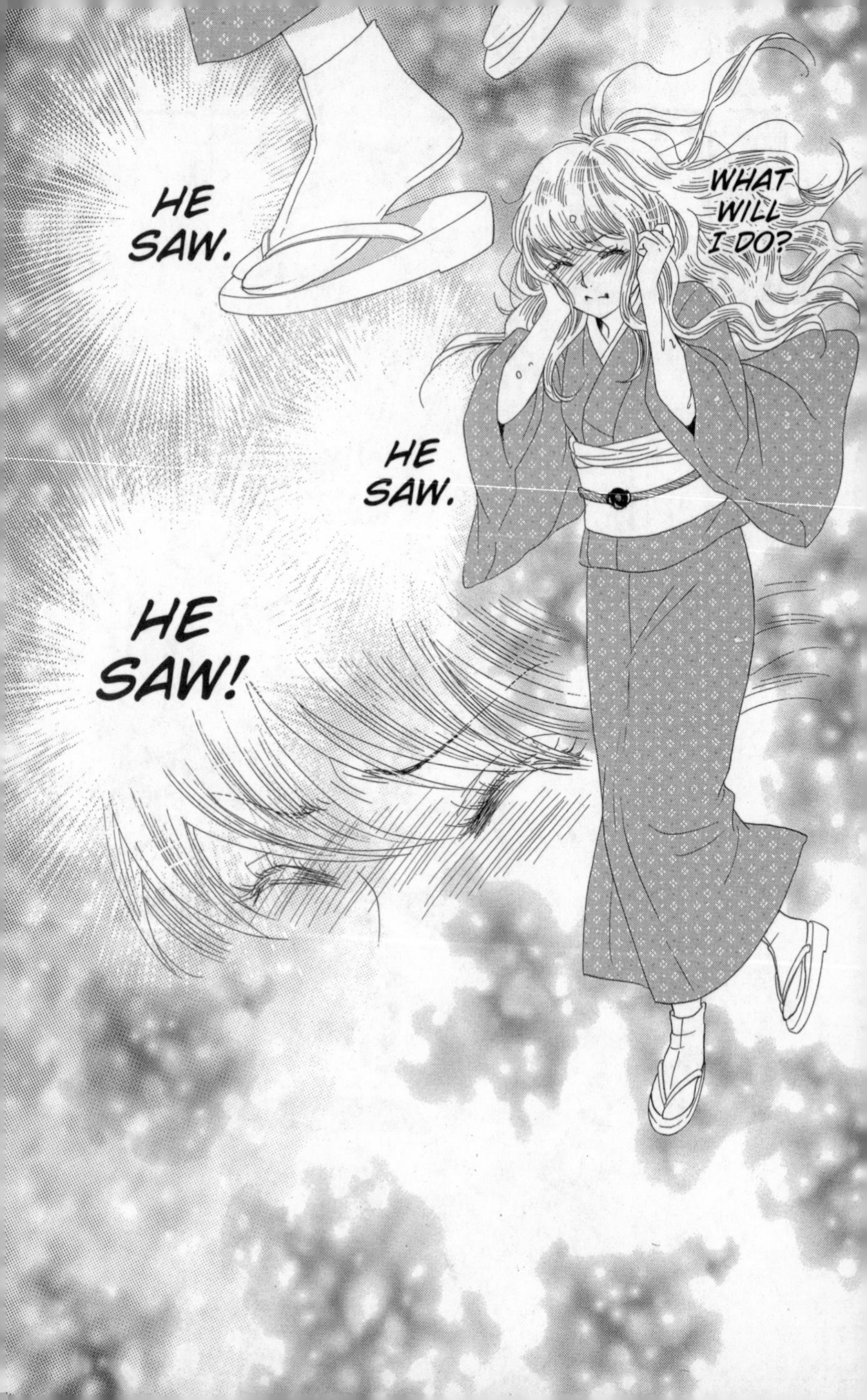
WHAT WILL I DO?
HE SAW.
HE SAW.
HE SAW!

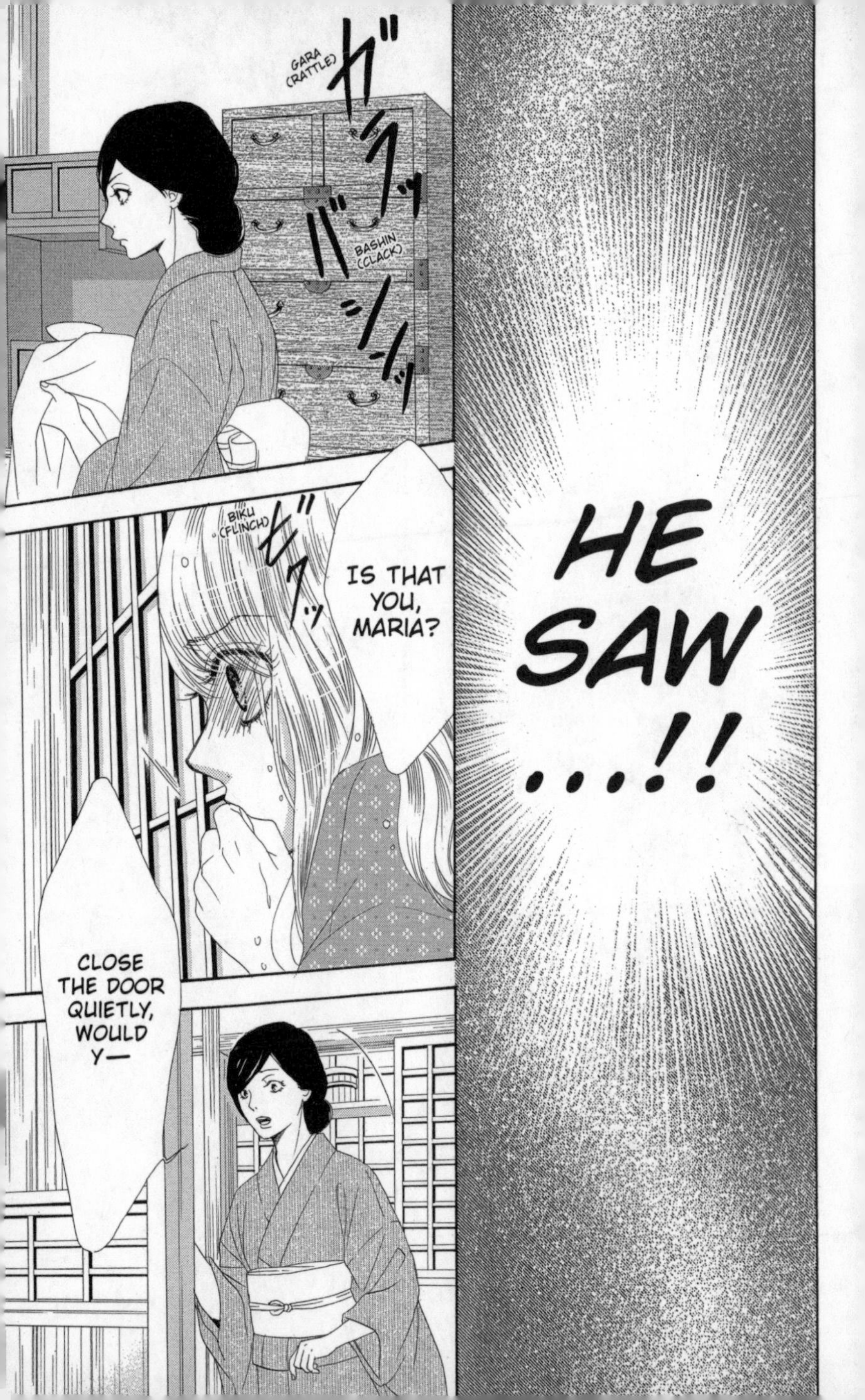
HE SAW ...!!
ガラッ
GARA (RATTLE)
バシーンッ
BASHIN (CLACK)
ビクッ
BIKU (FLINCH)
IS THAT YOU, MARIA?
CLOSE THE DOOR QUIETLY, WOULD Y—

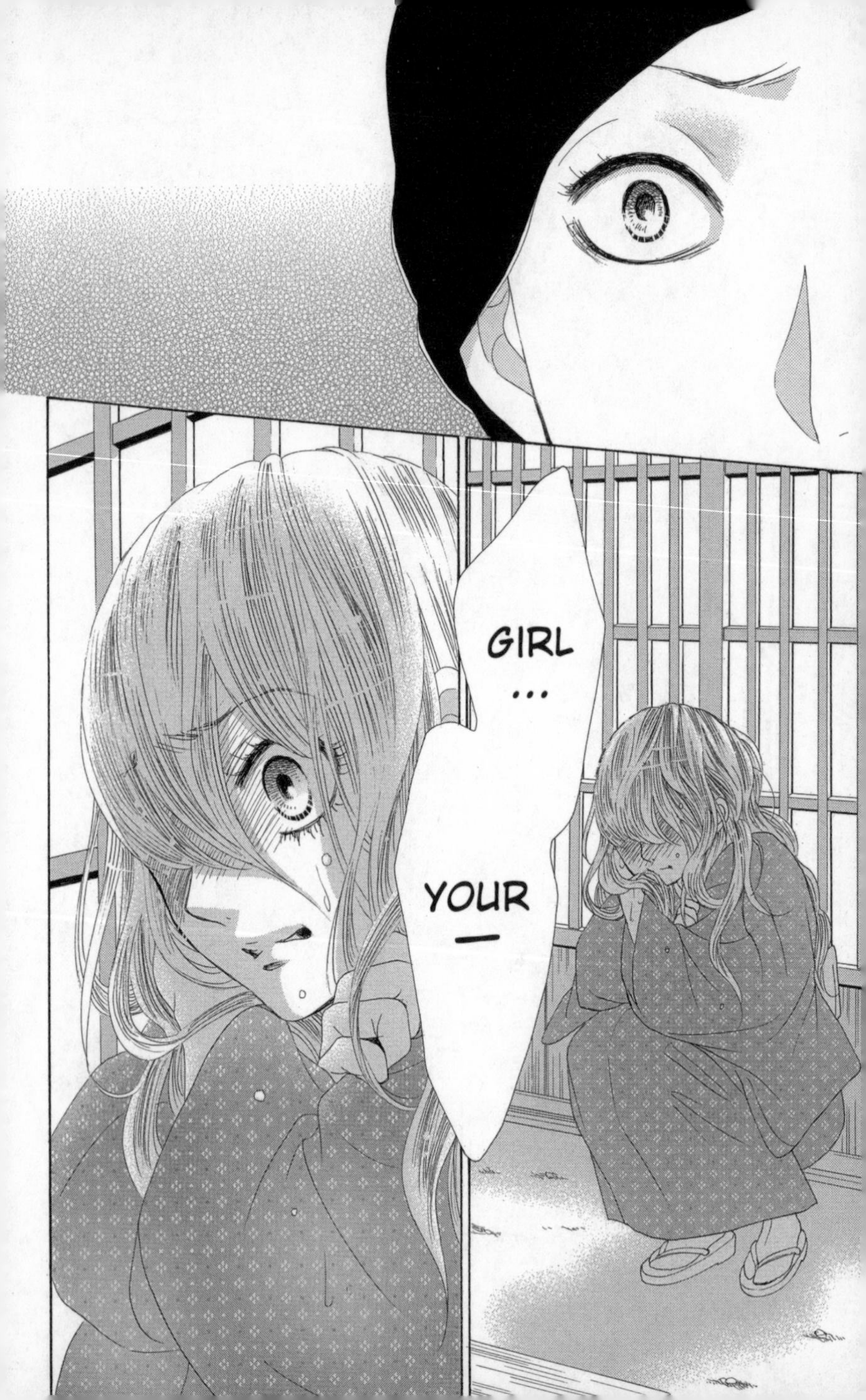
GIRL ...
YOUR —

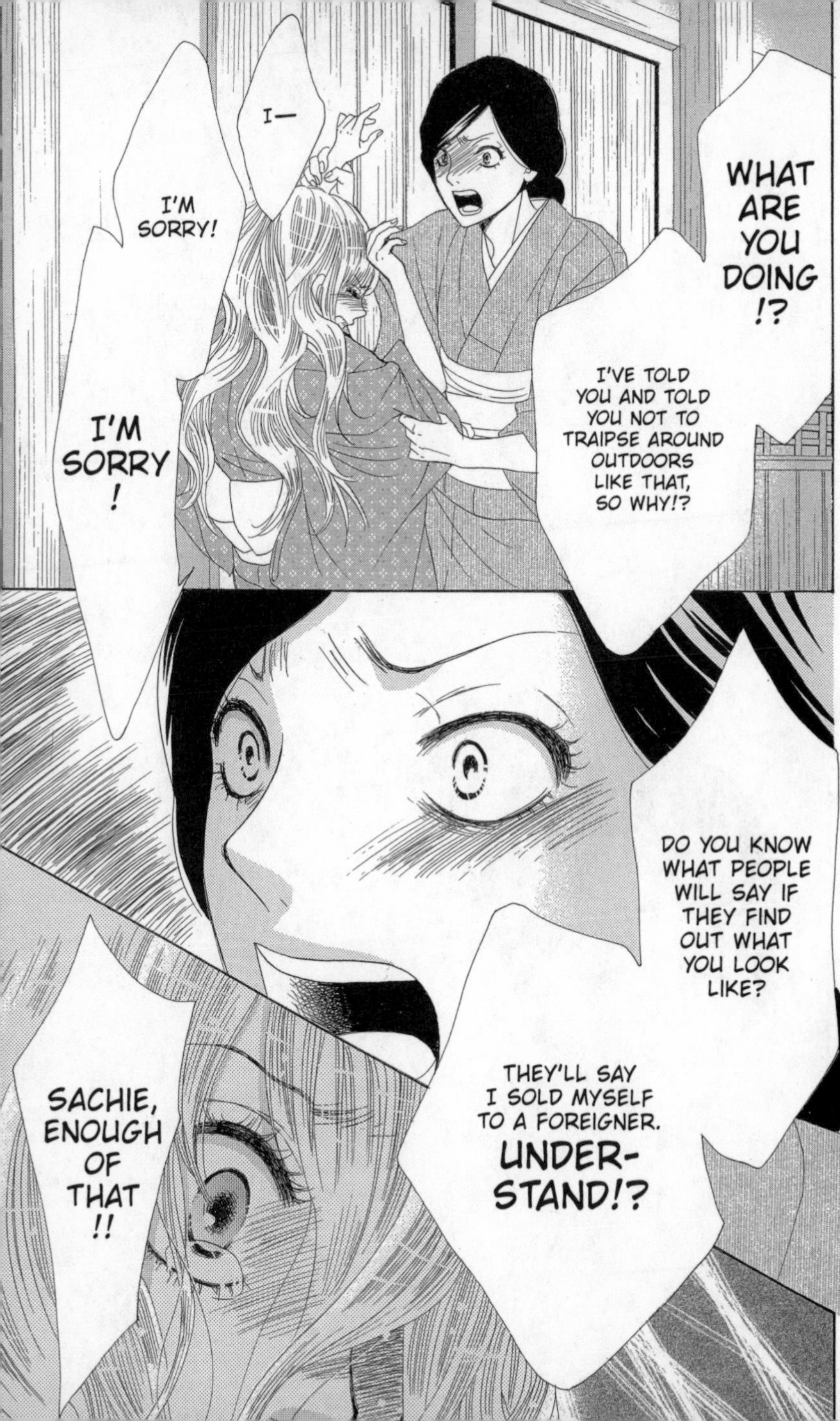
WHAT ARE YOU DOING!?
I'VE TOLD YOU AND TOLD YOU NOT TO TRAIPSE AROUND OUTDOORS LIKE THAT, SO WHY!?
I—
I'M SORRY!
I'M SORRY!
DO YOU KNOW WHAT PEOPLE WILL SAY IF THEY FIND OUT WHAT YOU LOOK LIKE?
THEY'LL SAY I SOLD MYSELF TO A FOREIGNER. UNDER-STAND!?
SACHIE, ENOUGH OF THAT!!

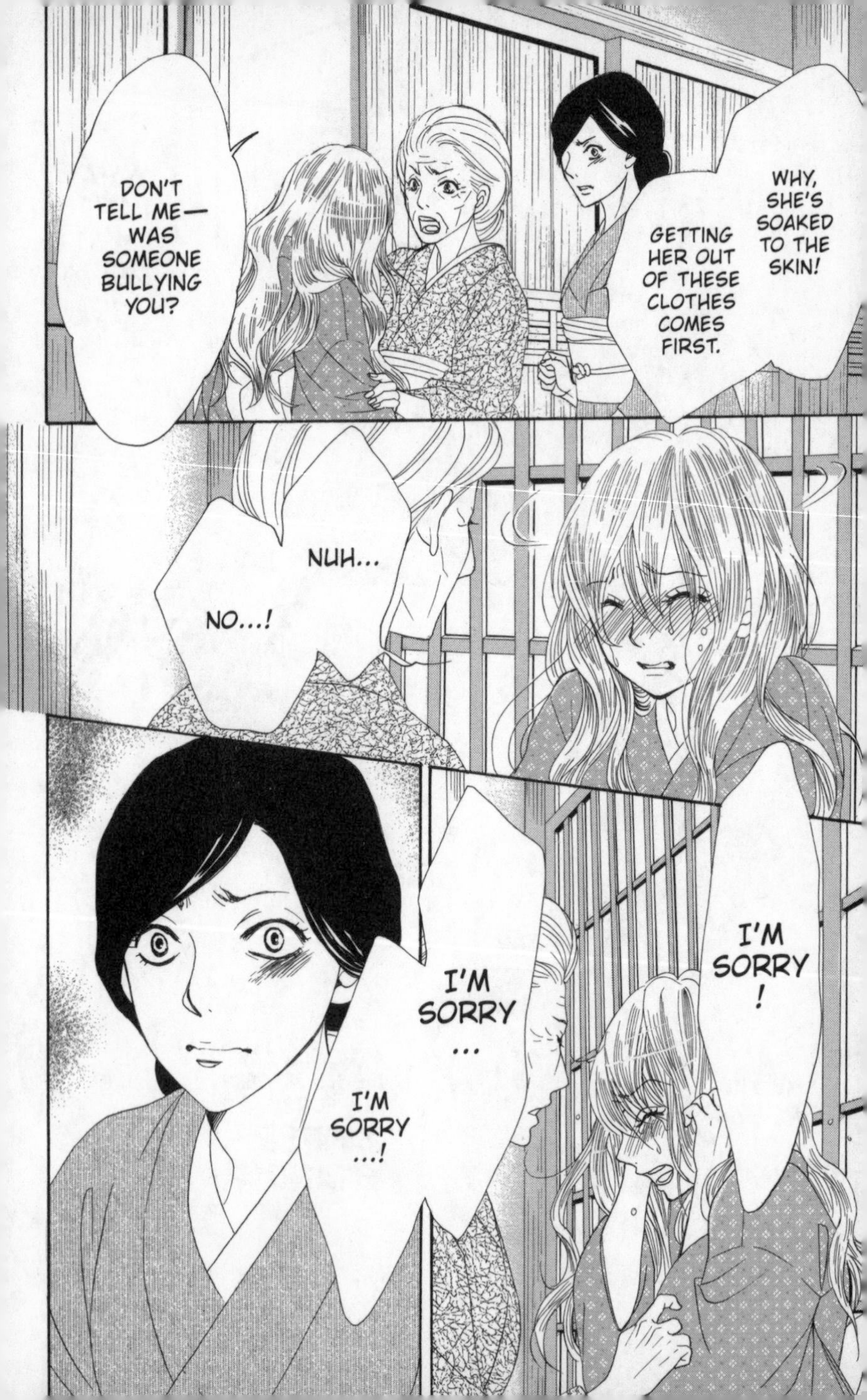
WHY, SHE'S SOAKED TO THE SKIN!
GETTING HER OUT OF THESE CLOTHES COMES FIRST.
DON'T TELL ME—WAS SOMEONE BULLYING YOU?
NUH...
NO...!
I'M SORRY!
I'M SORRY...
I'M SORRY...!

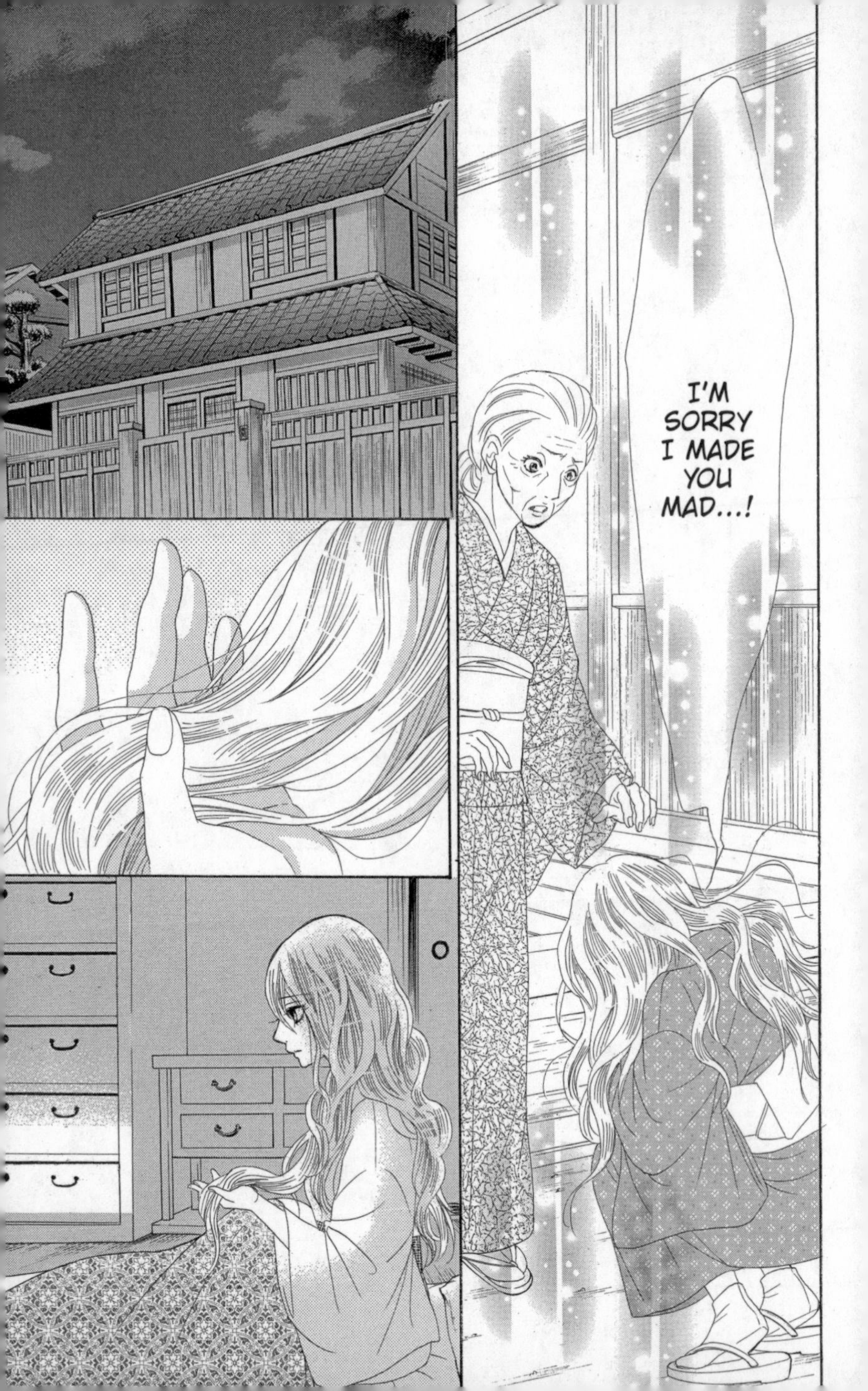
I'M SORRY I MADE YOU MAD...!

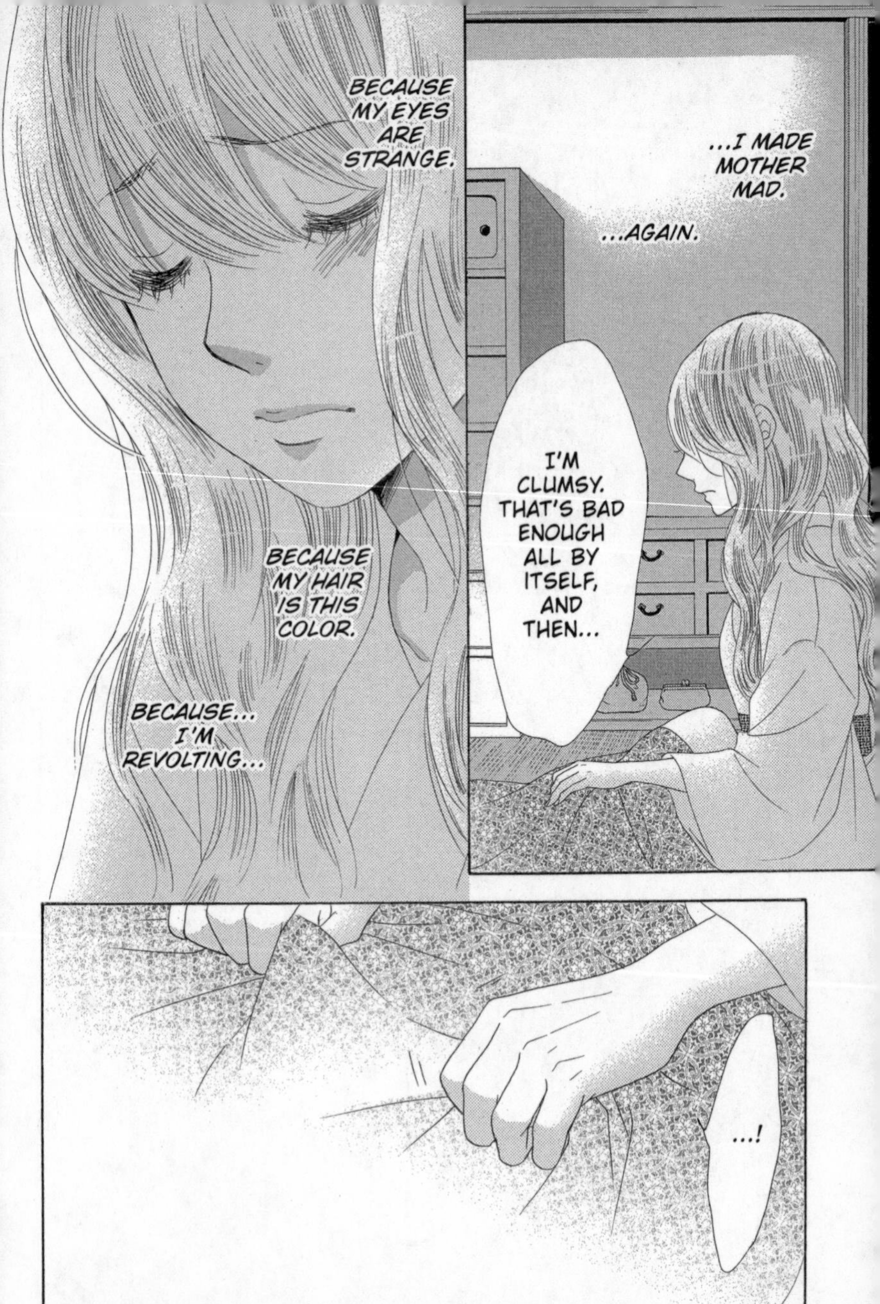
...I MADE MOTHER MAD.
...AGAIN.
I'M CLUMSY. THAT'S BAD ENOUGH ALL BY ITSELF, AND THEN...
BECAUSE MY EYES ARE STRANGE.
BECAUSE MY HAIR IS THIS COLOR.
BECAUSE... I'M REVOLTING...
...!

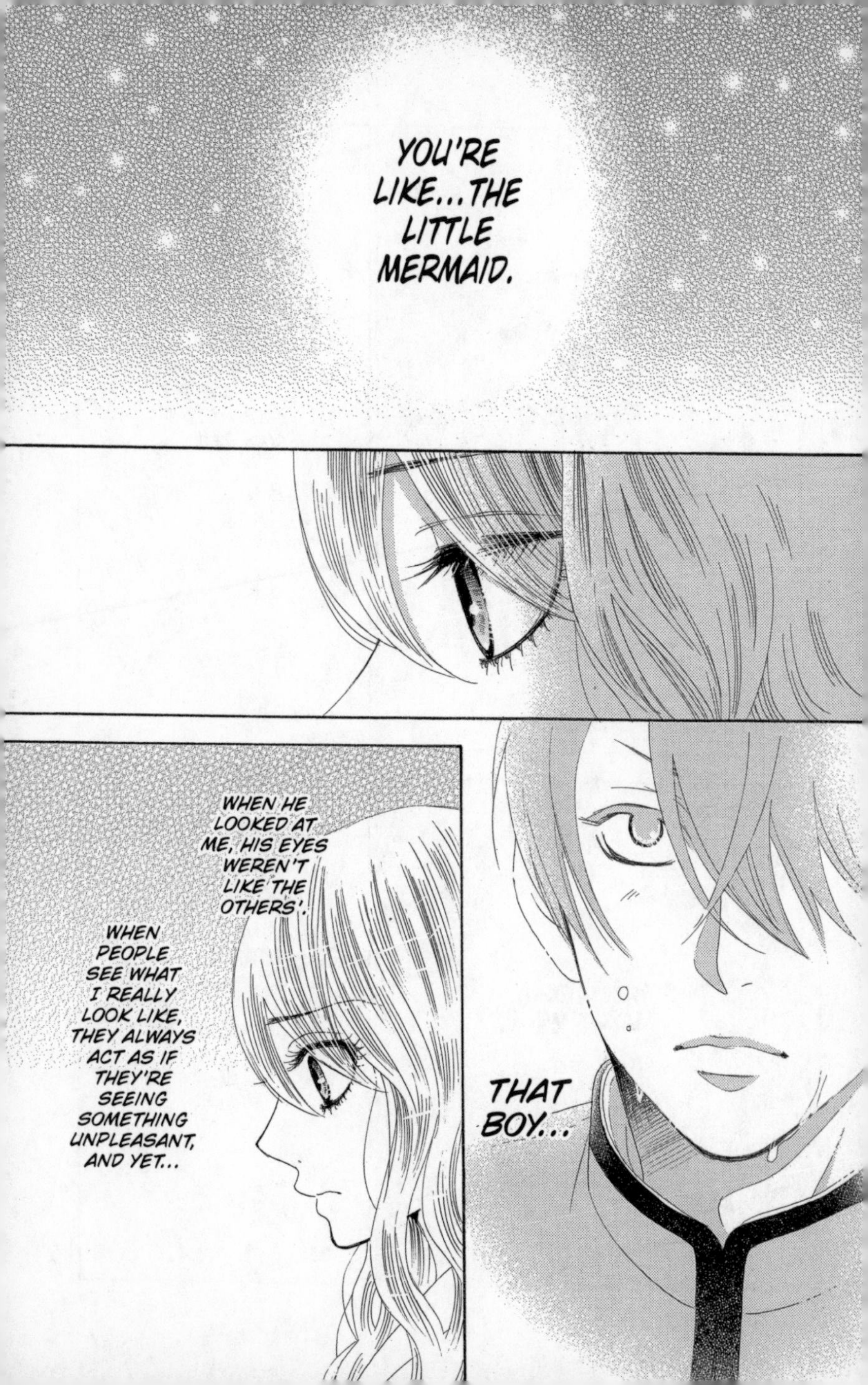
YOU'RE LIKE...THE LITTLE MERMAID.
THAT BOY...
WHEN HE LOOKED AT ME, HIS EYES WEREN'T LIKE THE OTHERS'.
WHEN PEOPLE SEE WHAT I REALLY LOOK LIKE, THEY ALWAYS ACT AS IF THEY'RE SEEING SOMETHING UNPLEASANT, AND YET...

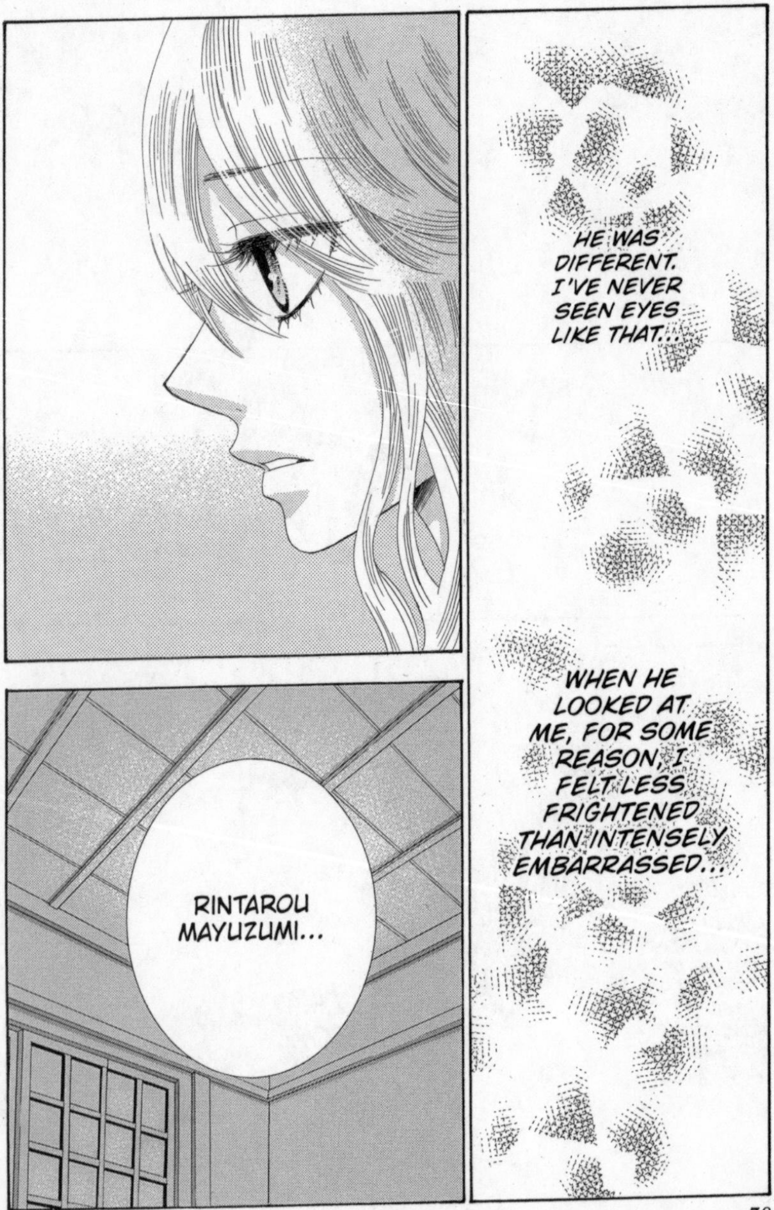
HE WAS DIFFERENT. I'VE NEVER SEEN EYES LIKE THAT...
WHEN HE LOOKED AT ME, FOR SOME REASON, I FELT LESS FRIGHTENED THAN INTENSELY EMBARRASSED...
RINTAROU MAYUZUMI...

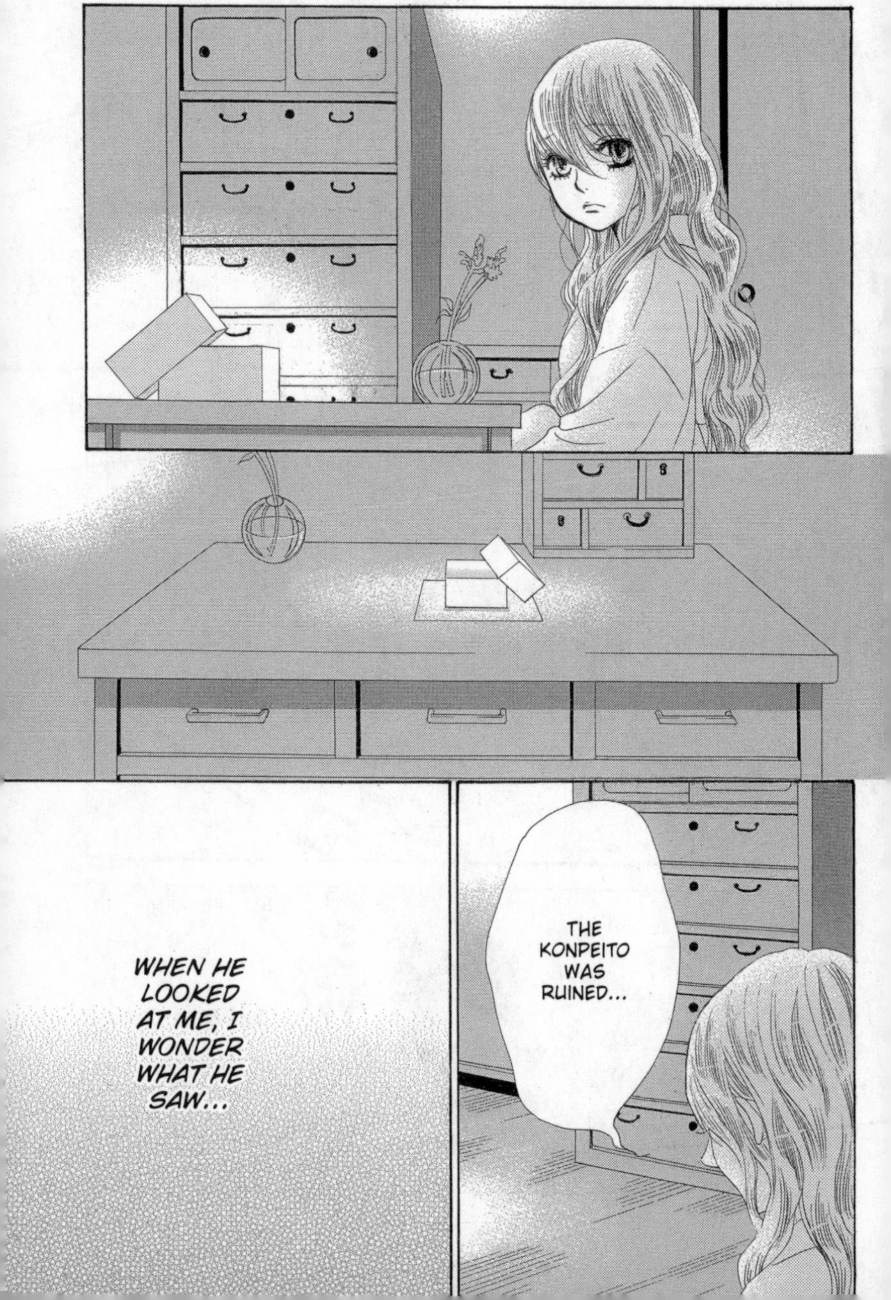
THE KONPEITO WAS RUINED...
WHEN HE LOOKED AT ME, I WONDER WHAT HE SAW...

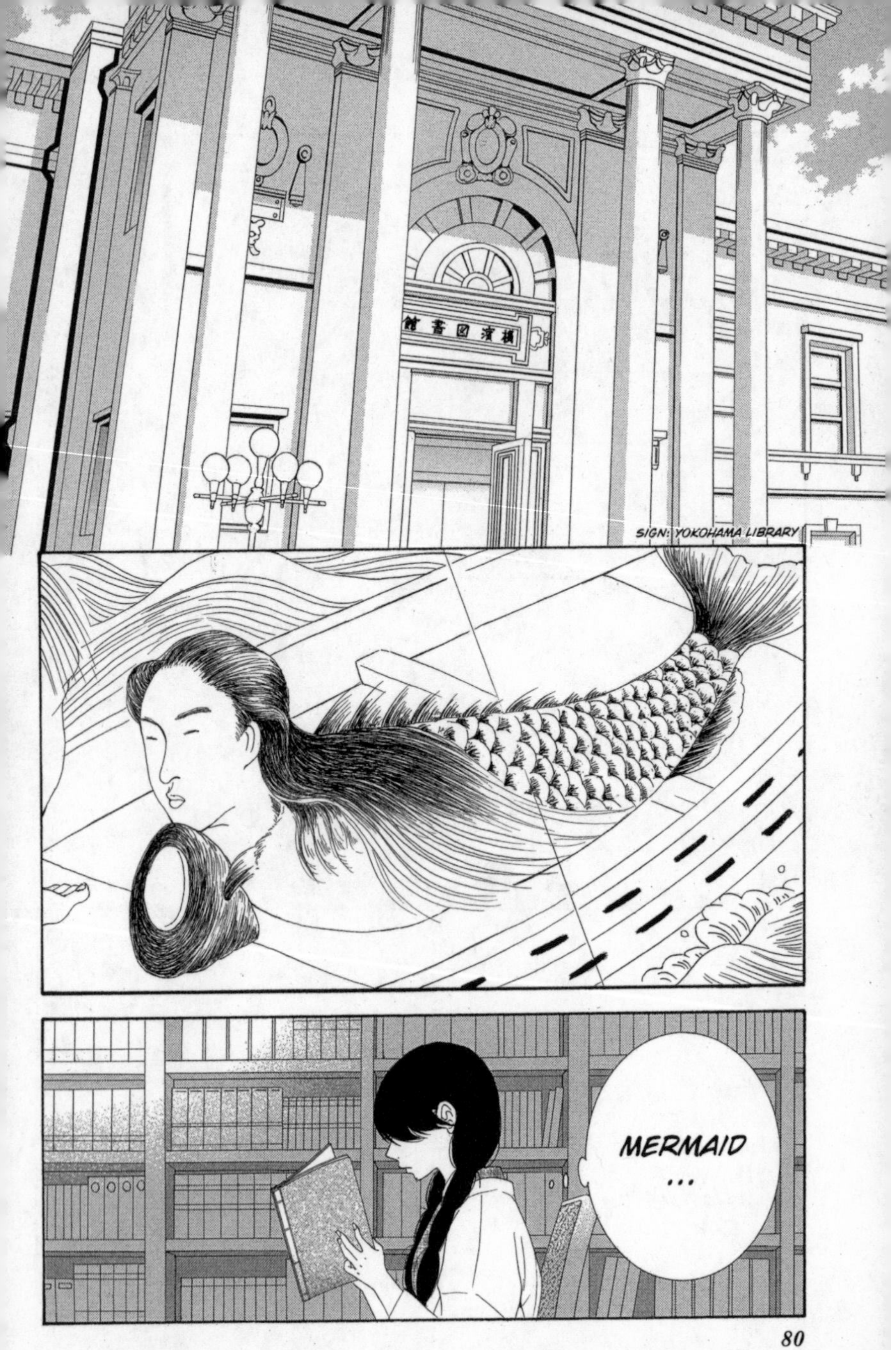
館書図濱横
SIGN: YOKOHAMA LIBRARY
MERMAID ...

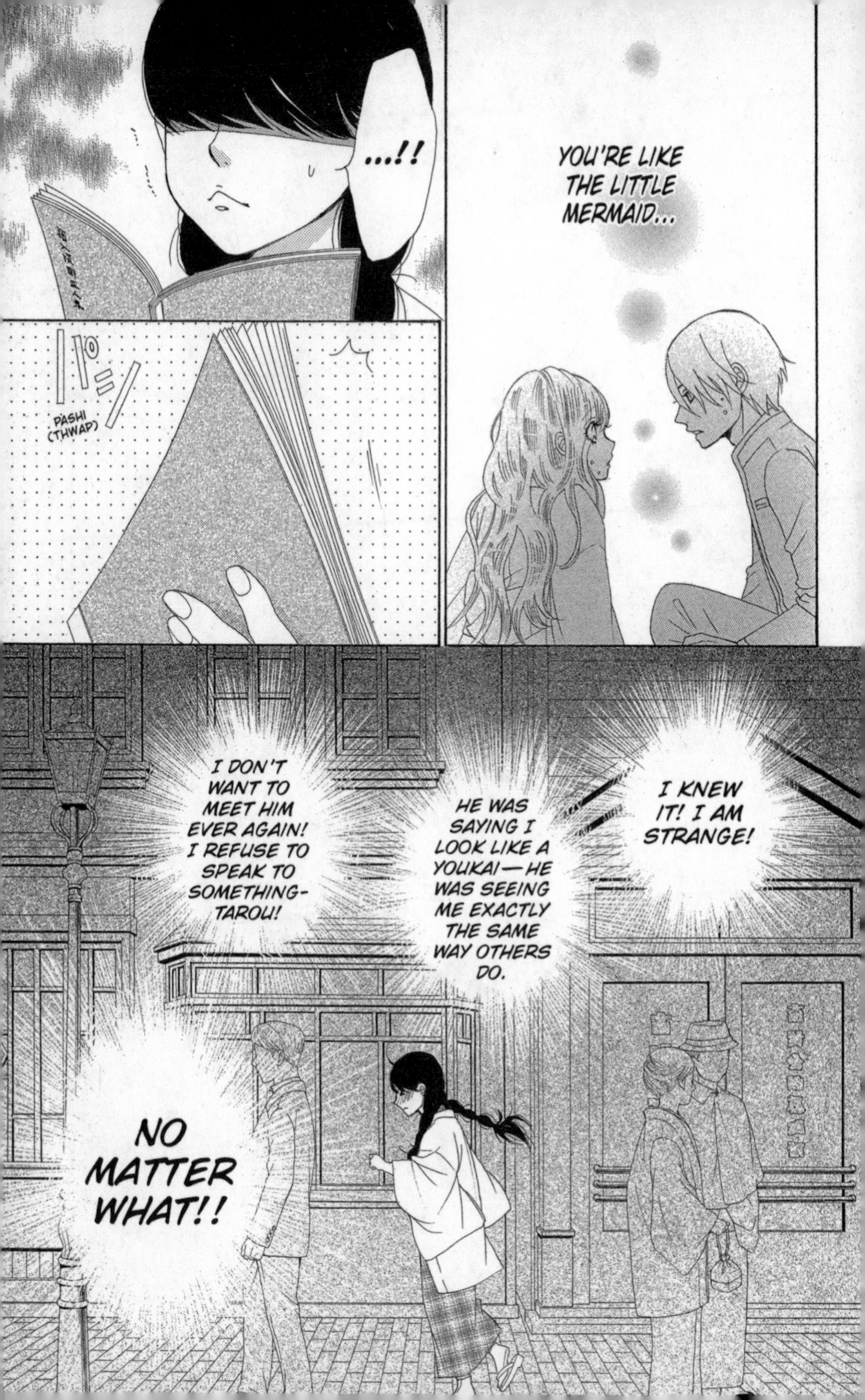
YOU'RE LIKE THE LITTLE MERMAID...
...!!
PASHI (THWAP)
I KNEW IT! I AM STRANGE!
HE WAS SAYING I LOOK LIKE A YOUKAI—HE WAS SEEING ME EXACTLY THE SAME WAY OTHERS DO.
I DON'T WANT TO MEET HIM EVER AGAIN! I REFUSE TO SPEAK TO SOMETHING-TAROU!
NO MATTER WHAT!!

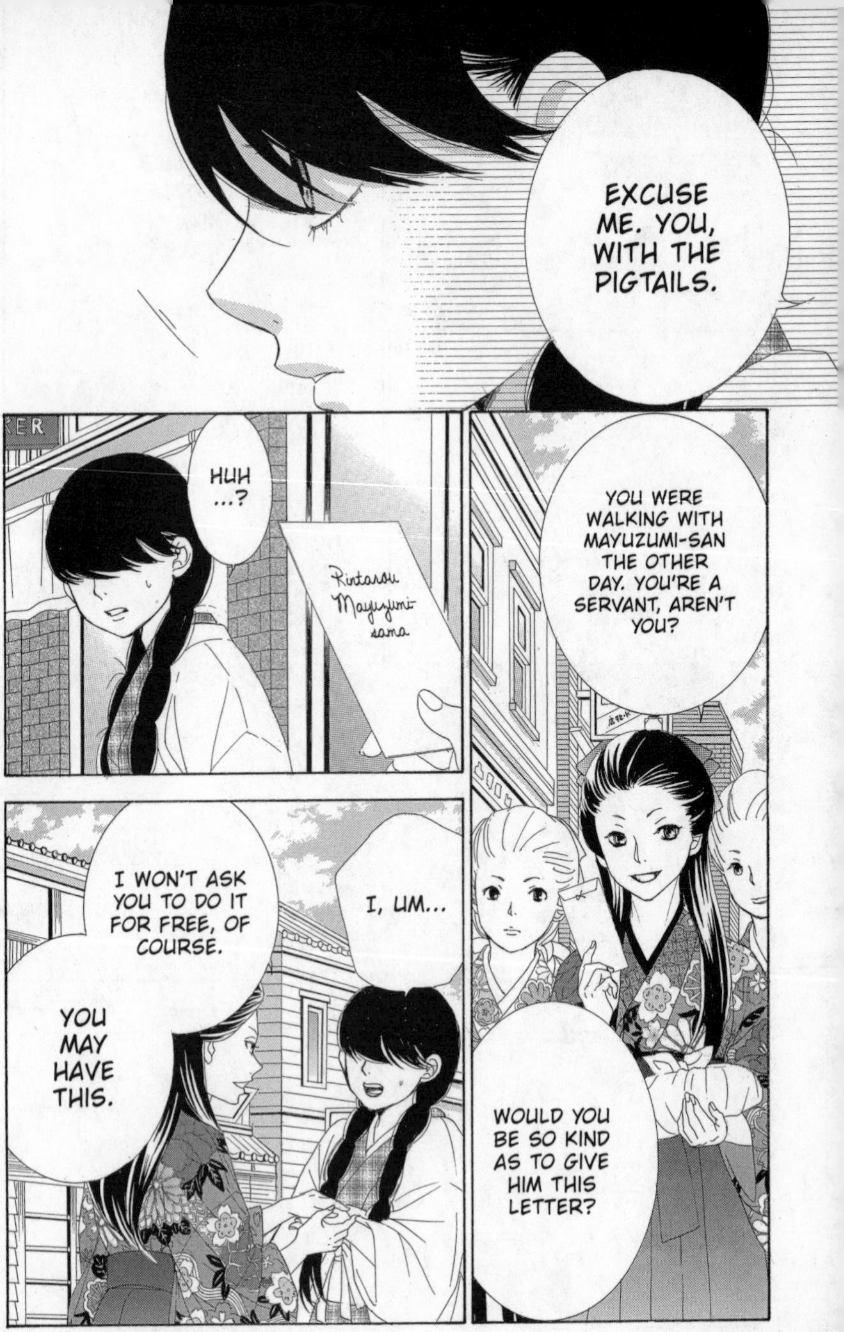
EXCUSE ME. YOU, WITH THE PIGTAILS.
YOU WERE WALKING WITH MAYUZUMI-SAN THE OTHER DAY. YOU'RE A SERVANT, AREN'T YOU?
WOULD YOU BE SO KIND AS TO GIVE HIM THIS LETTER?
HUH ...?
Rintarou Mayuzumi-sama
I, UM...
I WON'T ASK YOU TO DO IT FOR FREE, OF COURSE.
YOU MAY HAVE THIS.

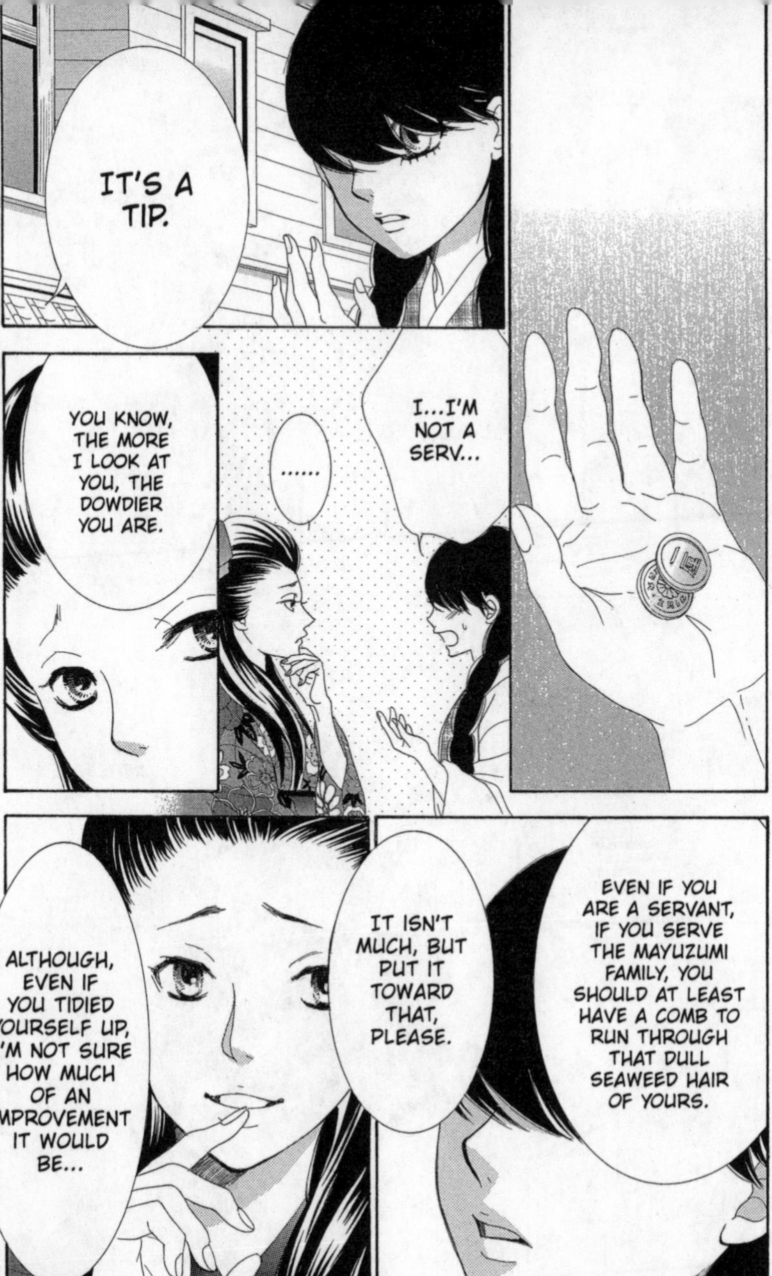
IT'S A TIP.
I...I'M NOT A SERV...
......
YOU KNOW, THE MORE I LOOK AT YOU, THE DOWDIER YOU ARE.
EVEN IF YOU ARE A SERVANT, IF YOU SERVE THE MAYUZUMI FAMILY, YOU SHOULD AT LEAST HAVE A COMB TO RUN THROUGH THAT DULL SEAWEED HAIR OF YOURS.
IT ISN'T MUCH, BUT PUT IT TOWARD THAT, PLEASE.
ALTHOUGH, EVEN IF YOU TIDIED YOURSELF UP, I'M NOT SURE HOW MUCH OF AN IMPROVEMENT IT WOULD BE...

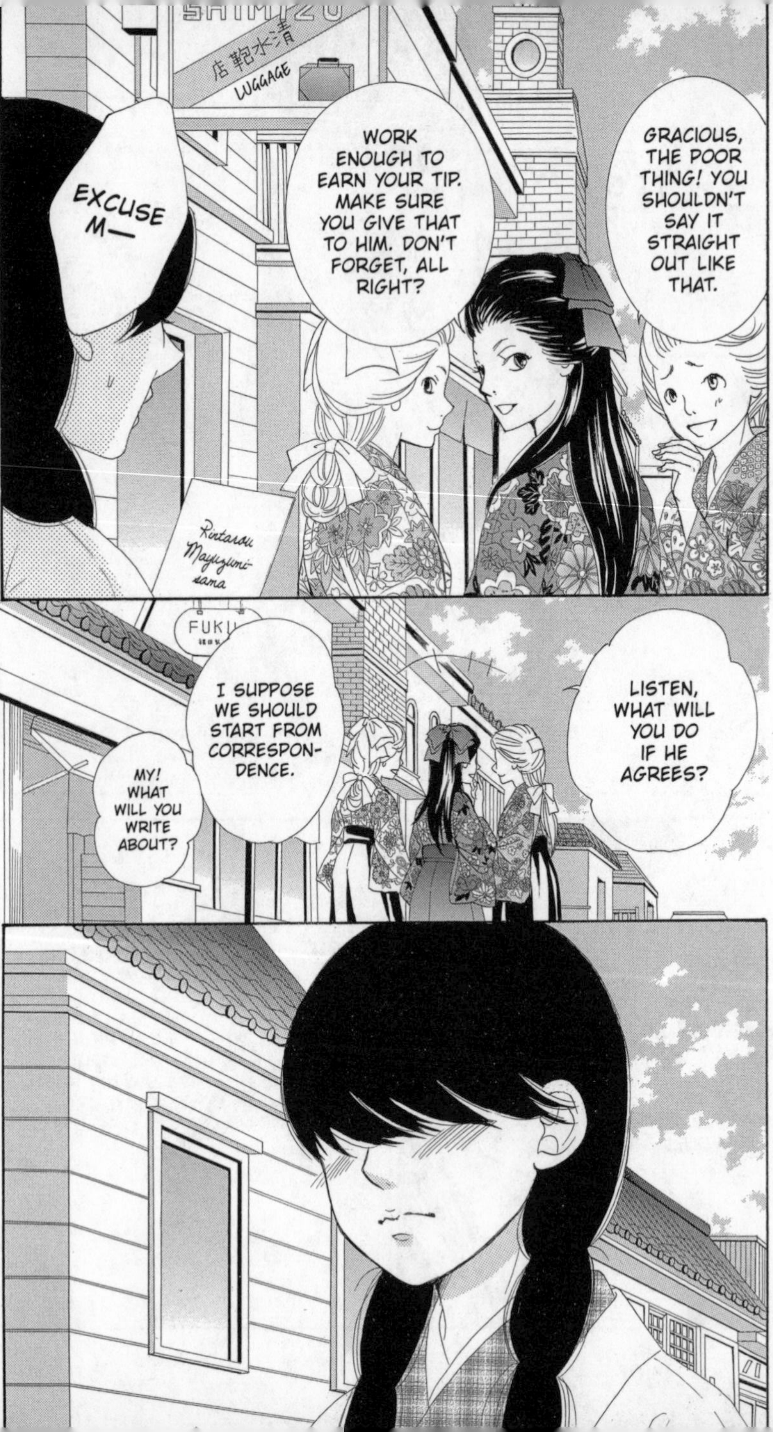
SHIMIZU
店鞄水清
LUGGAGE
GRACIOUS, THE POOR THING! YOU SHOULDN'T SAY IT STRAIGHT OUT LIKE THAT.
WORK ENOUGH TO EARN YOUR TIP. MAKE SURE YOU GIVE THAT TO HIM. DON'T FORGET, ALL RIGHT?
EXCUSE M—
Rintarou Mayuzumi-sama
LISTEN, WHAT WILL YOU DO IF HE AGREES?
I SUPPOSE WE SHOULD START FROM CORRESPONDENCE.
MY! WHAT WILL YOU WRITE ABOUT?

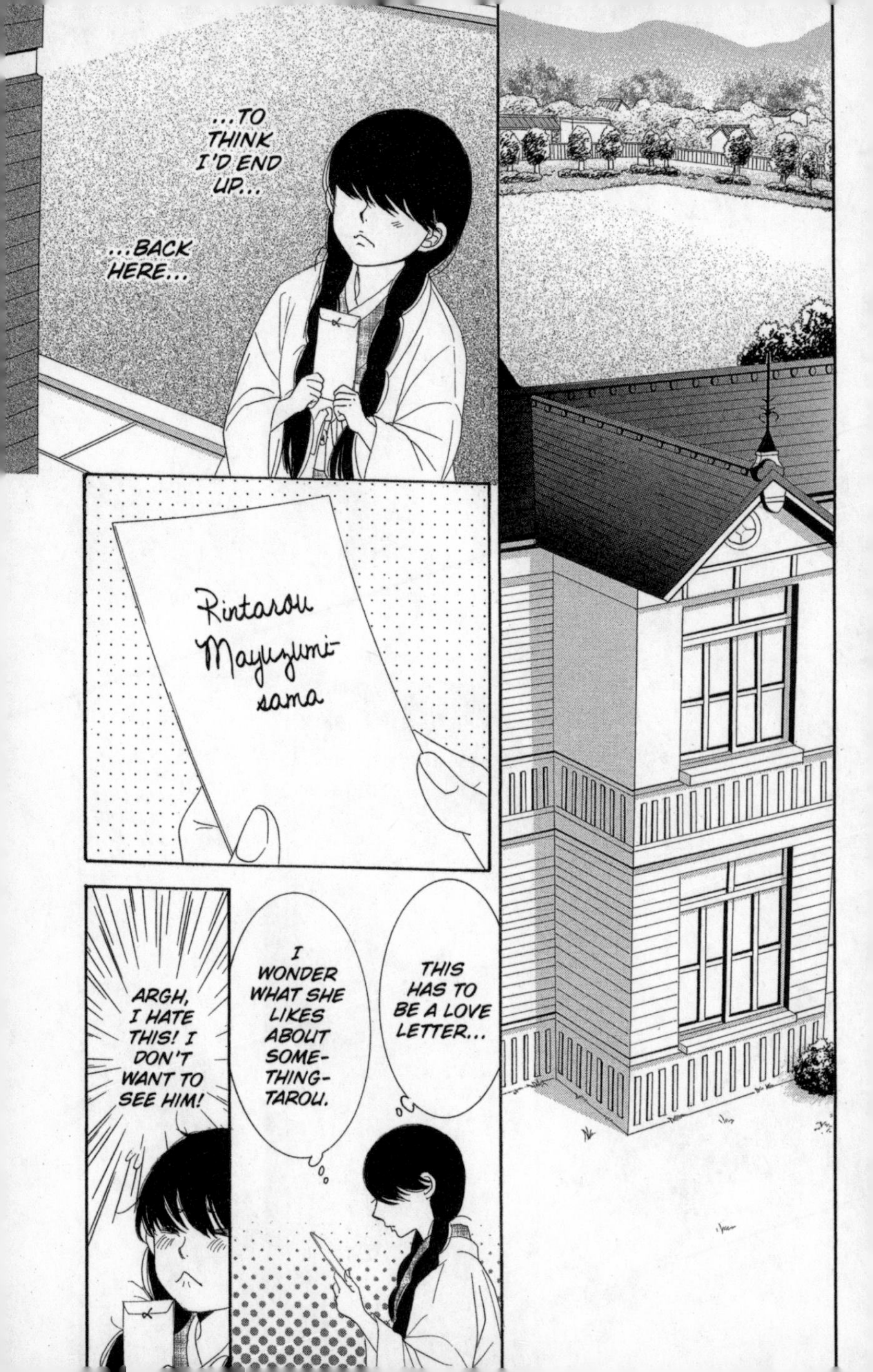
...TO THINK I'D END UP...
...BACK HERE...
Rintarou Mayuzumi-sama
THIS HAS TO BE A LOVE LETTER...
I WONDER WHAT SHE LIKES ABOUT SOME-THING-TAROU.
ARGH, I HATE THIS! I DON'T WANT TO SEE HIM!

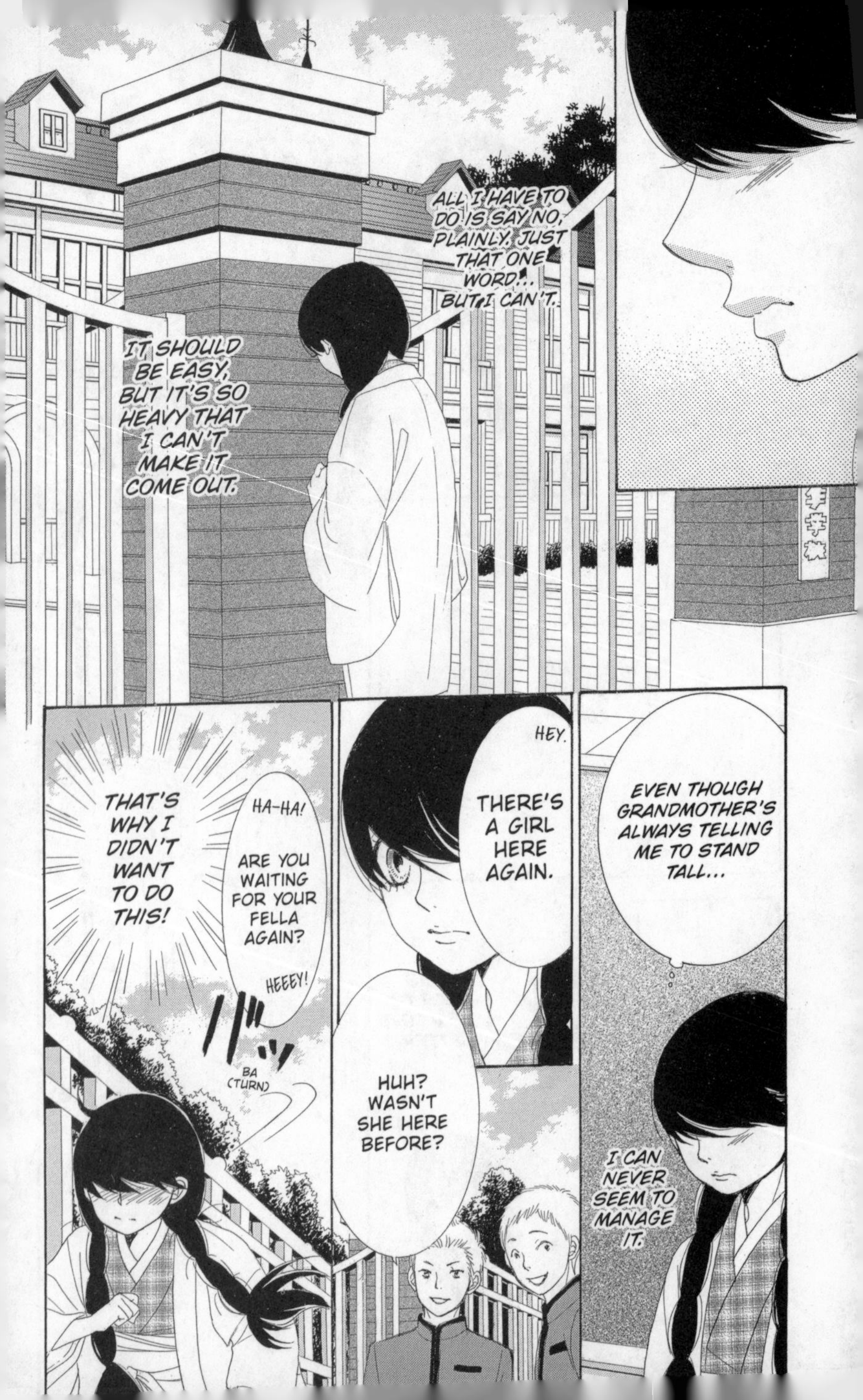
ALL I HAVE TO DO IS SAY NO, PLAINLY. JUST THAT ONE WORD... BUT I CAN'T.
IT SHOULD BE EASY, BUT IT'S SO HEAVY THAT I CAN'T MAKE IT COME OUT.
EVEN THOUGH GRANDMOTHER'S ALWAYS TELLING ME TO STAND TALL...
I CAN NEVER SEEM TO MANAGE IT.
HEY.
THERE'S A GIRL HERE AGAIN.
HUH? WASN'T SHE HERE BEFORE?
HA-HA!
ARE YOU WAITING FOR YOUR FELLA AGAIN?
HEEEY!
THAT'S WHY I DIDN'T WANT TO DO THIS!
BA (TURN)

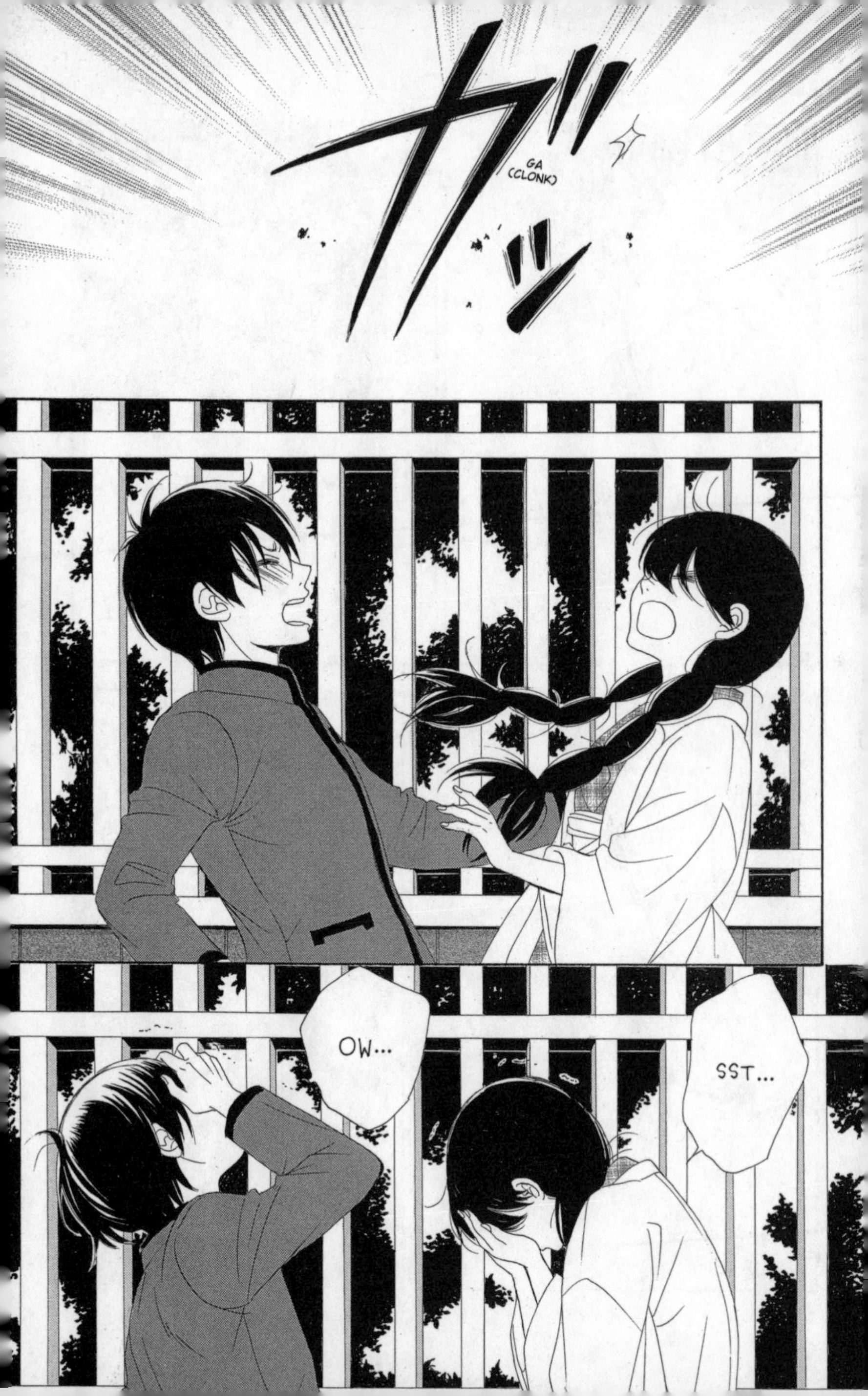
ガッ
GA (CLONK)
SST...
OW...

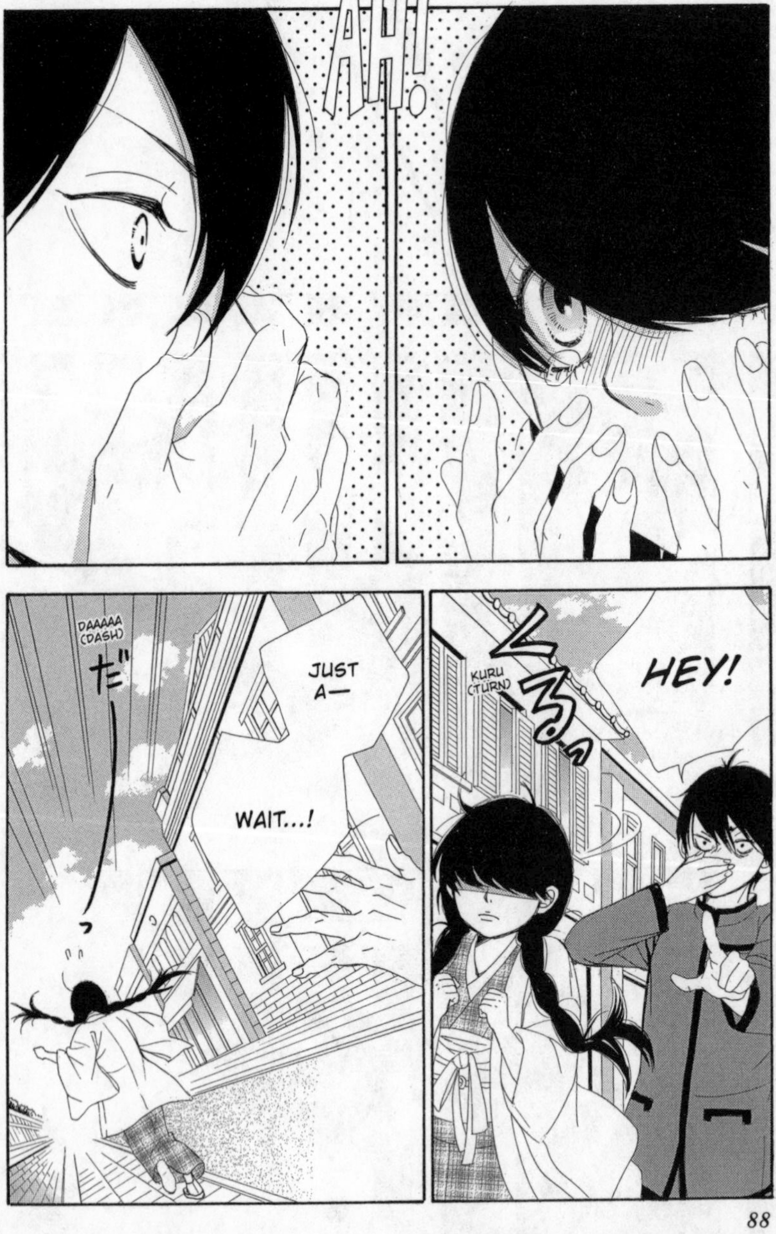
AH!
HEY!
KURU (TURN)
くる
JUST A—
WAIT...!
DAAAAA (DASH)
だー

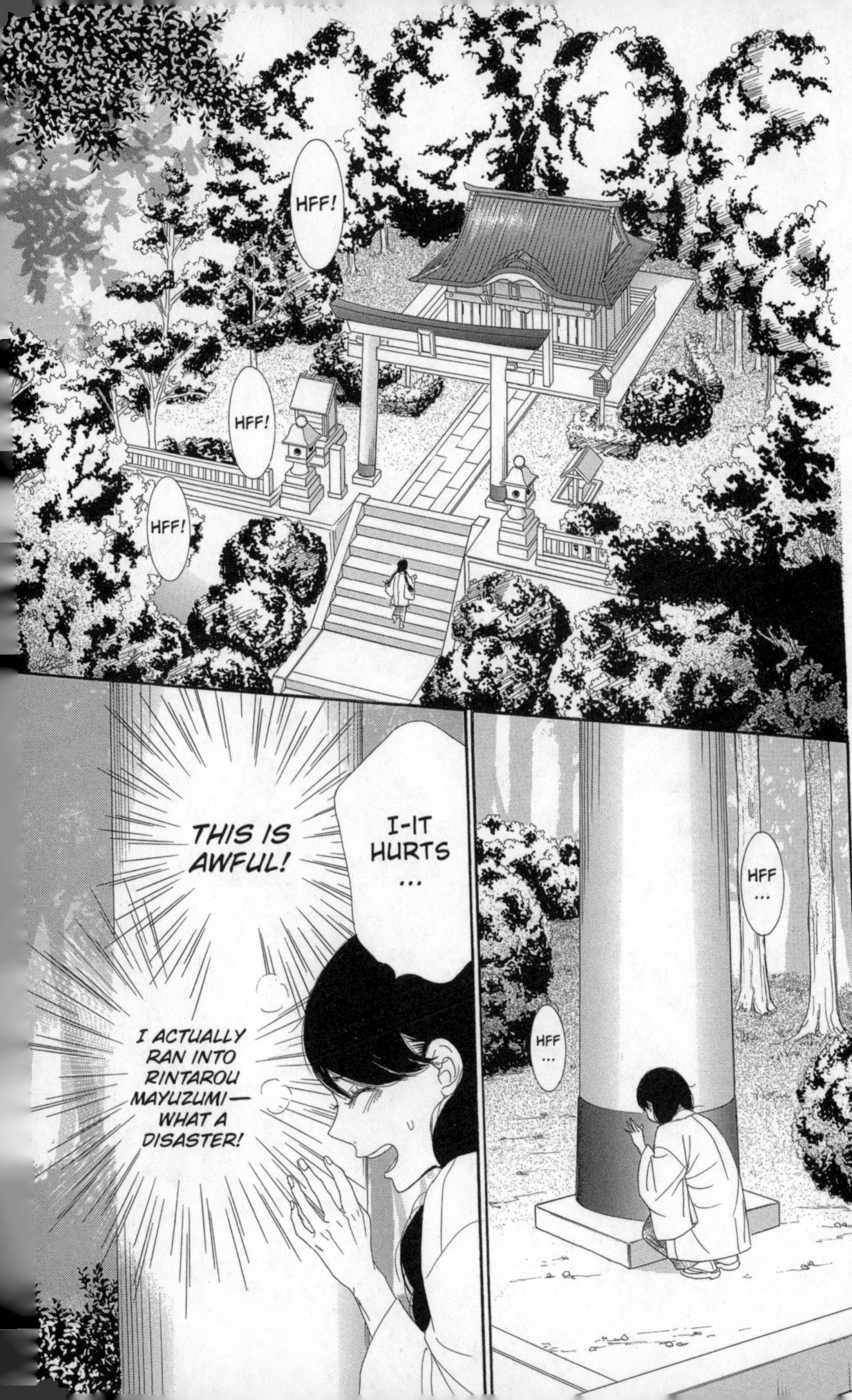
HFF!
HFF!
HFF!
HFF ...
HFF ...
I-IT HURTS ...
THIS IS AWFUL!
I ACTUALLY RAN INTO RINTAROU MAYUZUMI—WHAT A DISASTER!

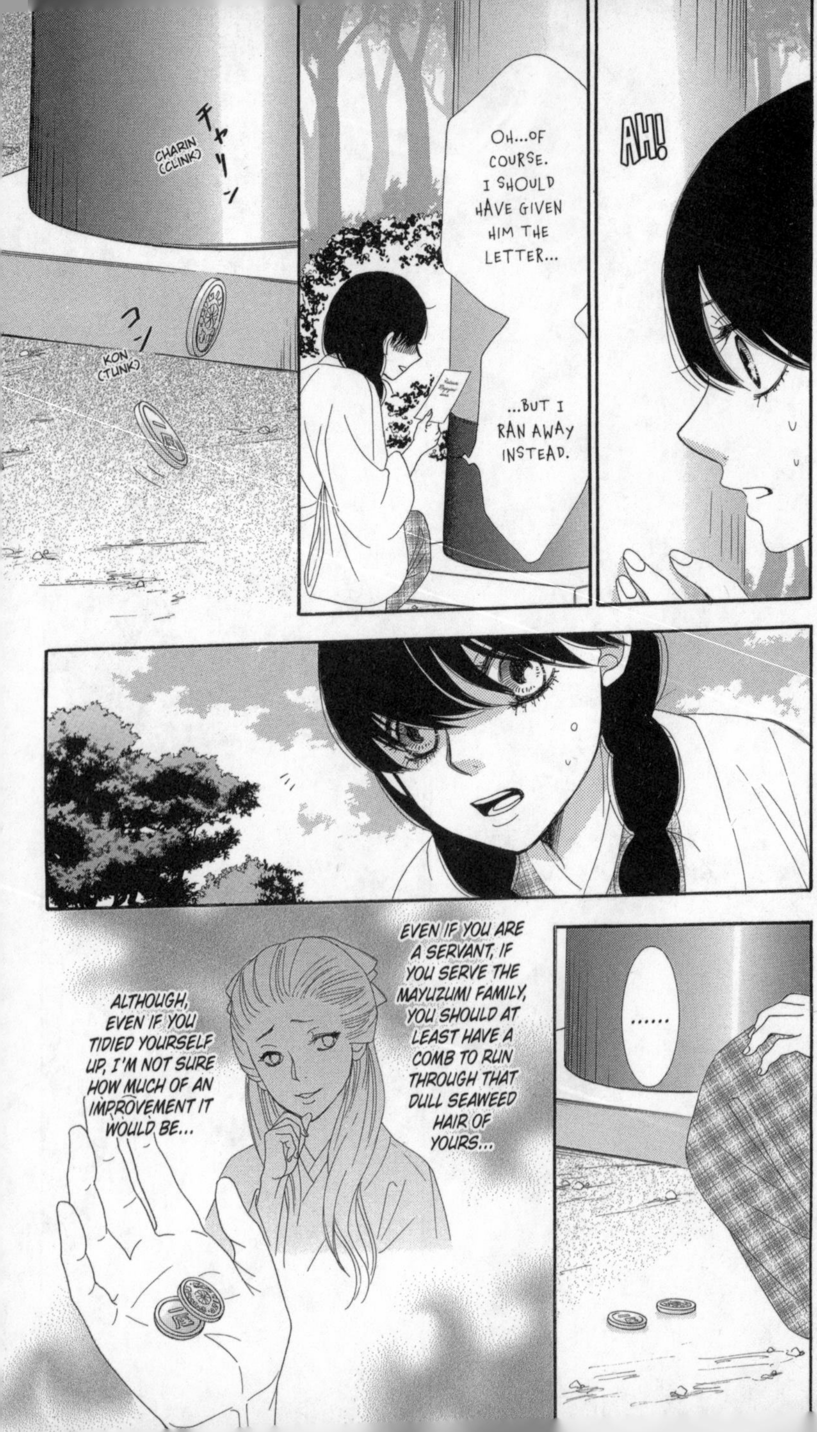
AH!
OH...OF COURSE. I SHOULD HAVE GIVEN HIM THE LETTER...
...BUT I RAN AWAY INSTEAD.
チャリーン
CHARIN (CLINK)
コン
KON (TUNK)
......
EVEN IF YOU ARE A SERVANT, IF YOU SERVE THE MAYUZUMI FAMILY, YOU SHOULD AT LEAST HAVE A COMB TO RUN THROUGH THAT DULL SEAWEED HAIR OF YOURS...
ALTHOUGH, EVEN IF YOU TIDIED YOURSELF UP, I'M NOT SURE HOW MUCH OF AN IMPROVEMENT IT WOULD BE...

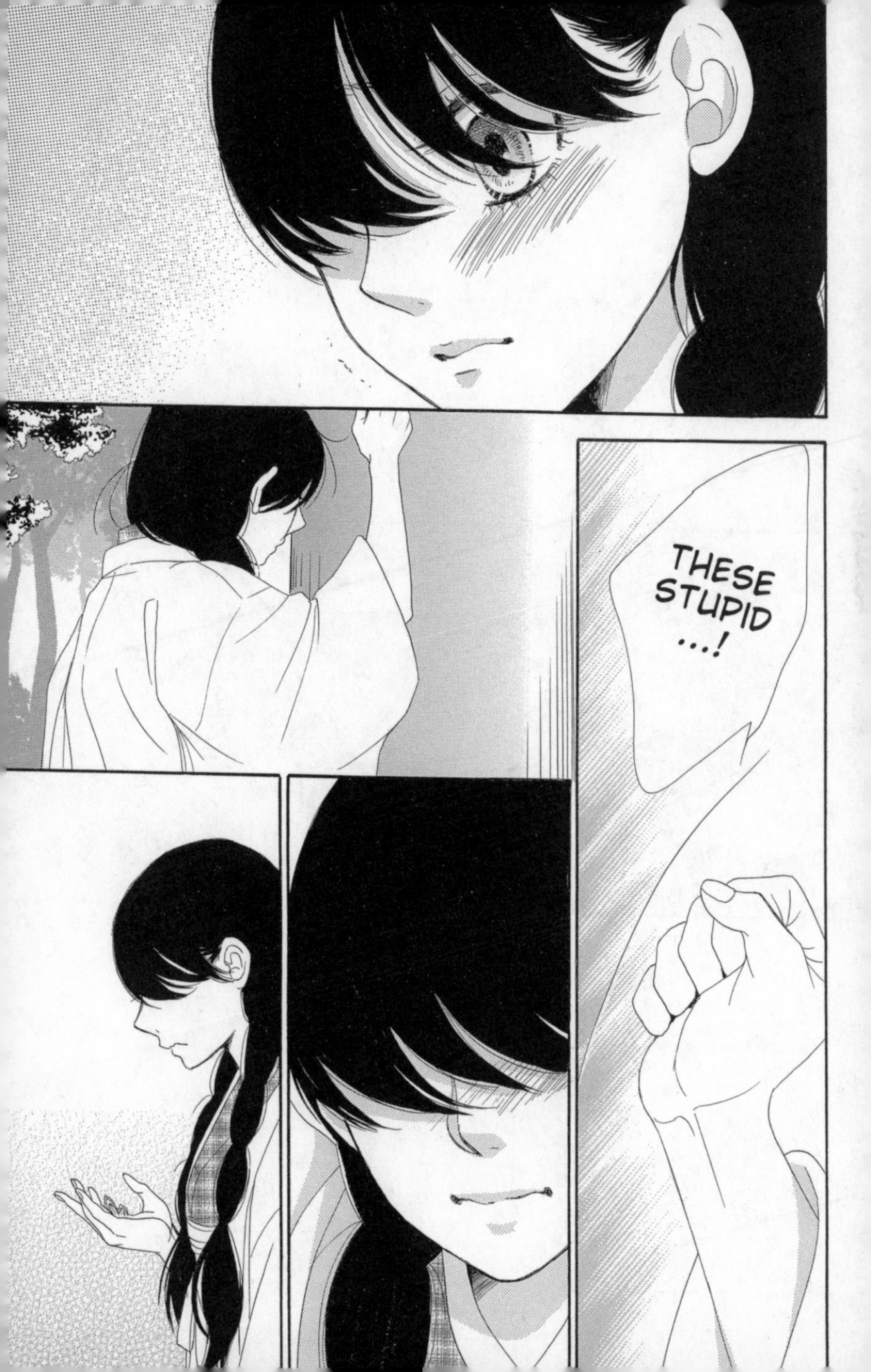
THESE STUPID ...!

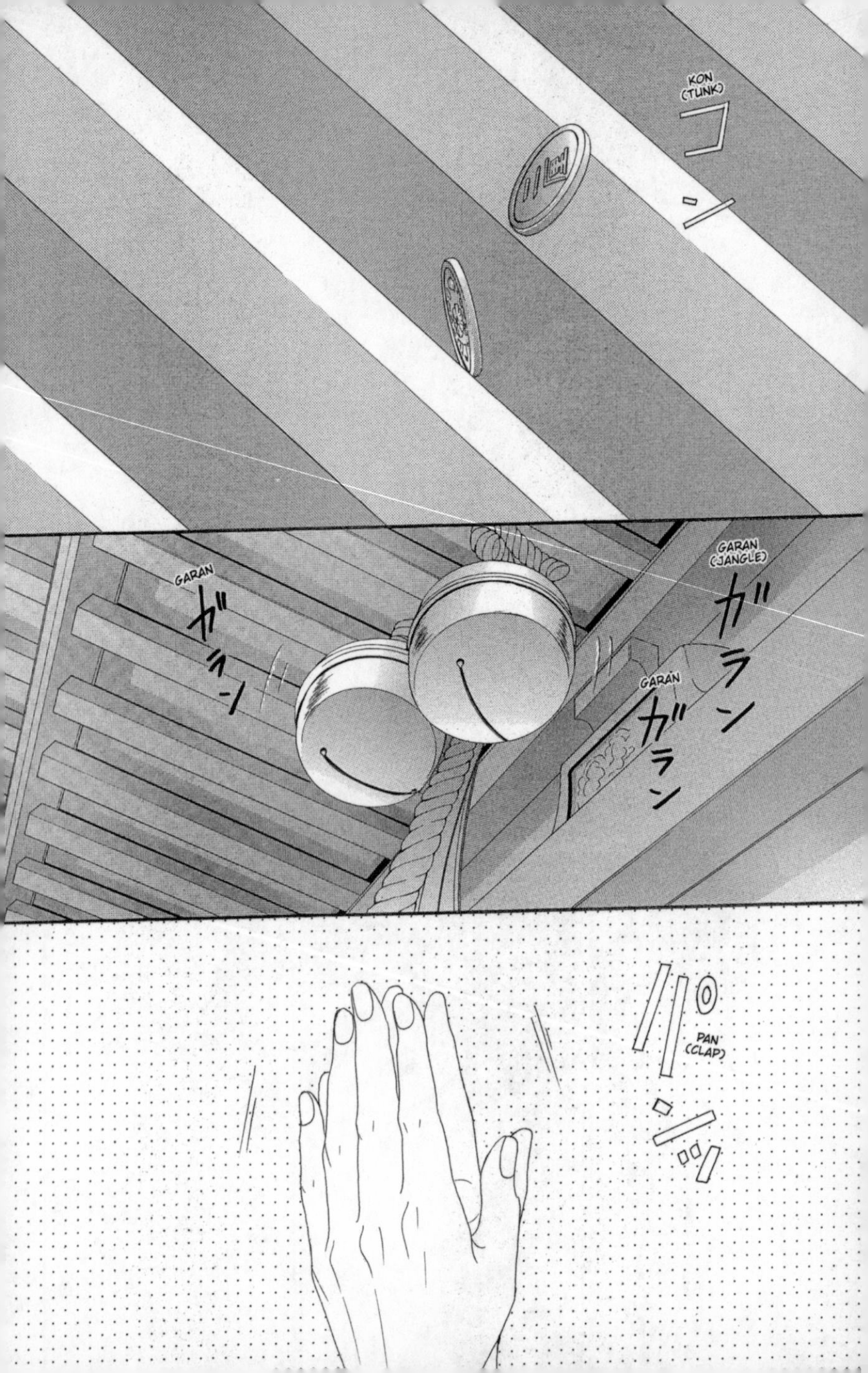
KON
(TUNK)
コン
GARAN
(JANGLE)
ガラン
GARAN
ガラン
GARAN
ガラン
PAN
(CLAP)
パン

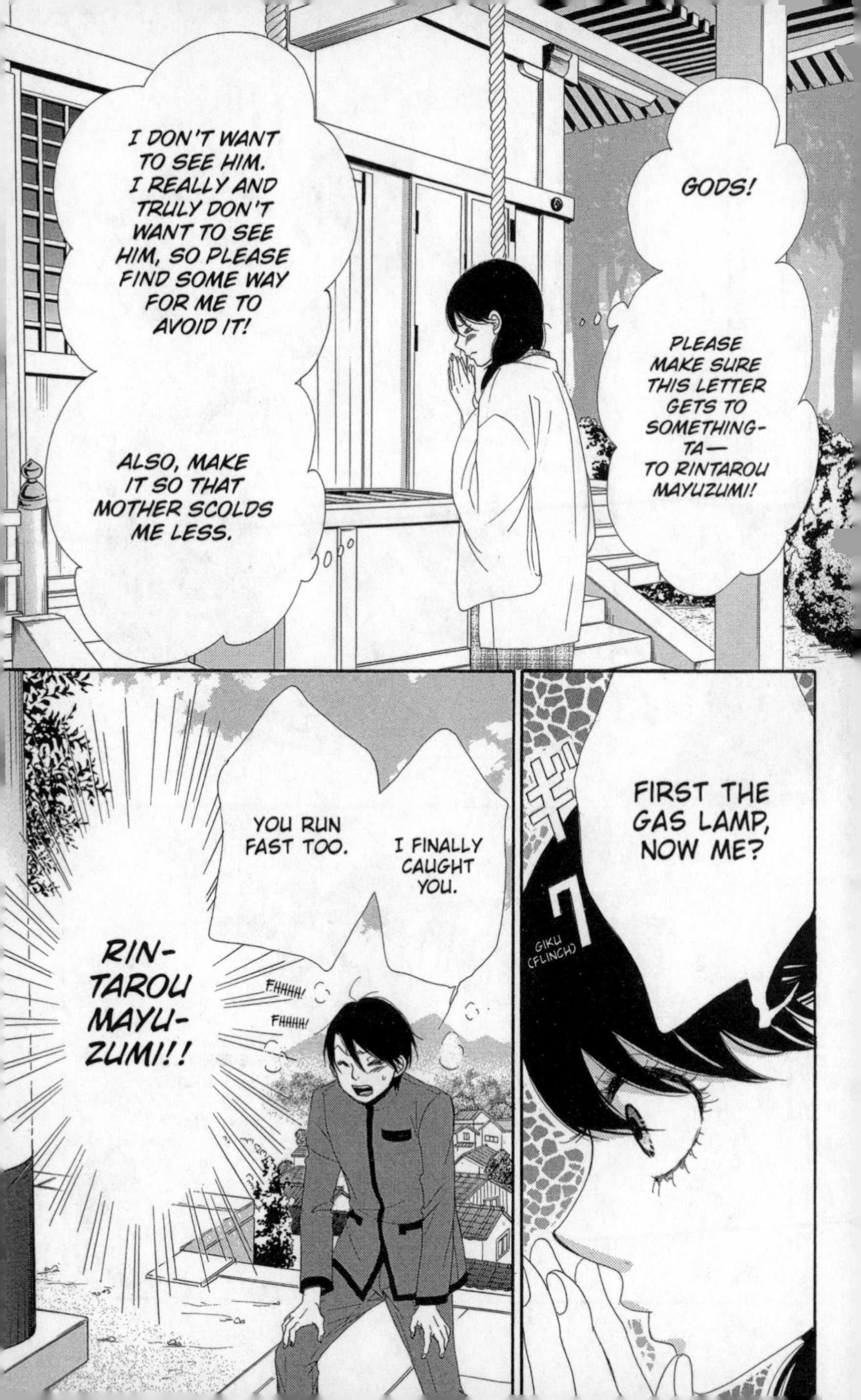
GODS!
PLEASE MAKE SURE THIS LETTER GETS TO SOMETHING-TA— TO RINTAROU MAYUZUMI!
I DON'T WANT TO SEE HIM. I REALLY AND TRULY DON'T WANT TO SEE HIM, SO PLEASE FIND SOME WAY FOR ME TO AVOID IT!
ALSO, MAKE IT SO THAT MOTHER SCOLDS ME LESS.
FIRST THE GAS LAMP, NOW ME?
GIKU (FLINCH)
I FINALLY CAUGHT YOU.
YOU RUN FAST TOO.
FHHHH!
FHHHH!
RIN-TAROU MAYU-ZUMI!!

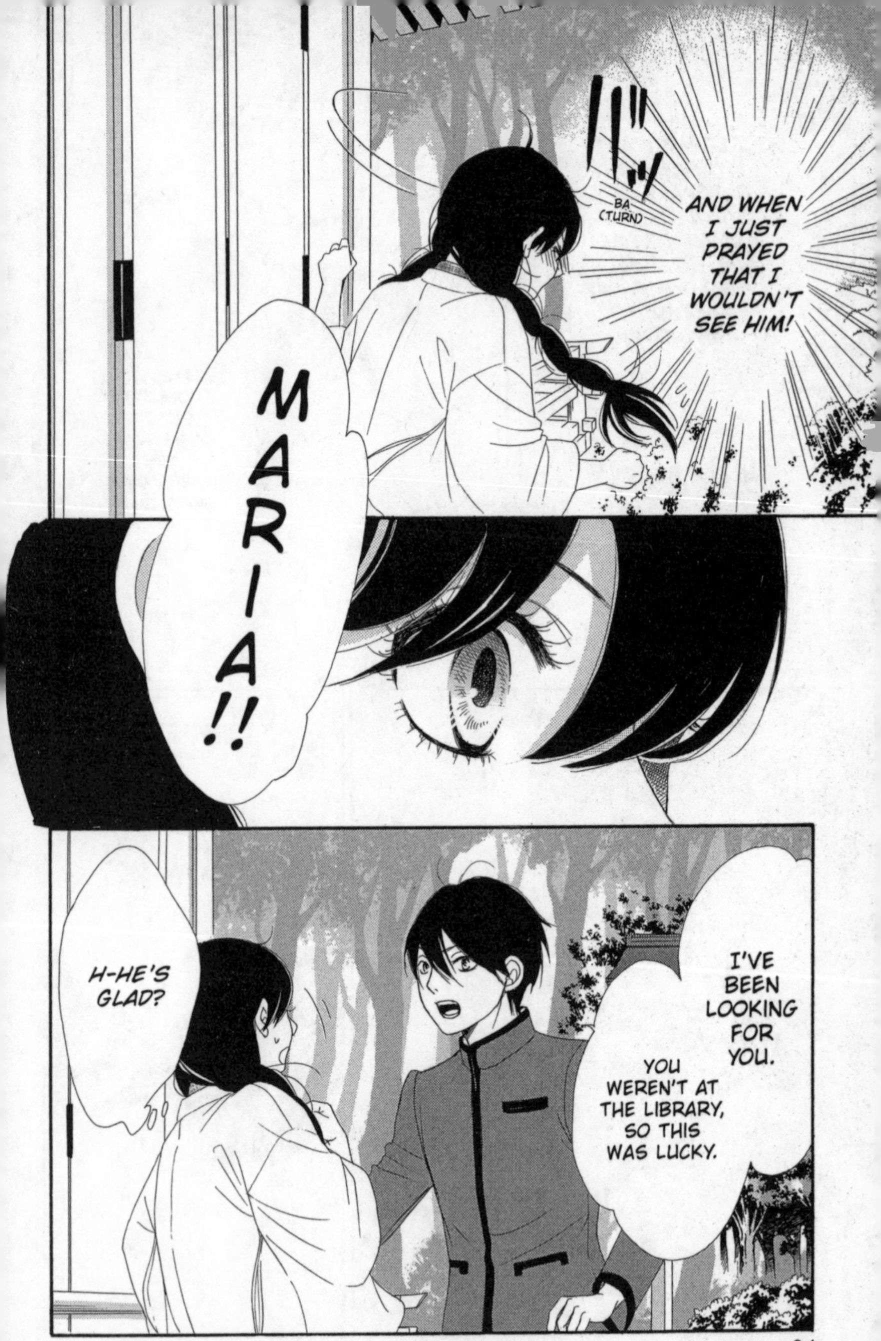
バッ
BA (TURN)
AND WHEN I JUST PRAYED THAT I WOULDN'T SEE HIM!
MARIA!!
I'VE BEEN LOOKING FOR YOU.
YOU WEREN'T AT THE LIBRARY, SO THIS WAS LUCKY.
H-HE'S GLAD?

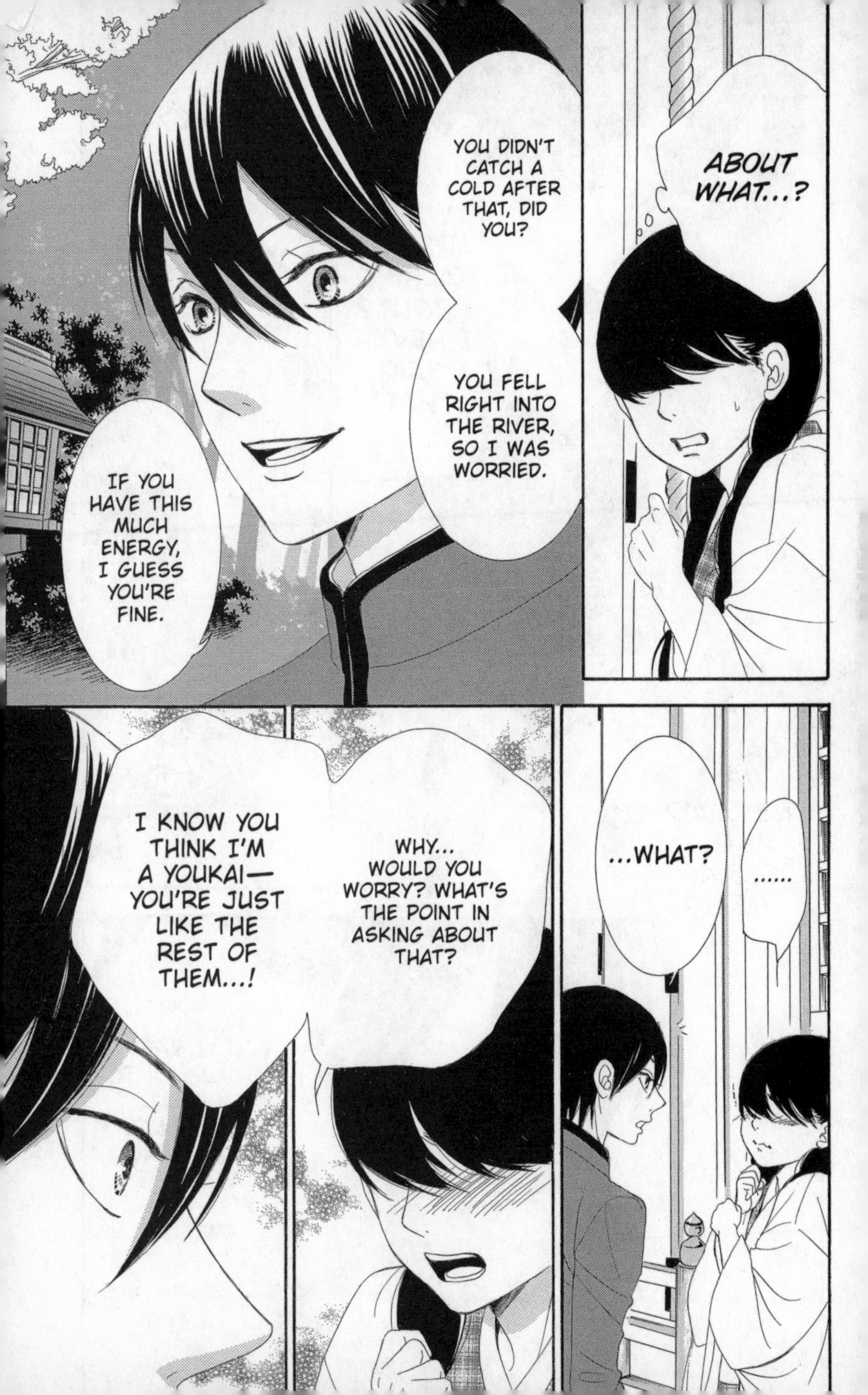
ABOUT WHAT...?
YOU DIDN'T CATCH A COLD AFTER THAT, DID YOU?
YOU FELL RIGHT INTO THE RIVER, SO I WAS WORRIED.
IF YOU HAVE THIS MUCH ENERGY, I GUESS YOU'RE FINE.
......
...WHAT?
WHY... WOULD YOU WORRY? WHAT'S THE POINT IN ASKING ABOUT THAT?
I KNOW YOU THINK I'M A YOUKAI—YOU'RE JUST LIKE THE REST OF THEM...!

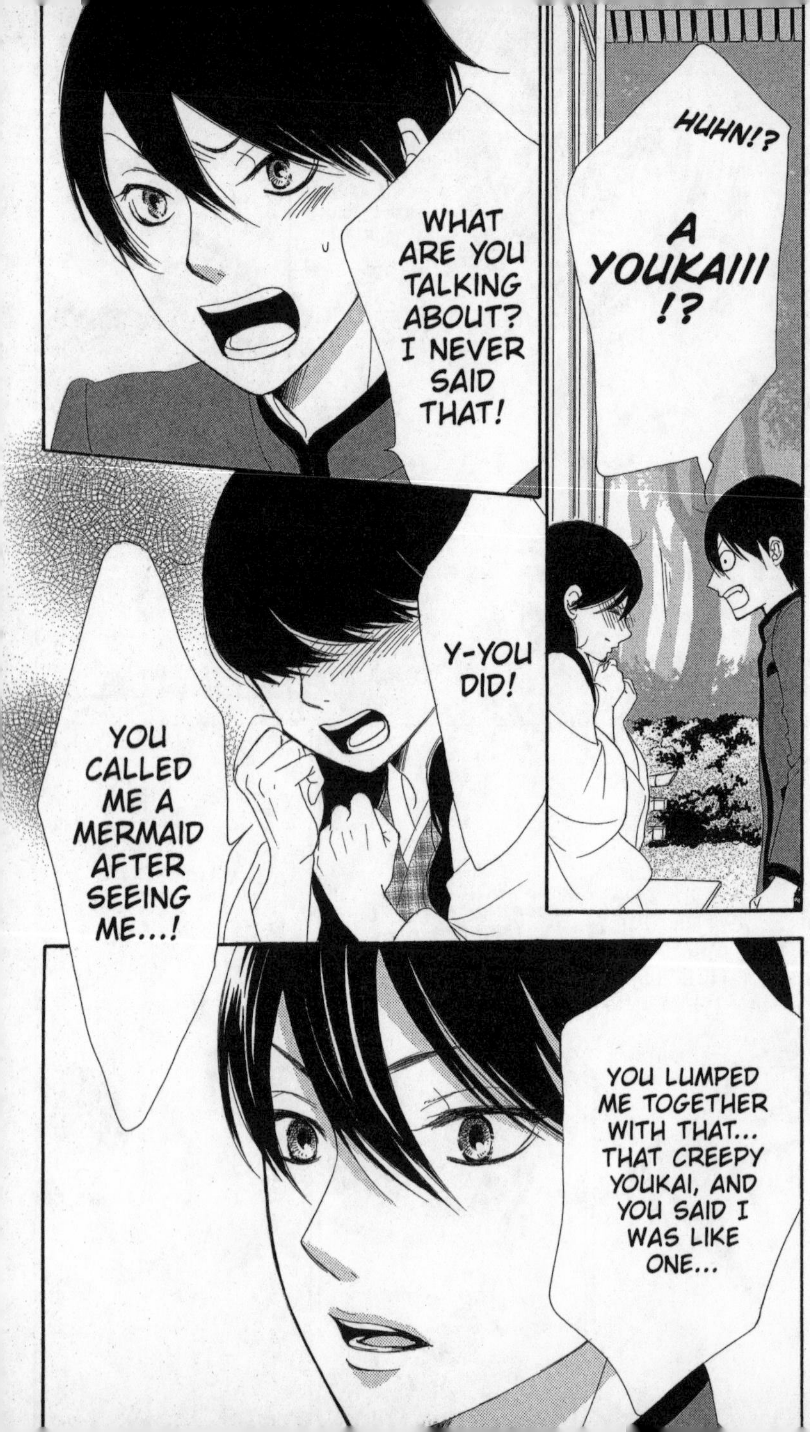
HUHN!?
A YOUKAIII!?
WHAT ARE YOU TALKING ABOUT? I NEVER SAID THAT!
Y-YOU DID!
YOU CALLED ME A MERMAID AFTER SEEING ME...!
YOU LUMPED ME TOGETHER WITH THAT... THAT CREEPY YOUKAI, AND YOU SAID I WAS LIKE ONE...

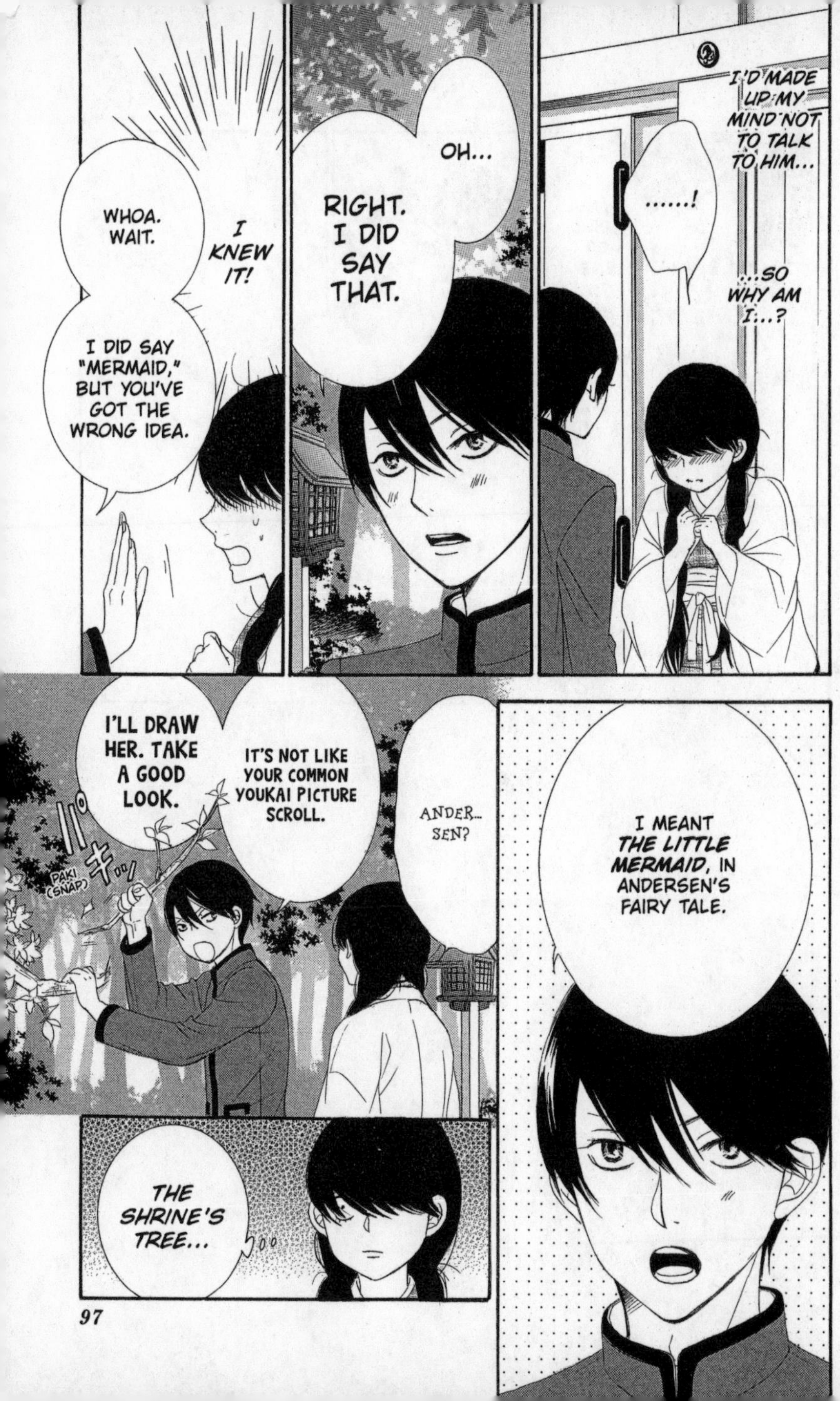
I'D MADE UP MY MIND NOT TO TALK TO HIM...
......!
...SO WHY AM I...?
OH...
RIGHT. I DID SAY THAT.
I KNEW IT!
WHOA. WAIT.
I DID SAY "MERMAID," BUT YOU'VE GOT THE WRONG IDEA.
I MEANT *THE LITTLE MERMAID*, IN ANDERSEN'S FAIRY TALE.
ANDER... SEN?
IT'S NOT LIKE YOUR COMMON YOUKAI PICTURE SCROLL.
I'LL DRAW HER. TAKE A GOOD LOOK.
PAKI (SNAP)
THE SHRINE'S TREE...

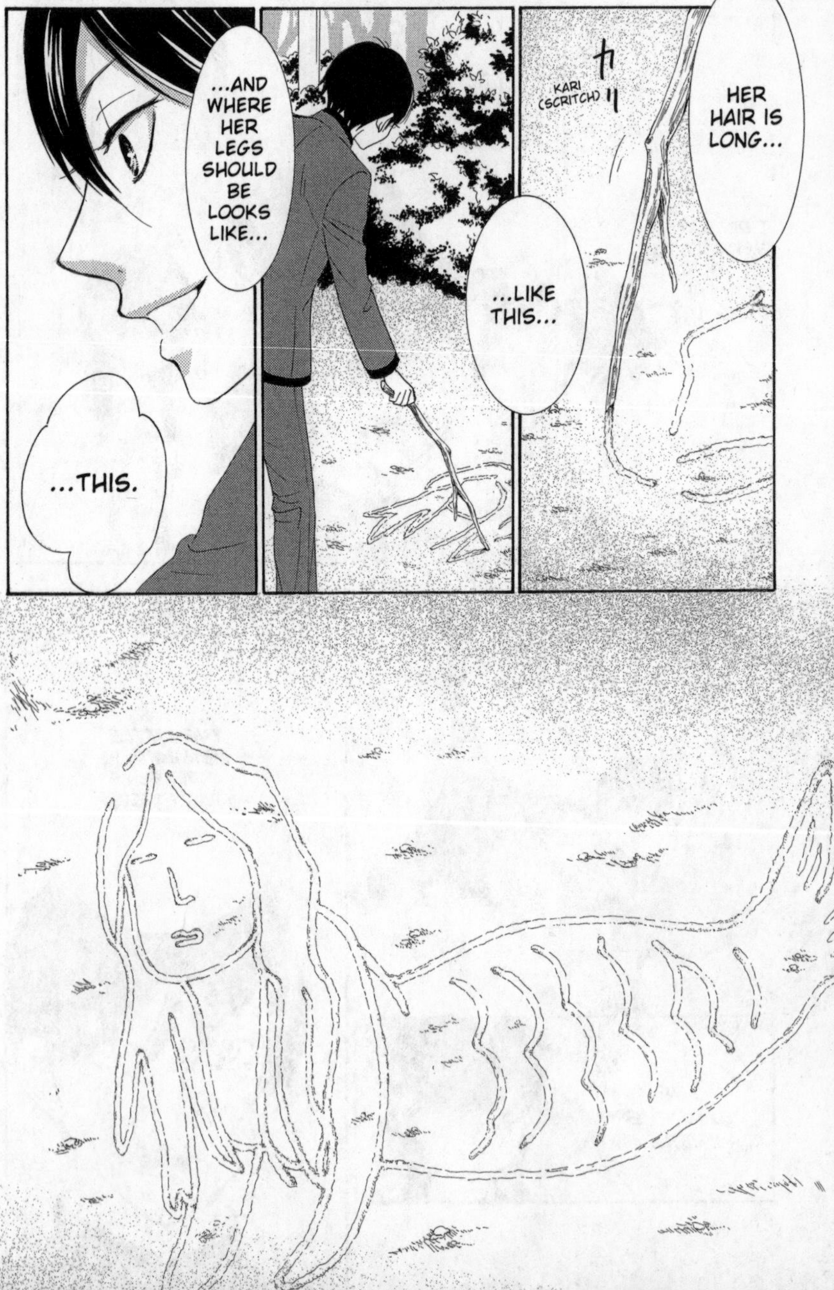
HER HAIR IS LONG...
カリ
KARI (SCRITCH)
...LIKE THIS...
...AND WHERE HER LEGS SHOULD BE LOOKS LIKE...
...THIS.

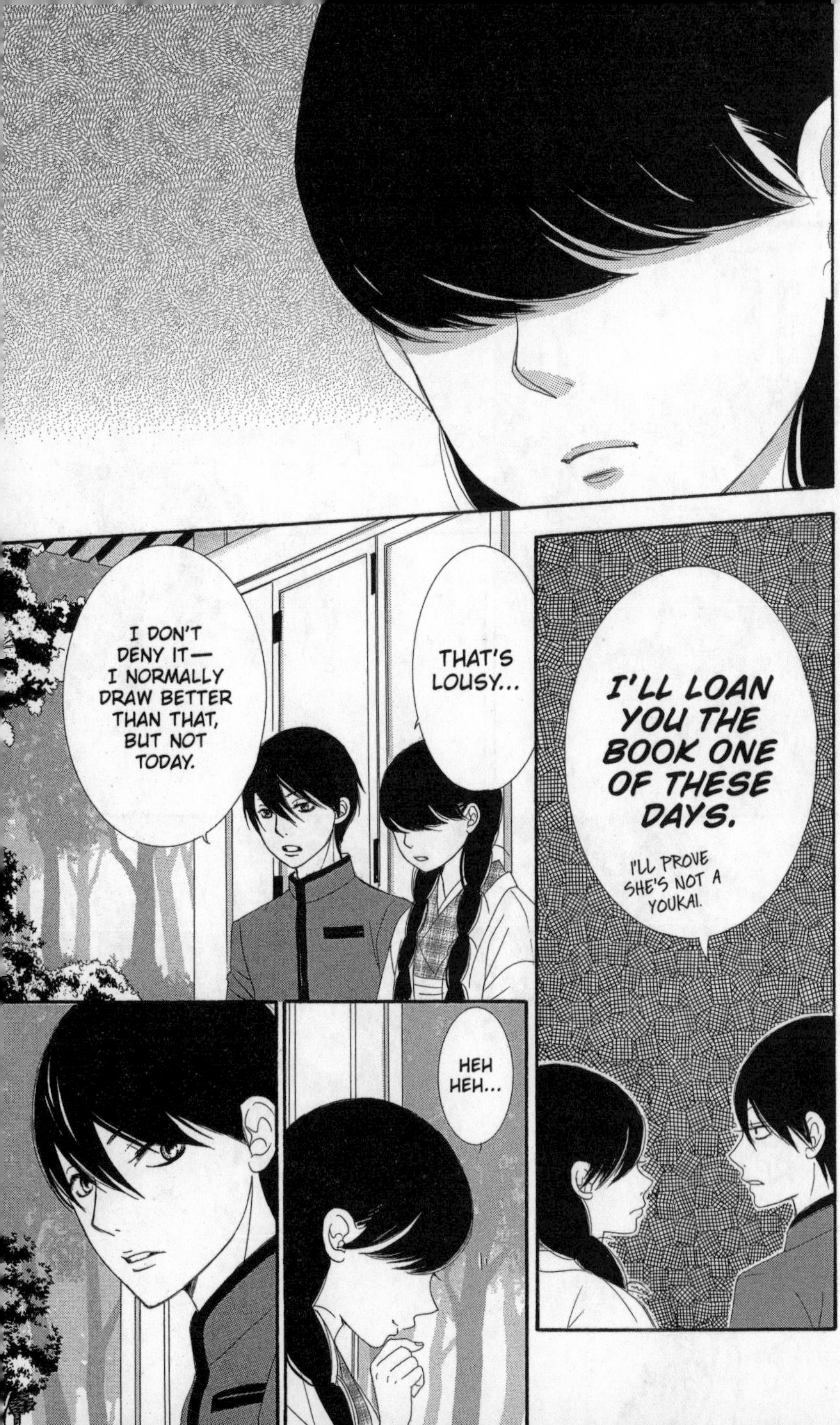
I'LL LOAN YOU THE BOOK ONE OF THESE DAYS.
I'LL PROVE SHE'S NOT A YOUKAI.
THAT'S LOUSY...
I DON'T DENY IT— I NORMALLY DRAW BETTER THAN THAT, BUT NOT TODAY.
HEH HEH...

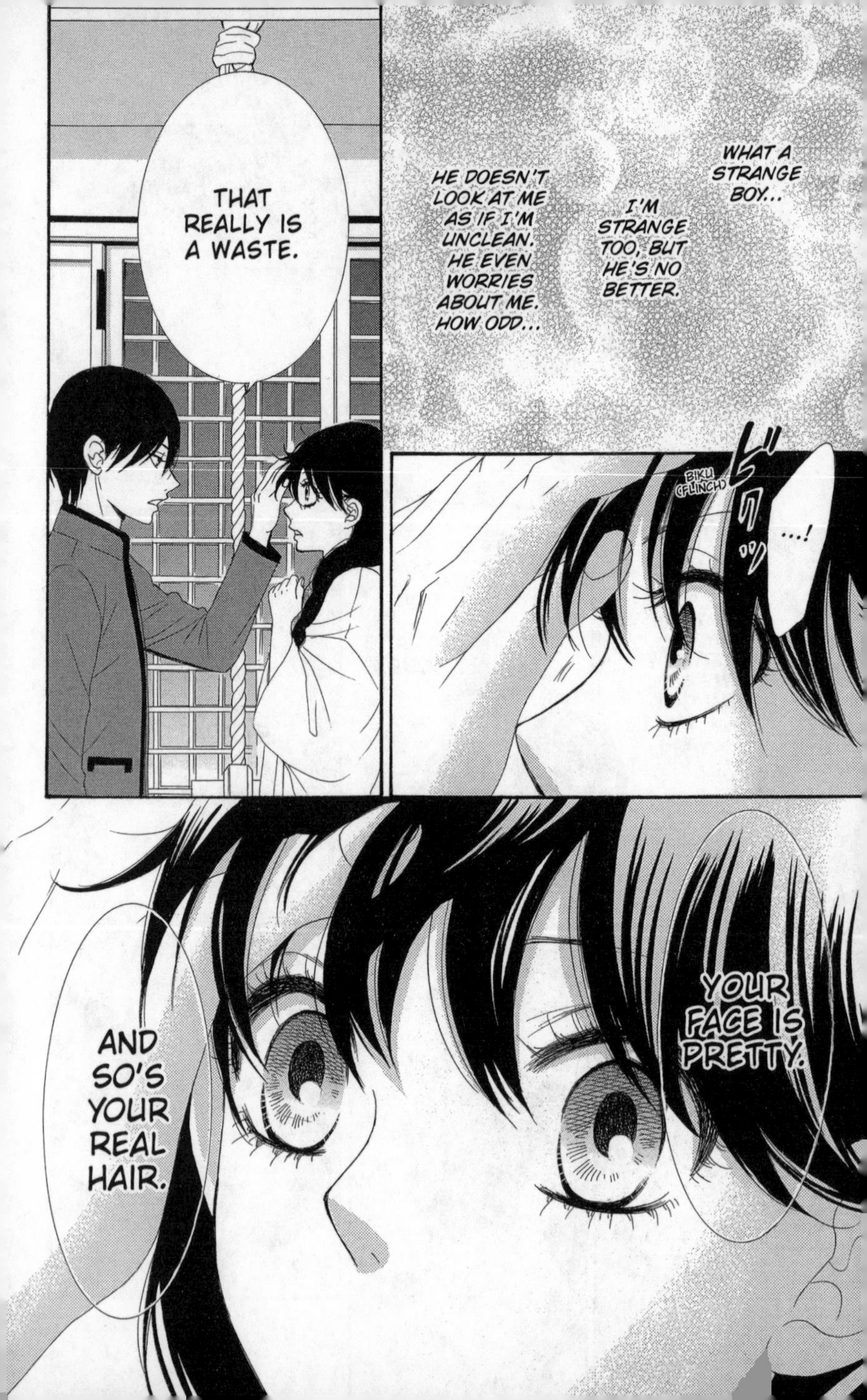
WHAT A STRANGE BOY...
I'M STRANGE TOO, BUT HE'S NO BETTER.
HE DOESN'T LOOK AT ME AS IF I'M UNCLEAN. HE EVEN WORRIES ABOUT ME. HOW ODD...
BIKU (FLINCH)
...!
THAT REALLY IS A WASTE.
YOUR FACE IS PRETTY.
AND SO'S YOUR REAL HAIR.

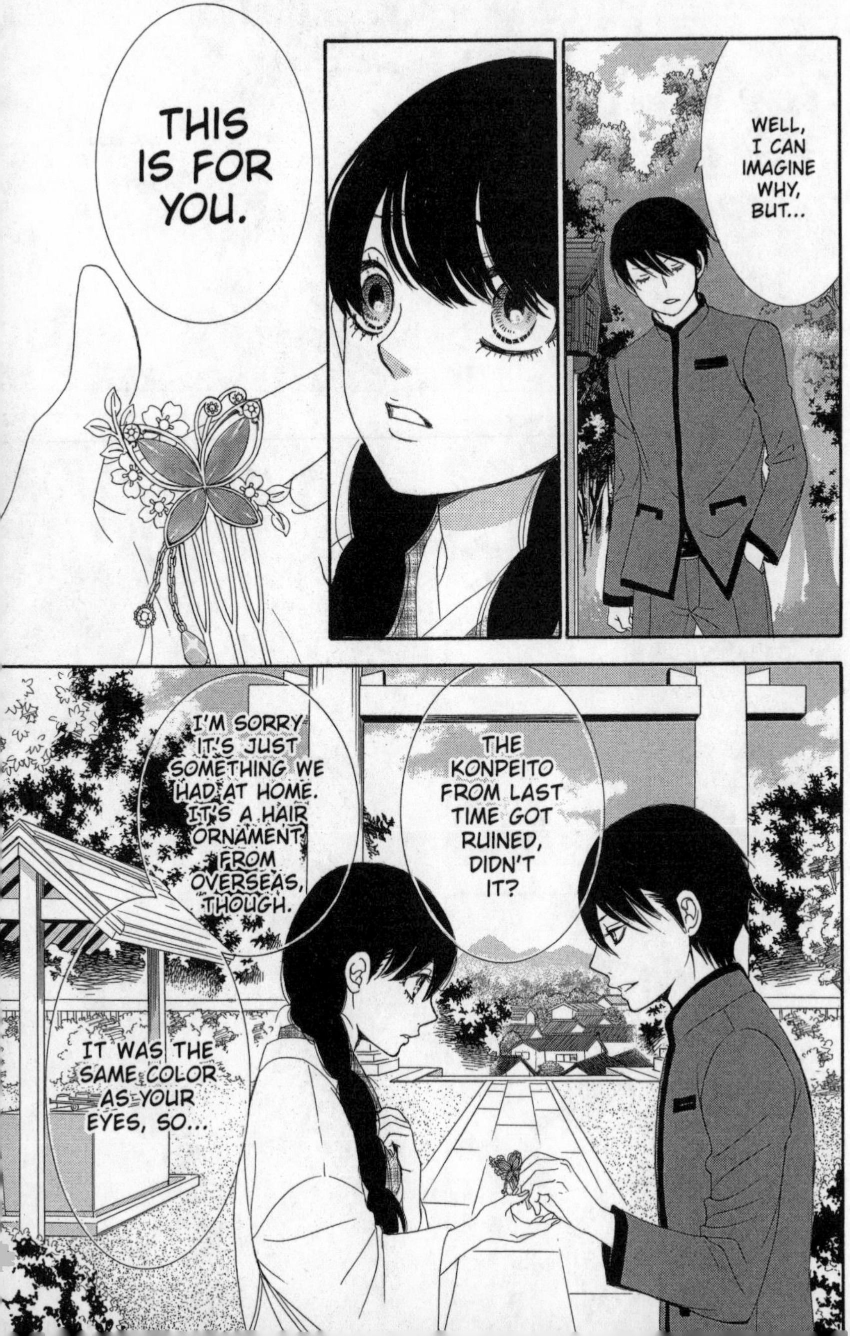
WELL, I CAN IMAGINE WHY, BUT...
THIS IS FOR YOU.
THE KONPEITO FROM LAST TIME GOT RUINED, DIDN'T IT?
I'M SORRY IT'S JUST SOMETHING WE HAD AT HOME. IT'S A HAIR ORNAMENT FROM OVERSEAS, THOUGH.
IT WAS THE SAME COLOR AS YOUR EYES, SO...

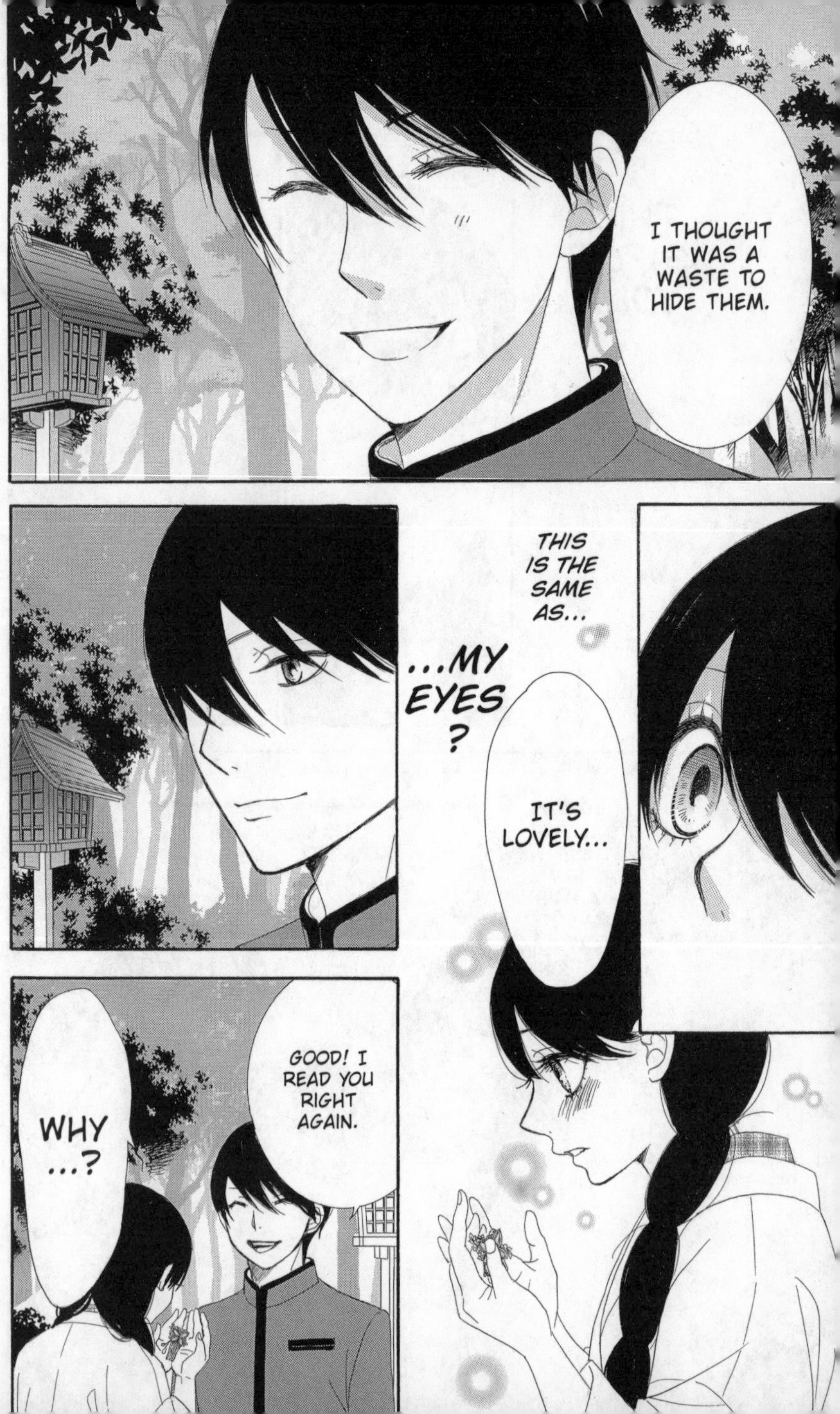
I THOUGHT IT WAS A WASTE TO HIDE THEM.
THIS IS THE SAME AS...
...MY EYES?
IT'S LOVELY...
GOOD! I READ YOU RIGHT AGAIN.
WHY...?

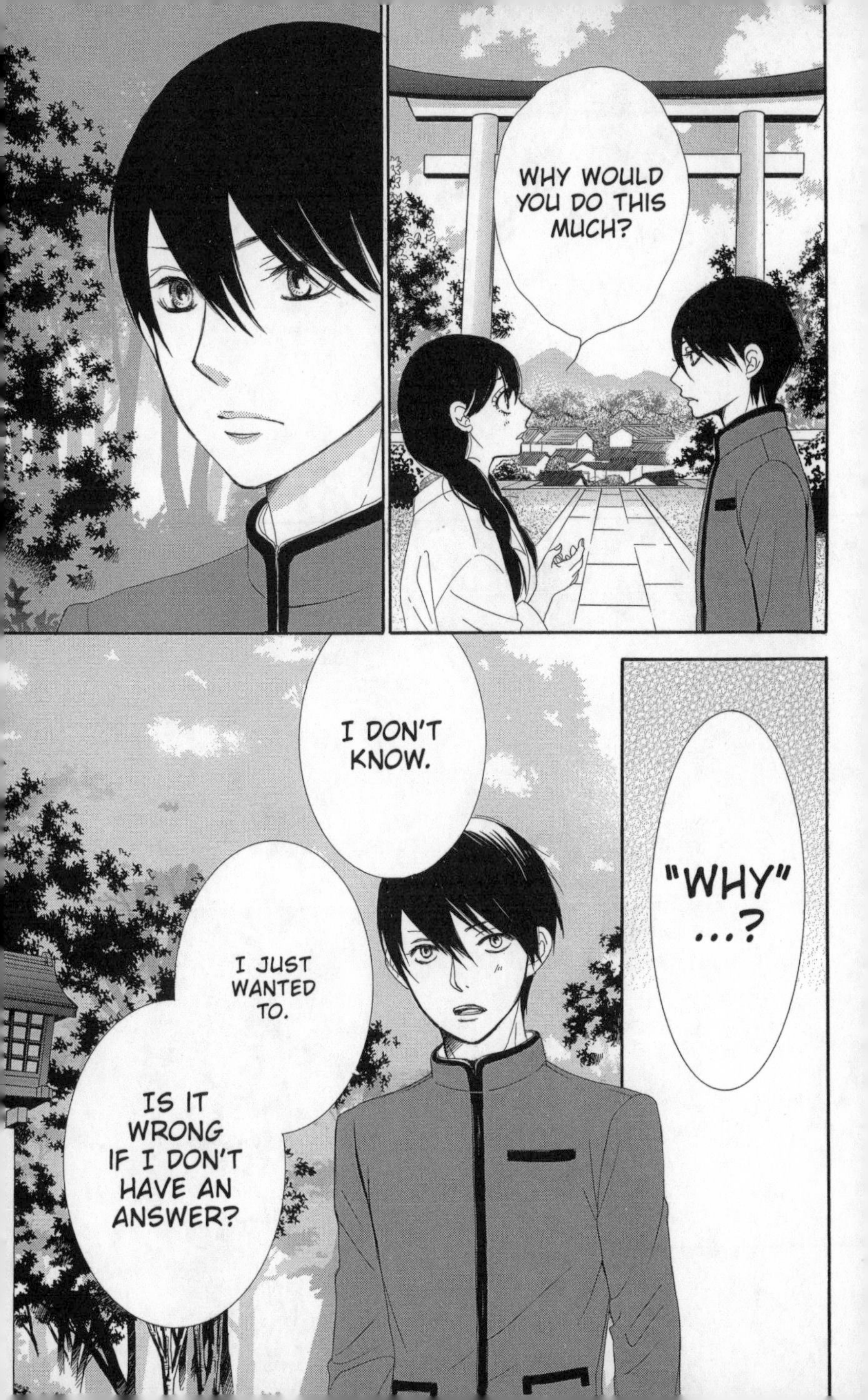
WHY WOULD YOU DO THIS MUCH?
"WHY"...?
I DON'T KNOW.
I JUST WANTED TO.
IS IT WRONG IF I DON'T HAVE AN ANSWER?

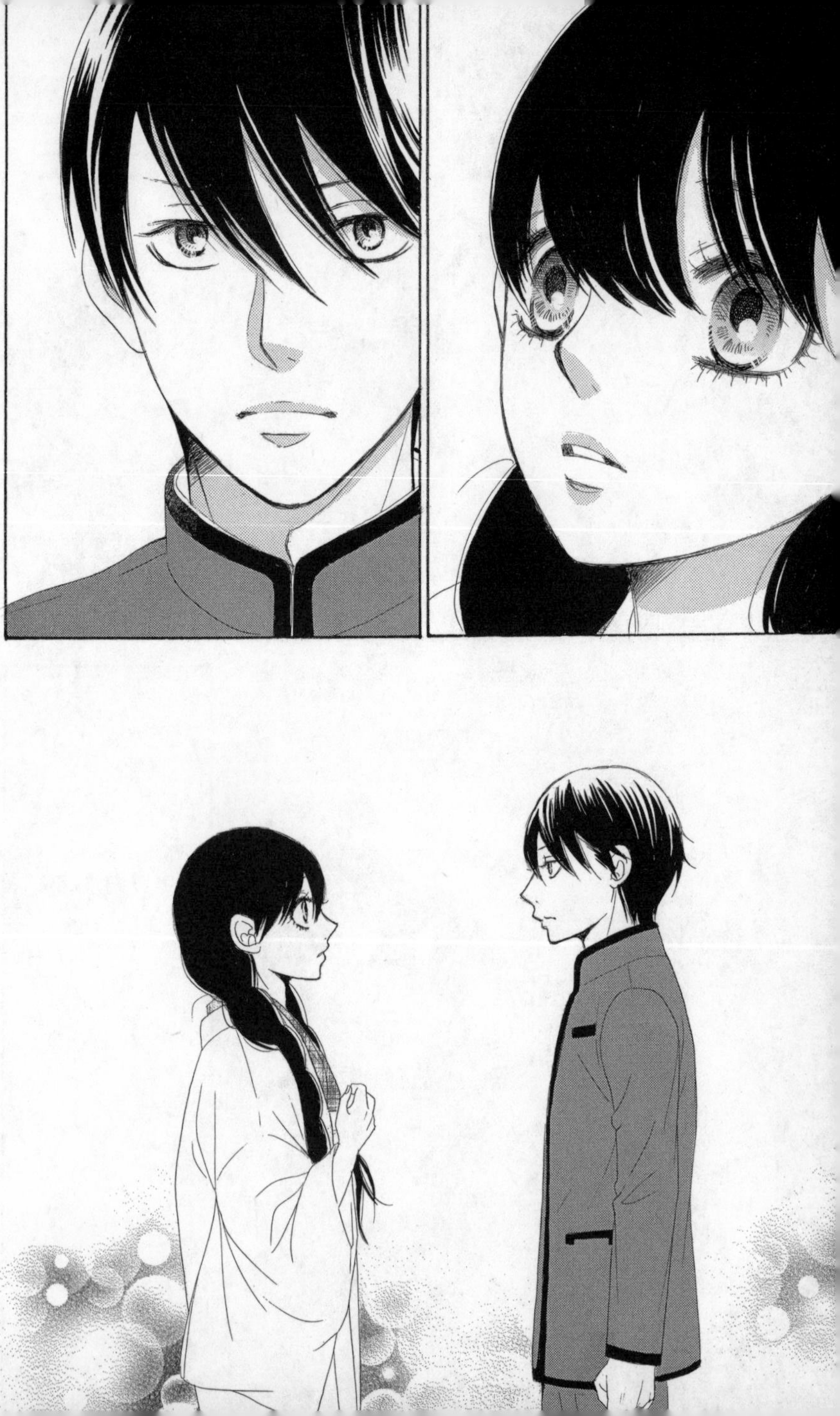

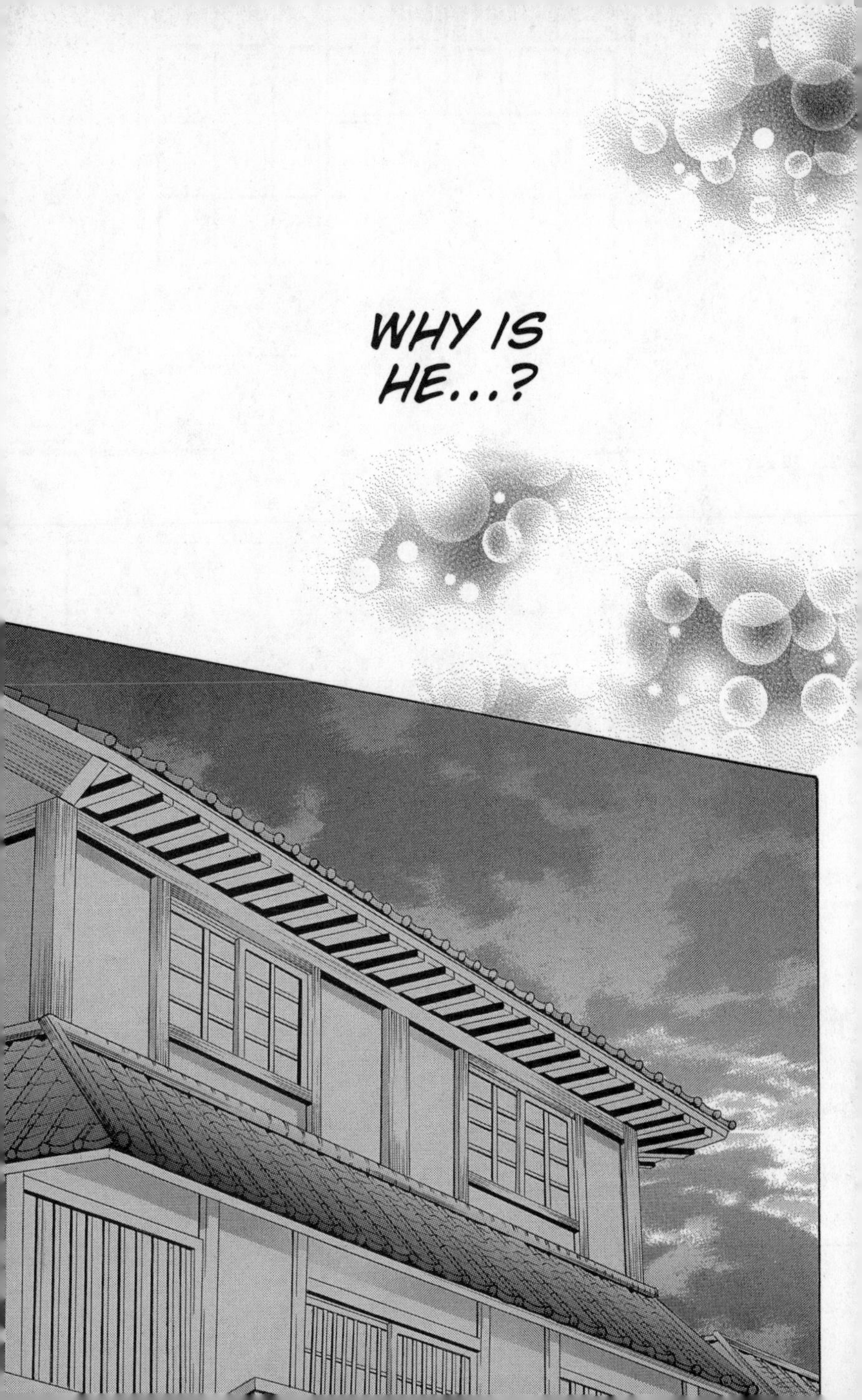
WHY IS
HE...?

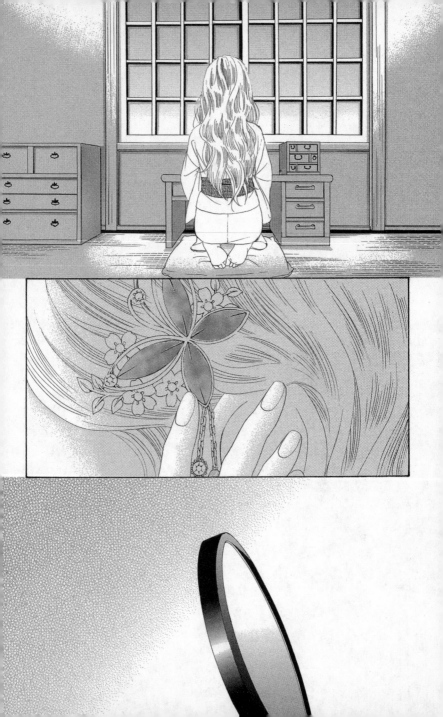

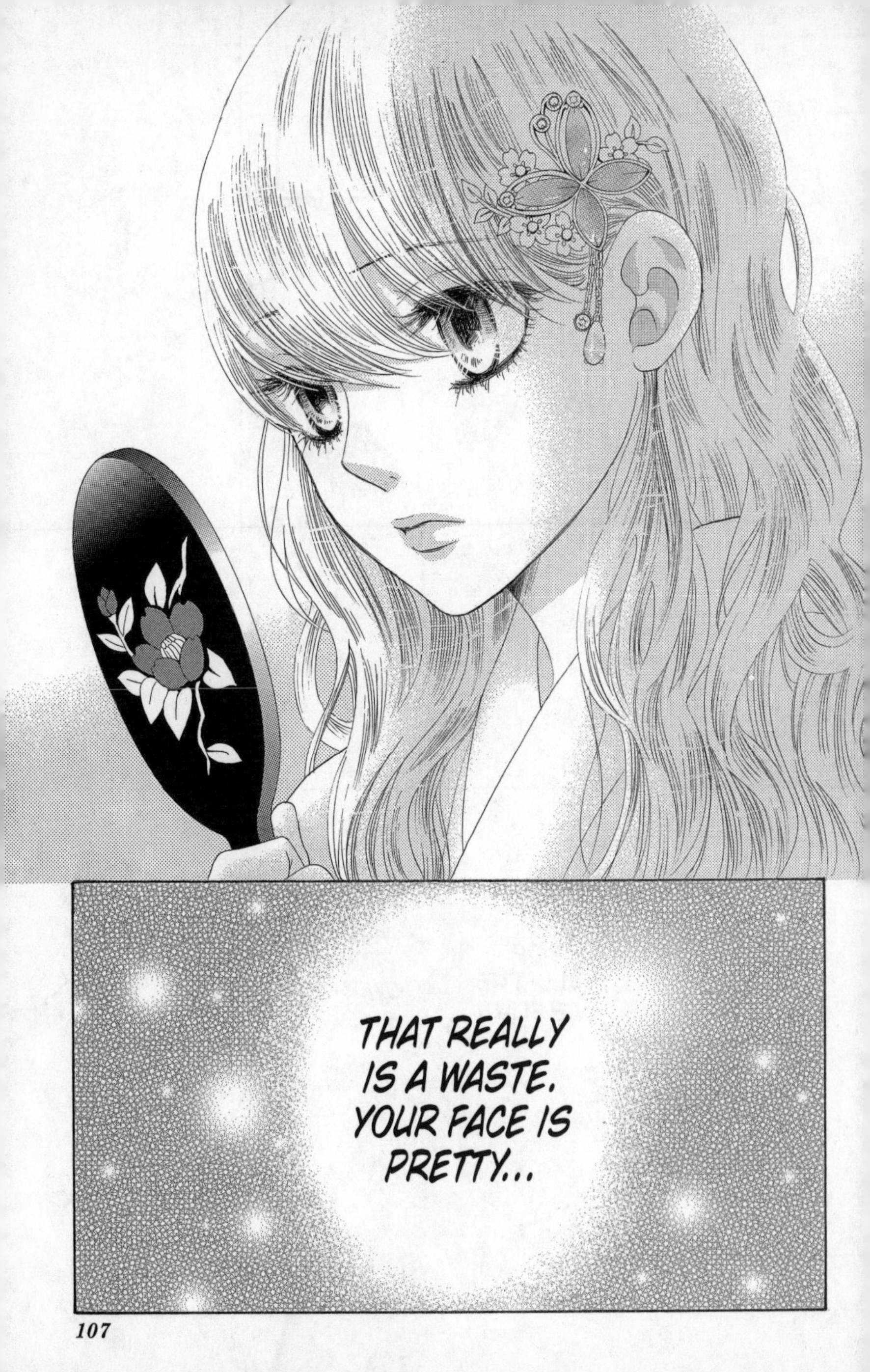
THAT REALLY IS A WASTE. YOUR FACE IS PRETTY...

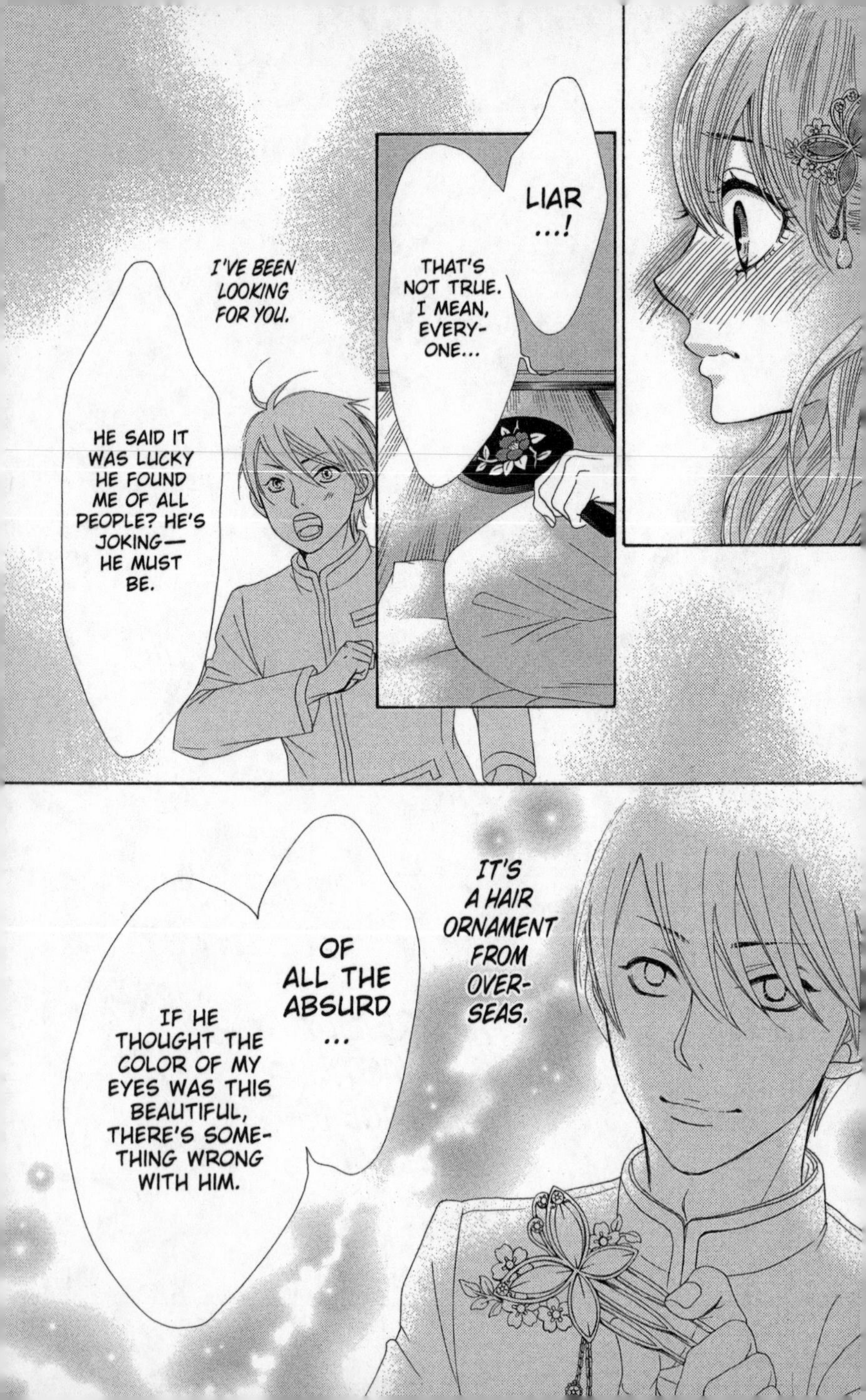

LIAR ...!
THAT'S NOT TRUE. I MEAN, EVERY-ONE...
I'VE BEEN LOOKING FOR YOU.
HE SAID IT WAS LUCKY HE FOUND ME OF ALL PEOPLE? HE'S JOKING— HE MUST BE.
IT'S A HAIR ORNAMENT FROM OVER-SEAS.
OF ALL THE ABSURD ...
IF HE THOUGHT THE COLOR OF MY EYES WAS THIS BEAUTIFUL, THERE'S SOME-THING WRONG WITH HIM.

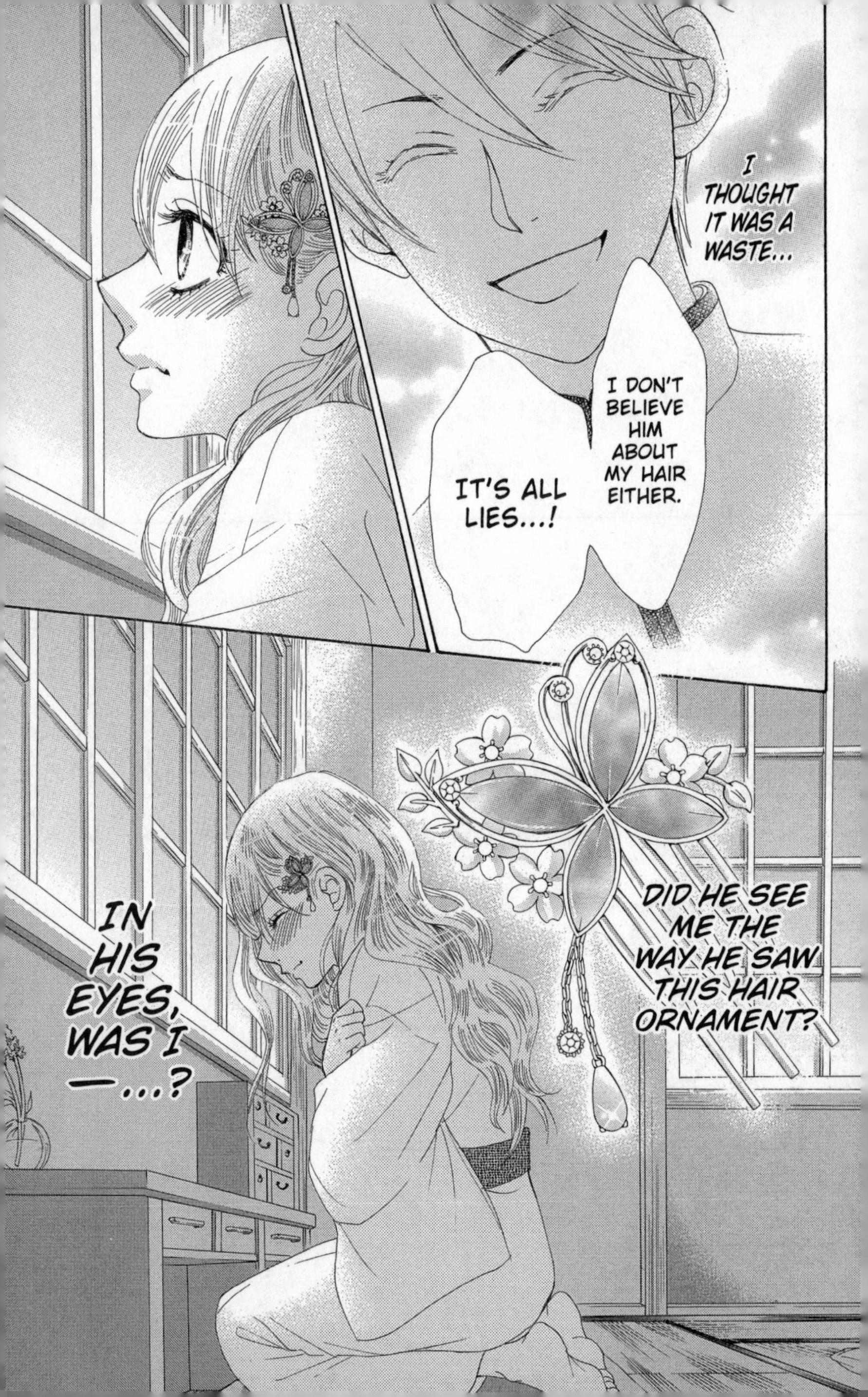
I THOUGHT IT WAS A WASTE...
I DON'T BELIEVE HIM ABOUT MY HAIR EITHER.
IT'S ALL LIES...!
DID HE SEE ME THE WAY HE SAW THIS HAIR ORNAMENT?
IN HIS EYES, WAS I —...?

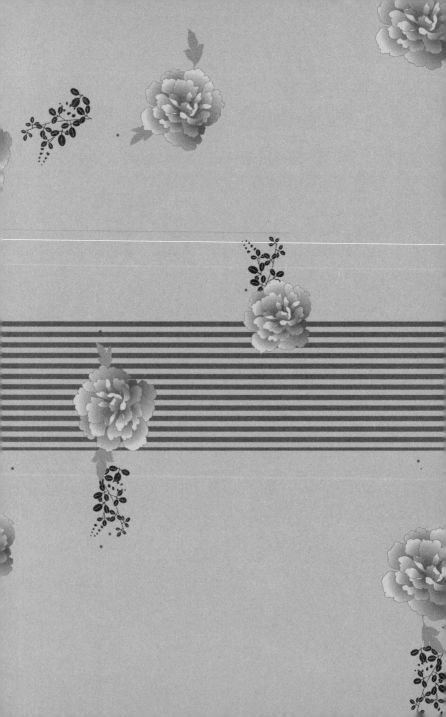

Episode 3

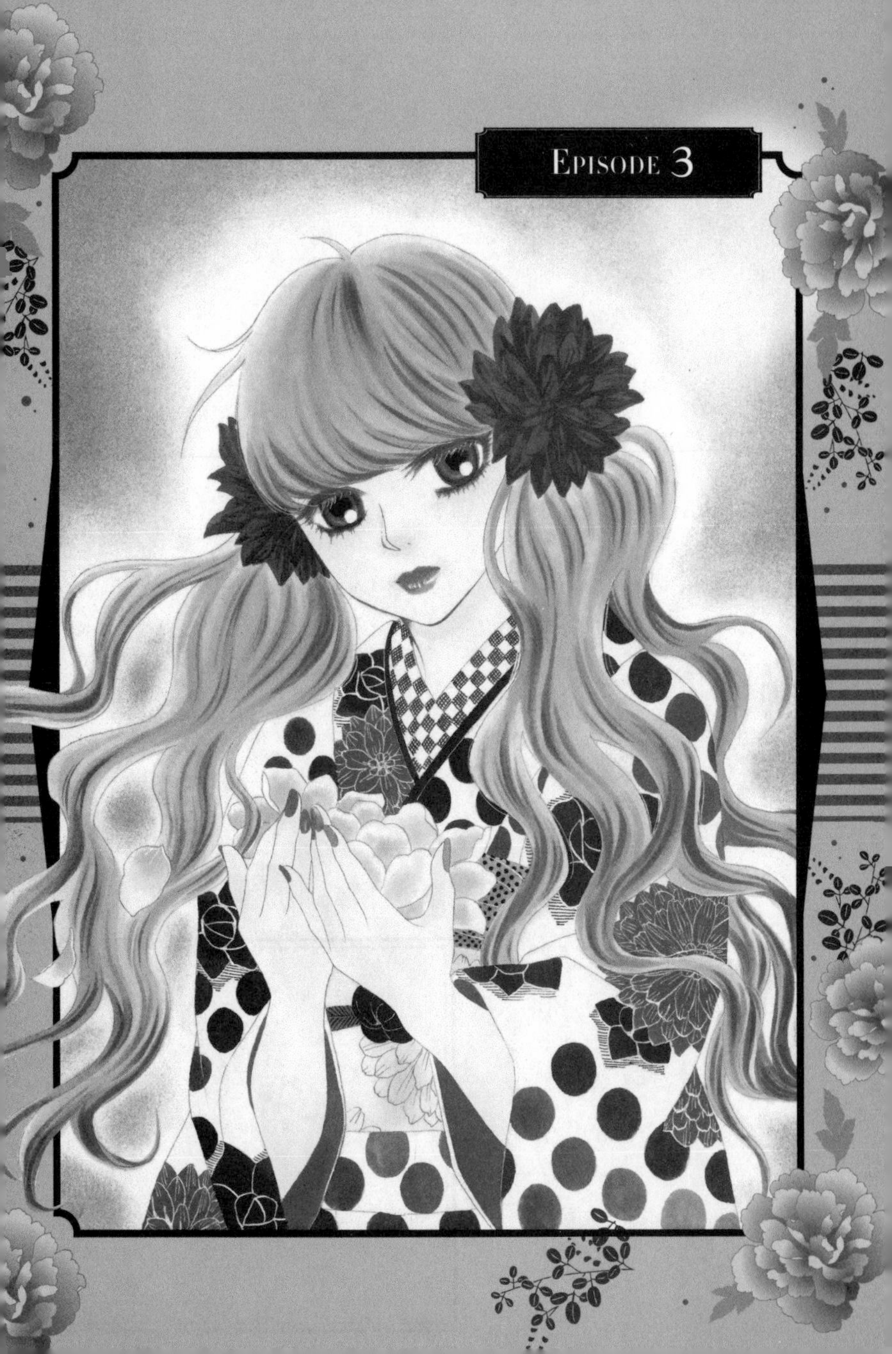

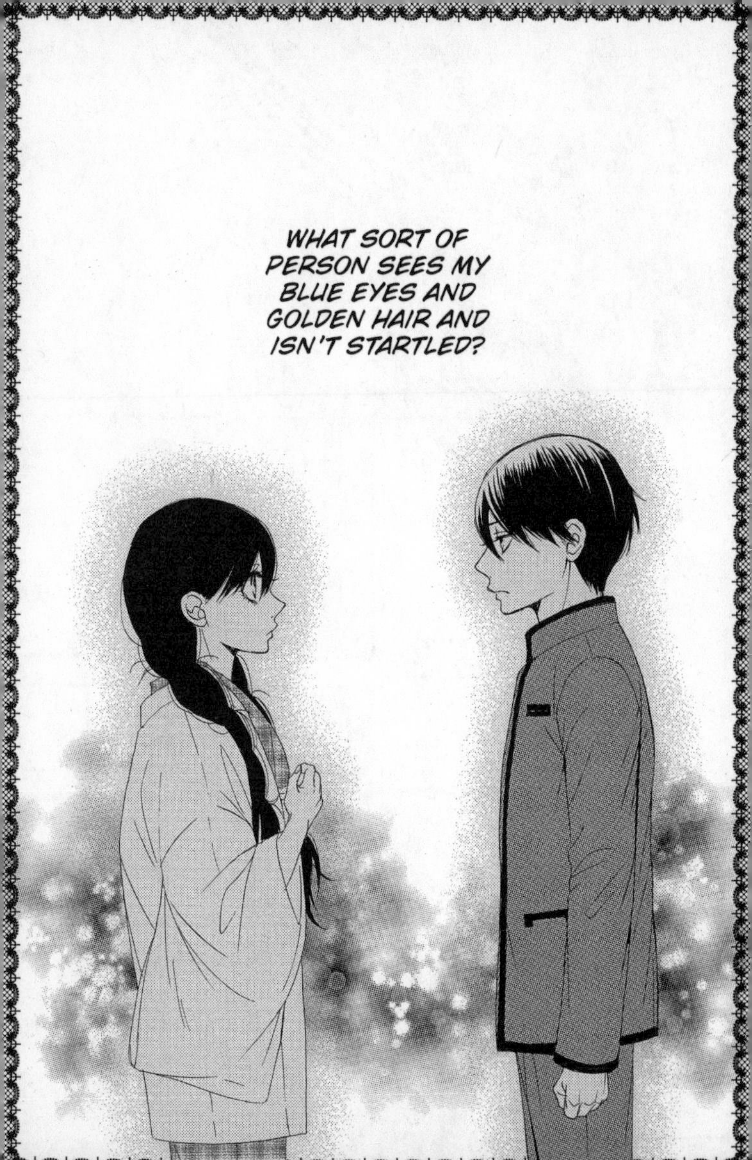
WHAT SORT OF PERSON SEES MY BLUE EYES AND GOLDEN HAIR AND ISN'T STARTLED?

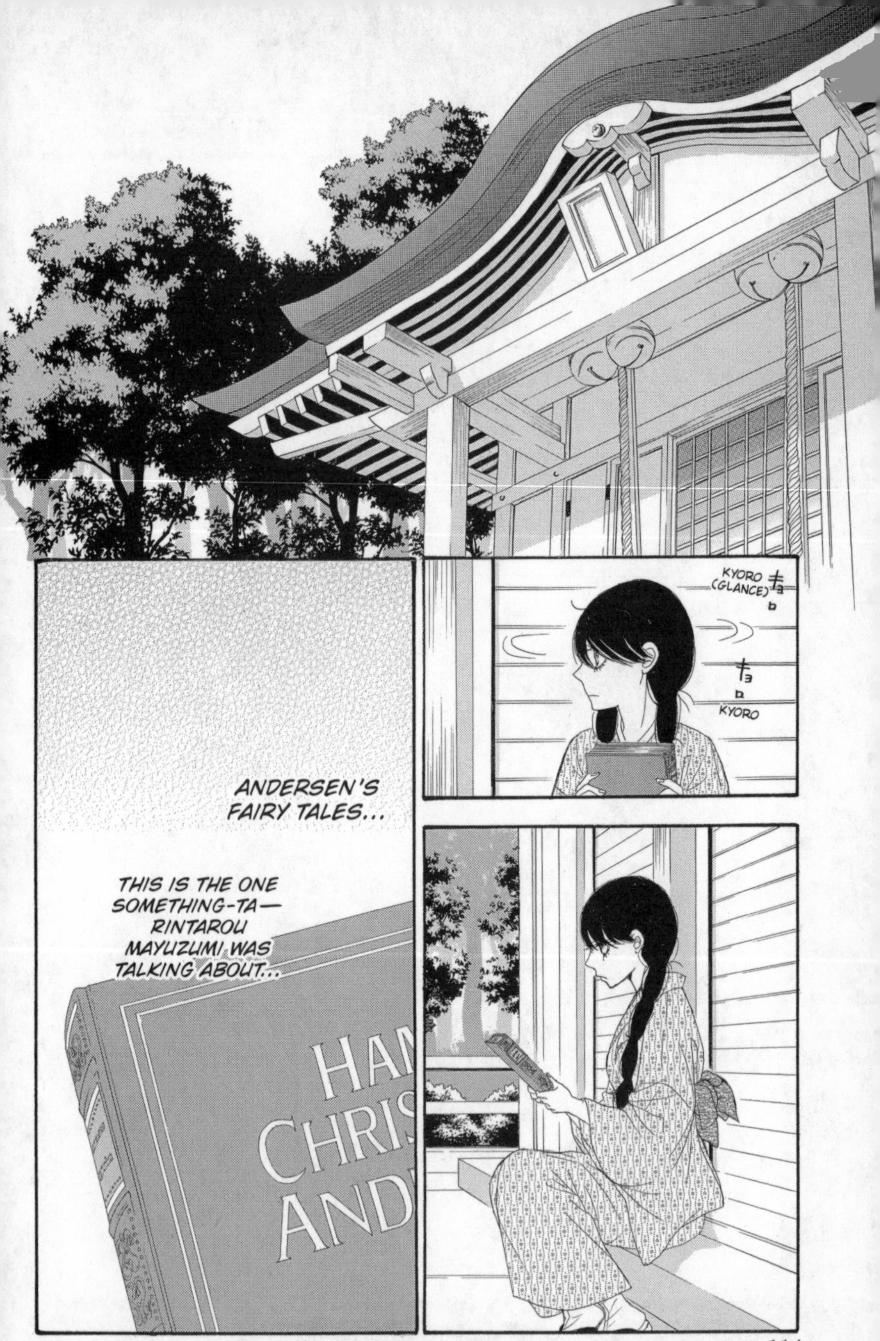

KYORO (GLANCE)
KYORO
ANDERSEN'S FAIRY TALES...
THIS IS THE ONE SOMETHING-TA— RINTAROU MAYUZUMI WAS TALKING ABOUT...

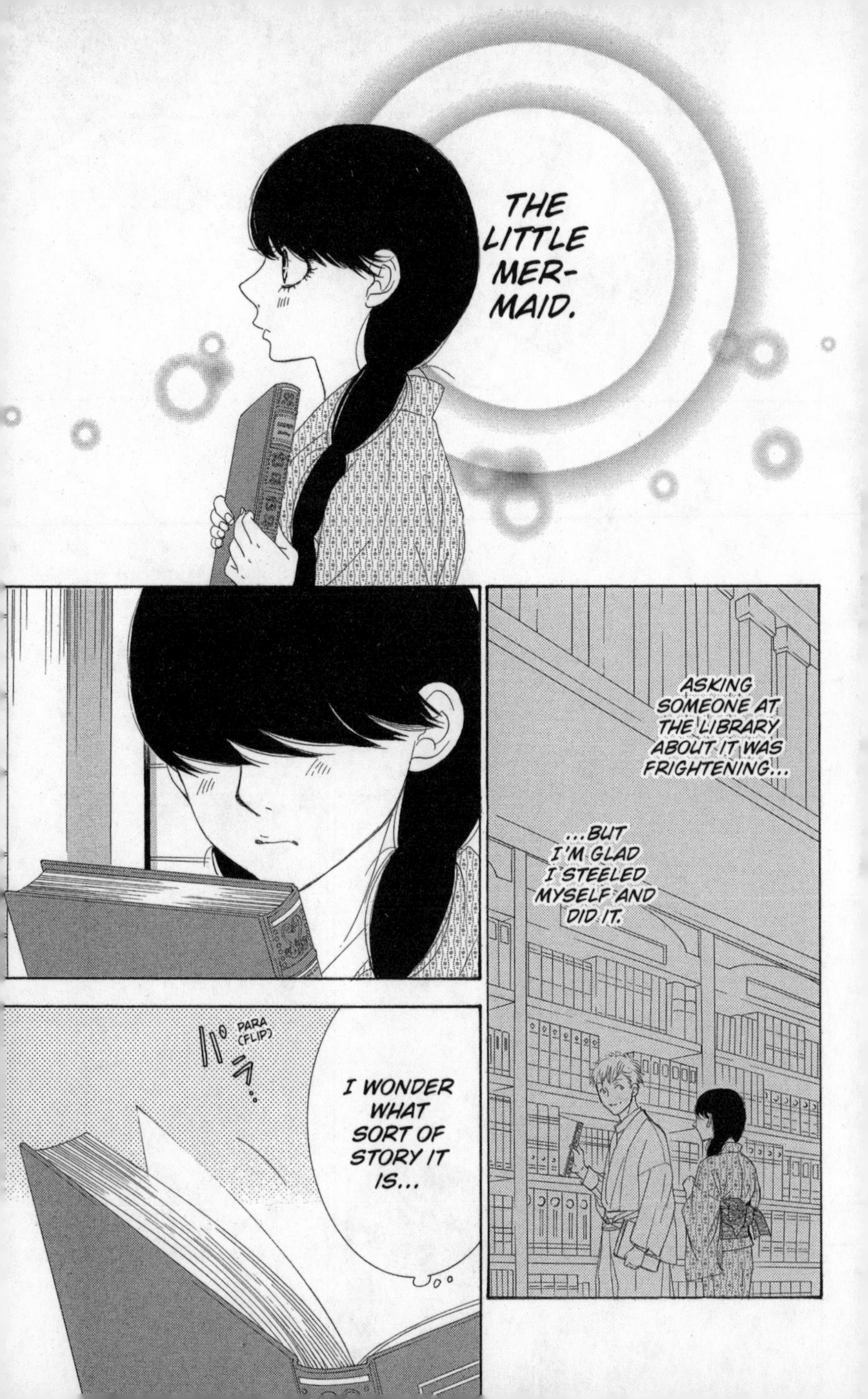
THE LITTLE MERMAID.
ASKING SOMEONE AT THE LIBRARY ABOUT IT WAS FRIGHTENING...
...BUT I'M GLAD I STEELED MYSELF AND DID IT.
PARA (FLIP)
I WONDER WHAT SORT OF STORY IT IS...

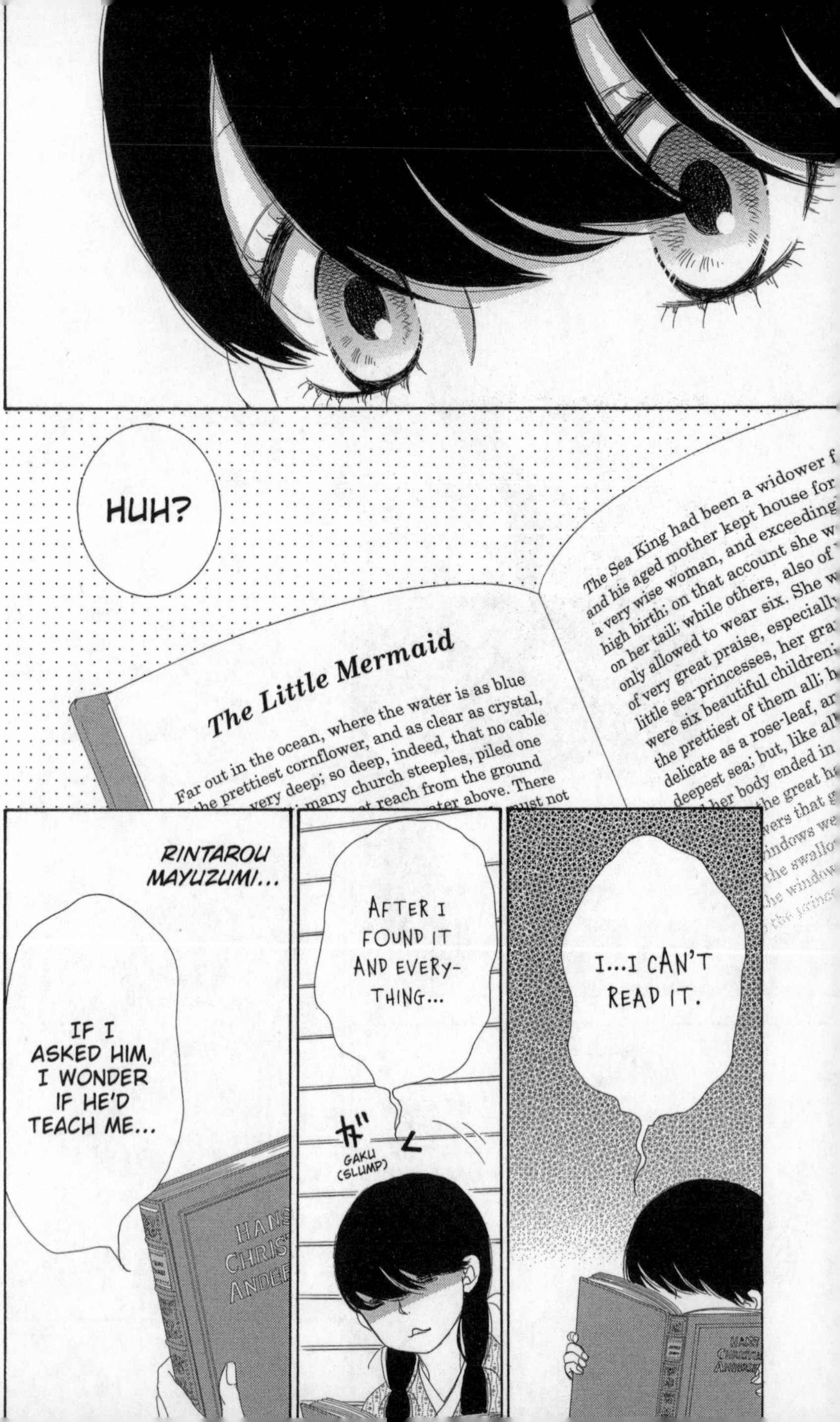
HUH?
The Sea King had been a widower
and his aged mother kept house for
a very wise woman, and exceeding
high birth; on that account she
on her tail; while others, also of
only allowed to wear six. She
of very great praise, especially
little sea-princesses, her
were six beautiful children;
the prettiest of them all;
delicate as a rose-leaf,
deepest sea; but, like all
The Little Mermaid
Far out in the ocean, where the water is as blue
the prettiest cornflower, and as clear as crystal,
very deep; so deep, indeed, that no cable
many church steeples, piled one
reach from the ground
I...I CAN'T READ IT.
AFTER I FOUND IT AND EVERYTHING...
ガく
GAKU (SLUMP)
RINTAROU MAYUZUMI...
IF I ASKED HIM, I WONDER IF HE'D TEACH ME...

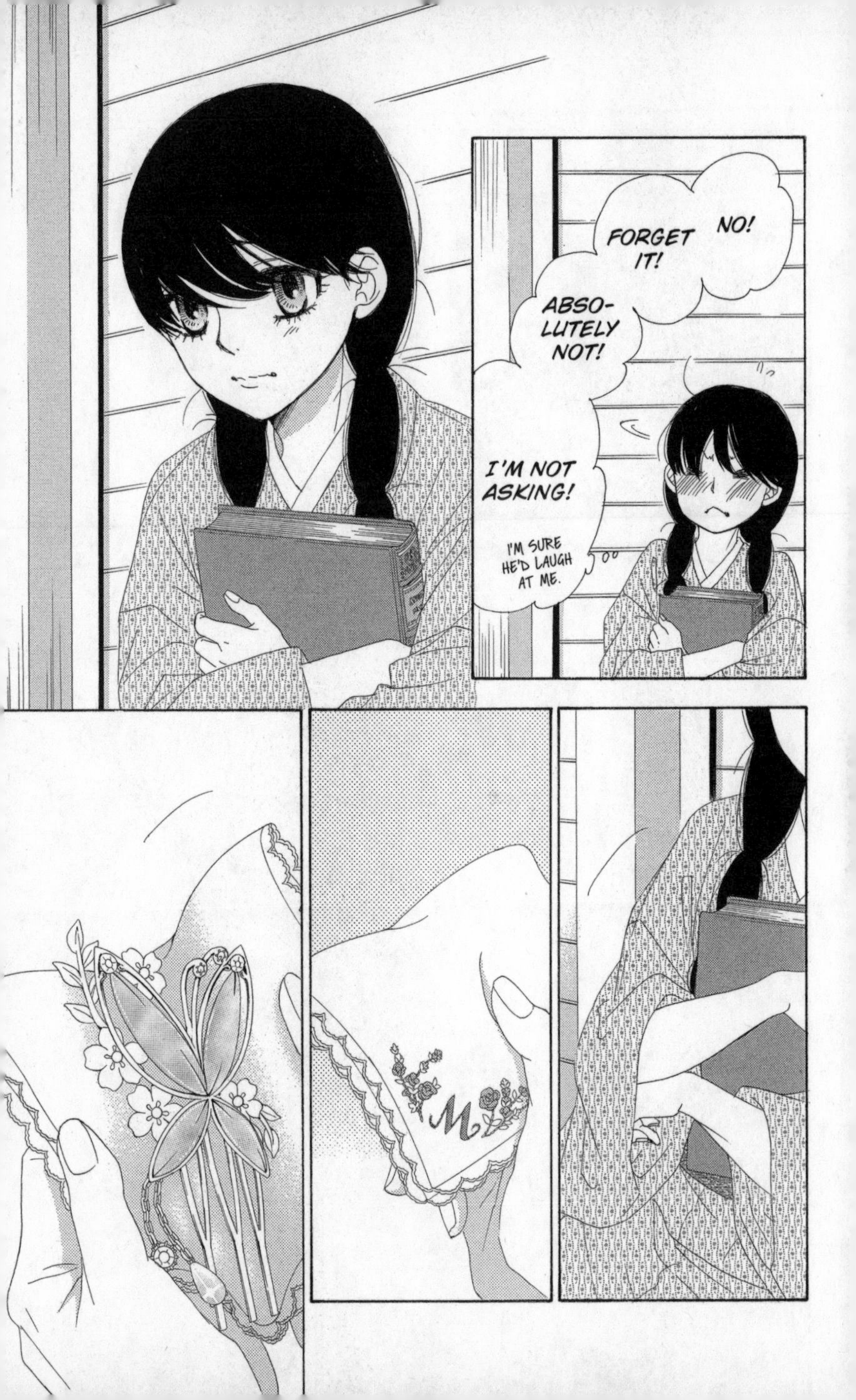
NO!
FORGET IT!
ABSOLUTELY NOT!
I'M NOT ASKING!
I'M SURE HE'D LAUGH AT ME.

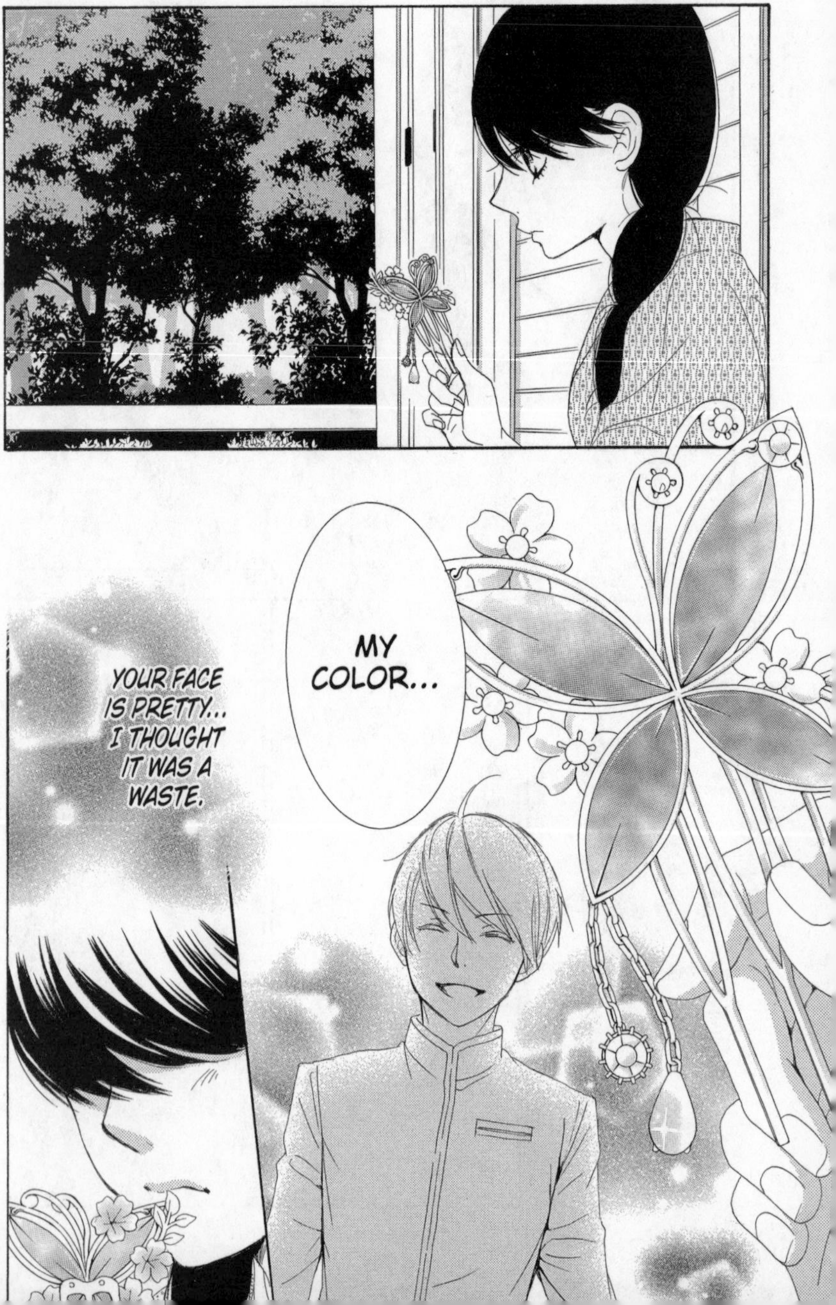
MY COLOR...
YOUR FACE IS PRETTY... I THOUGHT IT WAS A WASTE.

IF I WORE THIS IN FRONT OF HIM...I WONDER WHAT HE'D SAY...
WOULD HE REALLY THINK IT SUITED ME?
WOULD HE SMILE THAT WAY AND TELL ME SO?
IF I WORE THIS...
WHY IS HE ON MY MIND...
...SO VERY MUCH?

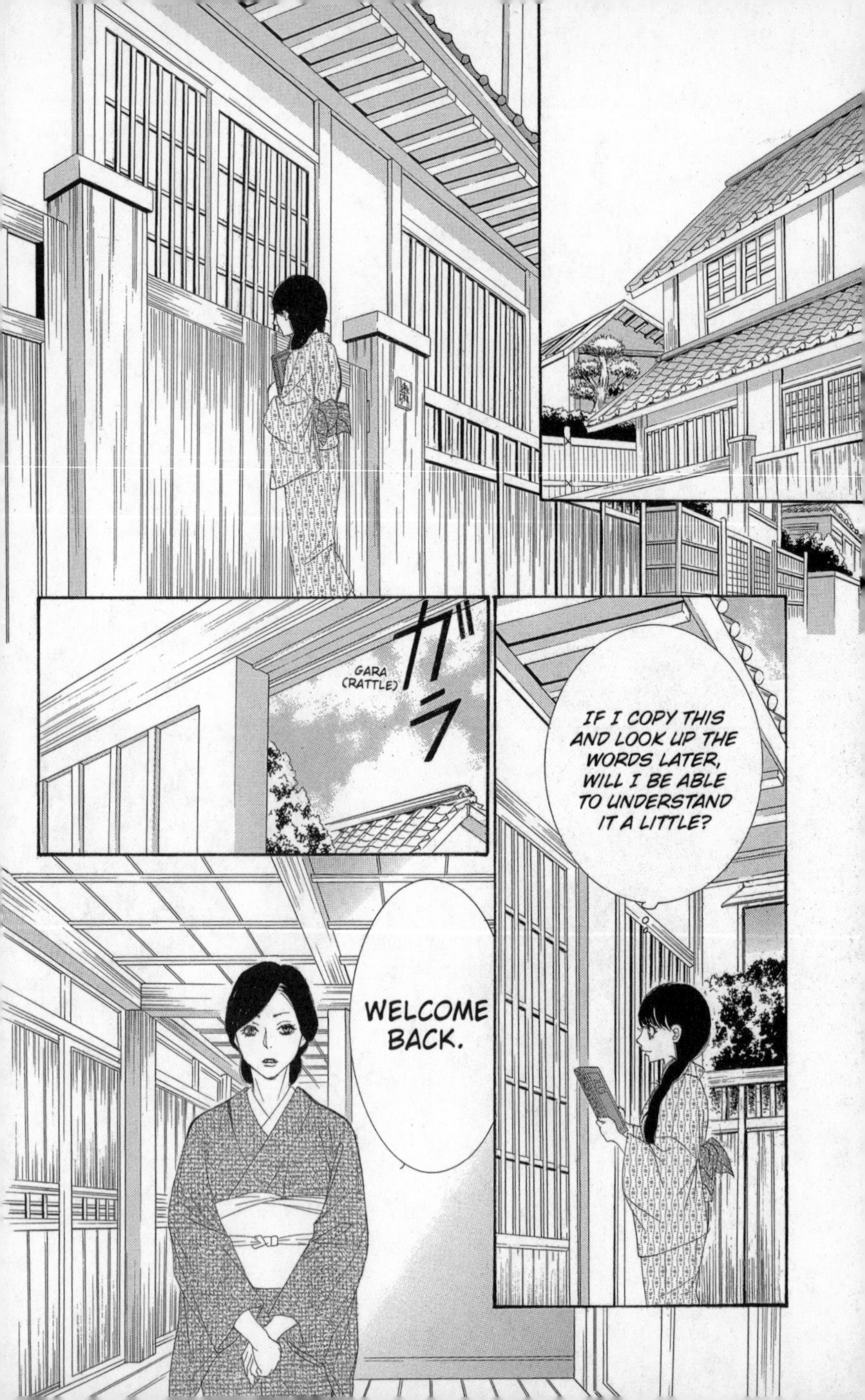
IF I COPY THIS AND LOOK UP THE WORDS LATER, WILL I BE ABLE TO UNDERSTAND IT A LITTLE?
ガラ
GARA (RATTLE)
WELCOME BACK.

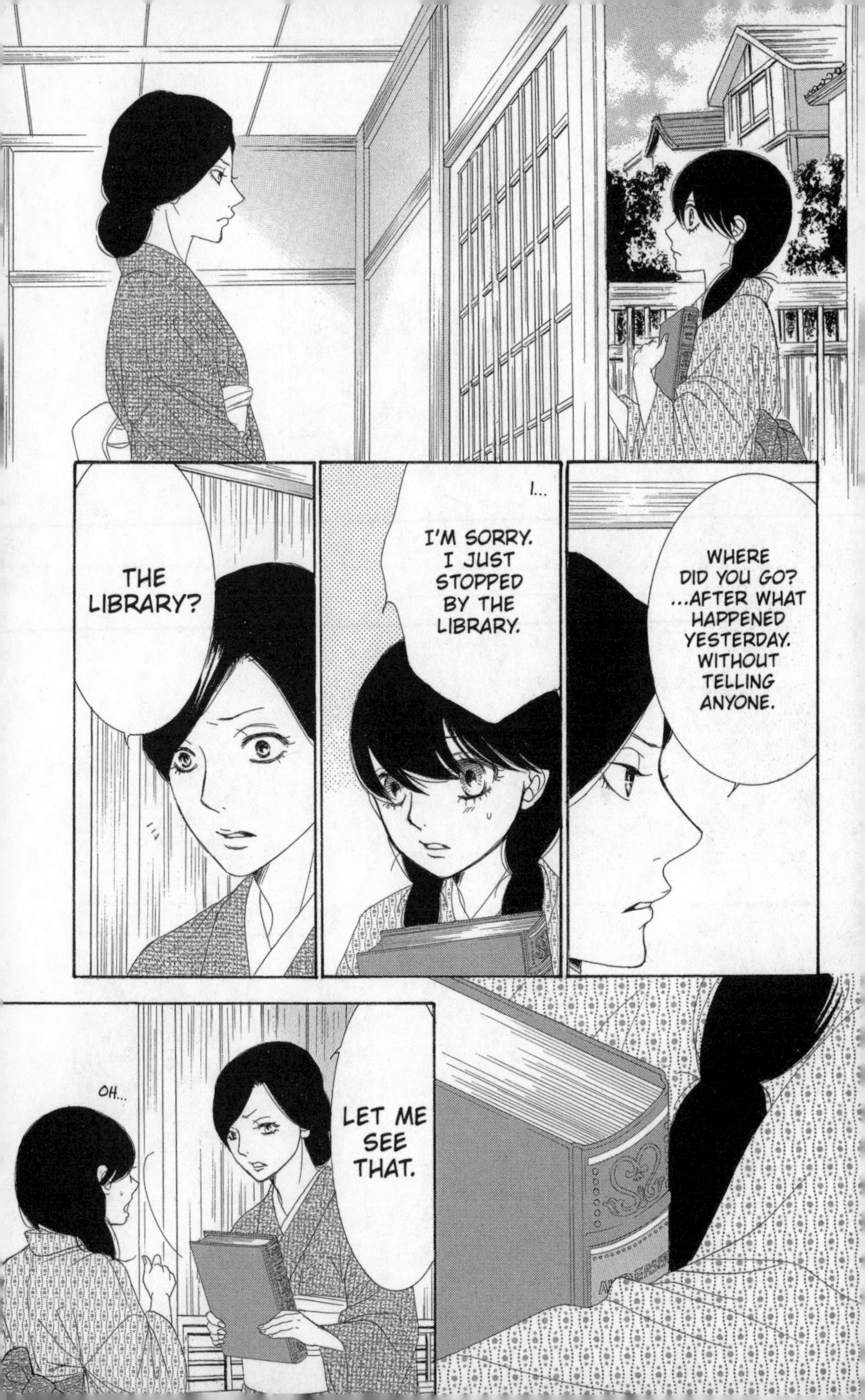
WHERE DID YOU GO? ...AFTER WHAT HAPPENED YESTERDAY. WITHOUT TELLING ANYONE.
I...
I'M SORRY. I JUST STOPPED BY THE LIBRARY.
THE LIBRARY?
LET ME SEE THAT.
OH...

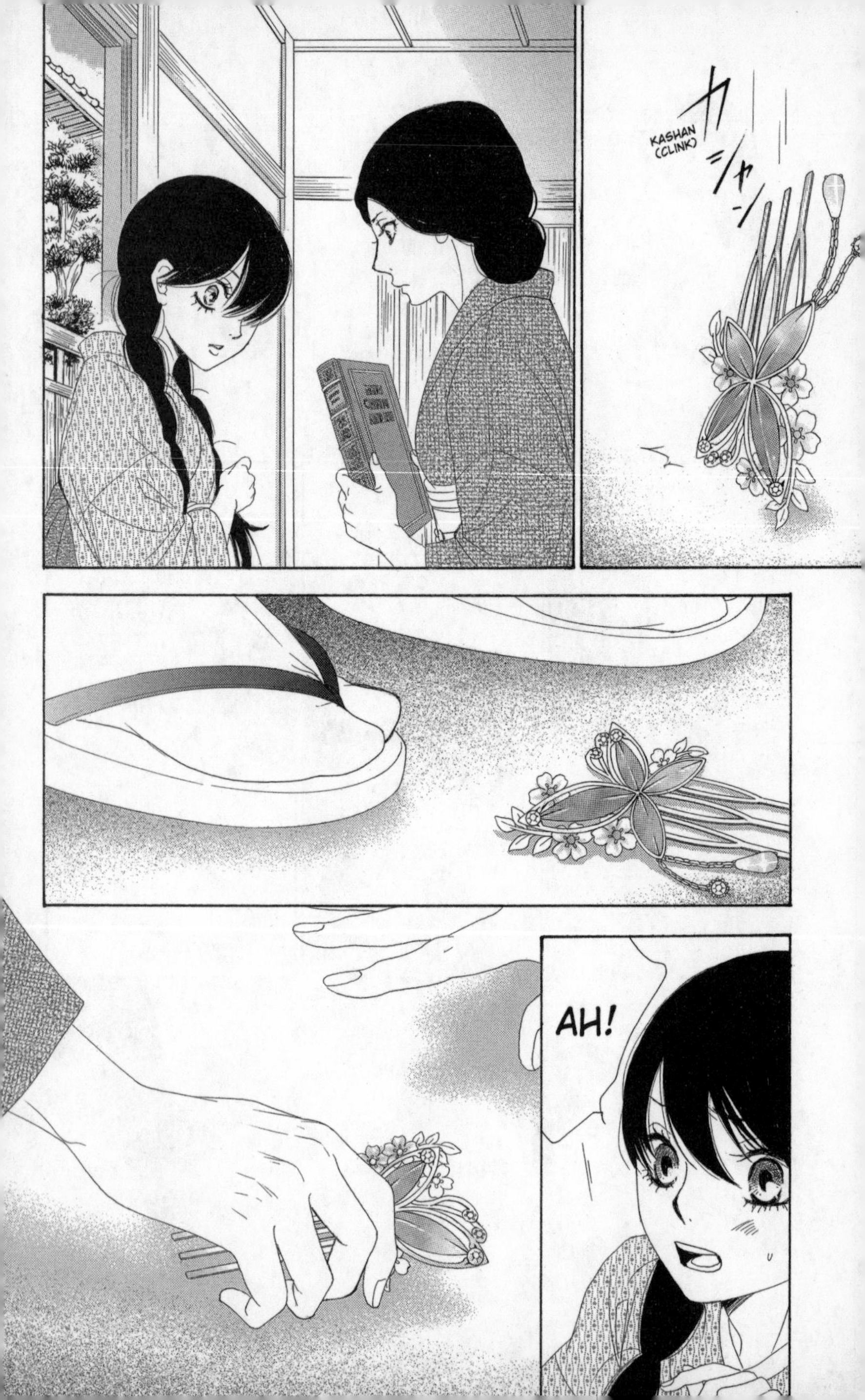
KASHAN (CLINK)
AH!

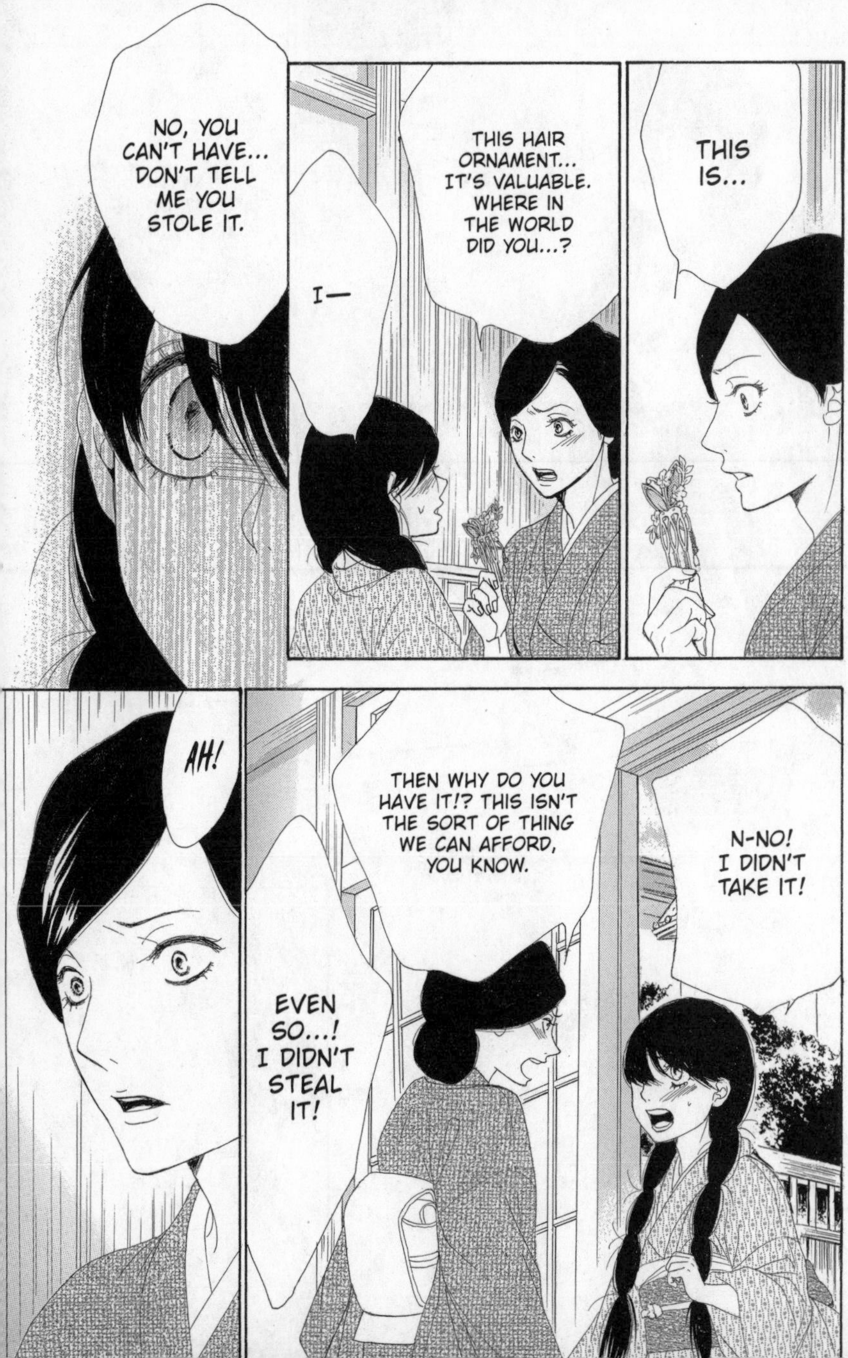
THIS IS...
THIS HAIR ORNAMENT... IT'S VALUABLE. WHERE IN THE WORLD DID YOU...?
I—
NO, YOU CAN'T HAVE... DON'T TELL ME YOU STOLE IT.
N-NO! I DIDN'T TAKE IT!
THEN WHY DO YOU HAVE IT!? THIS ISN'T THE SORT OF THING WE CAN AFFORD, YOU KNOW.
EVEN SO...! I DIDN'T STEAL IT!
AH!

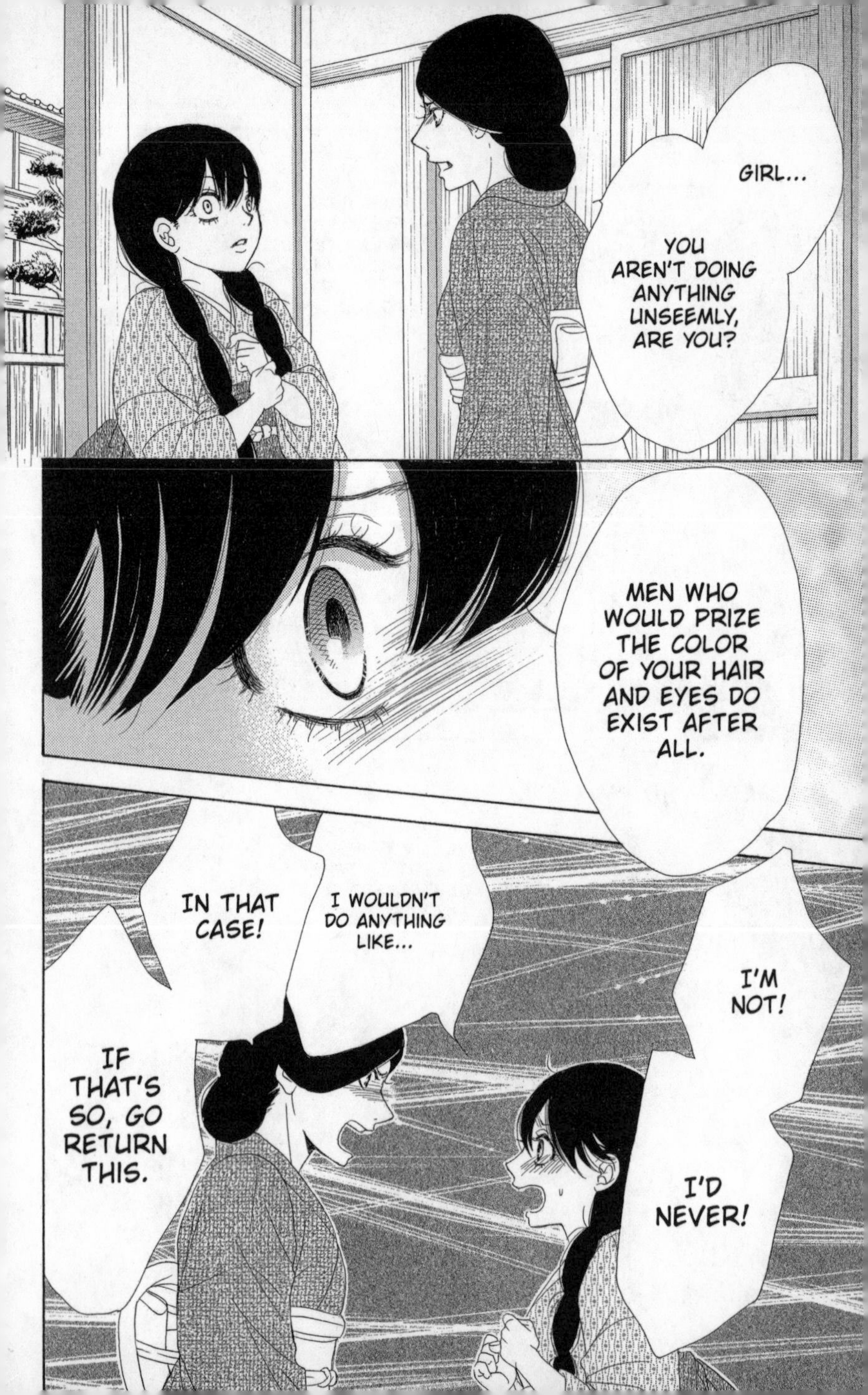
GIRL...
YOU AREN'T DOING ANYTHING UNSEEMLY, ARE YOU?
MEN WHO WOULD PRIZE THE COLOR OF YOUR HAIR AND EYES DO EXIST AFTER ALL.
I'M NOT!
I'D NEVER!
I WOULDN'T DO ANYTHING LIKE...
IN THAT CASE!
IF THAT'S SO, GO RETURN THIS.

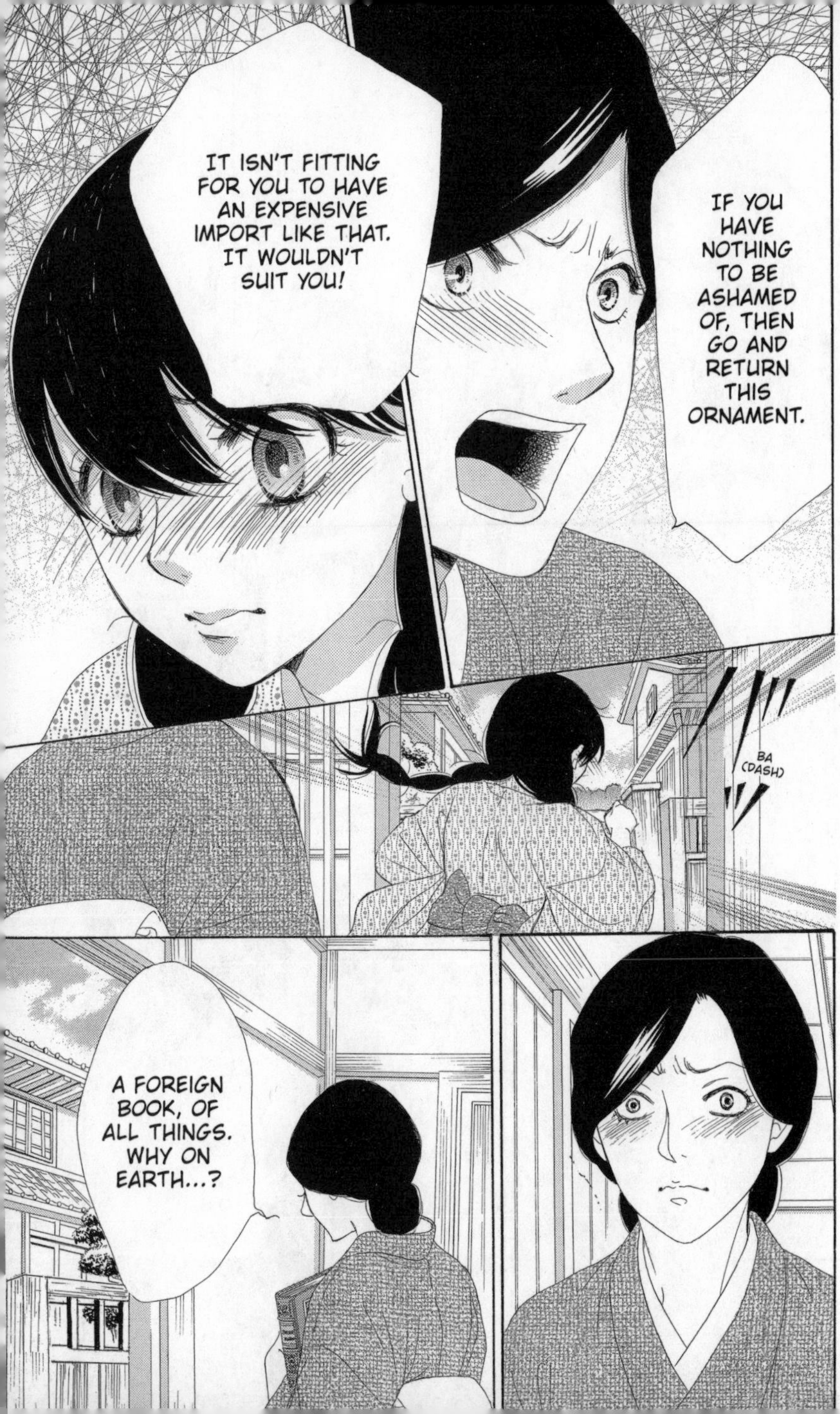
IF YOU HAVE NOTHING TO BE ASHAMED OF, THEN GO AND RETURN THIS ORNAMENT.
IT ISN'T FITTING FOR YOU TO HAVE AN EXPENSIVE IMPORT LIKE THAT. IT WOULDN'T SUIT YOU!
BA (DASH)
A FOREIGN BOOK, OF ALL THINGS. WHY ON EARTH...?

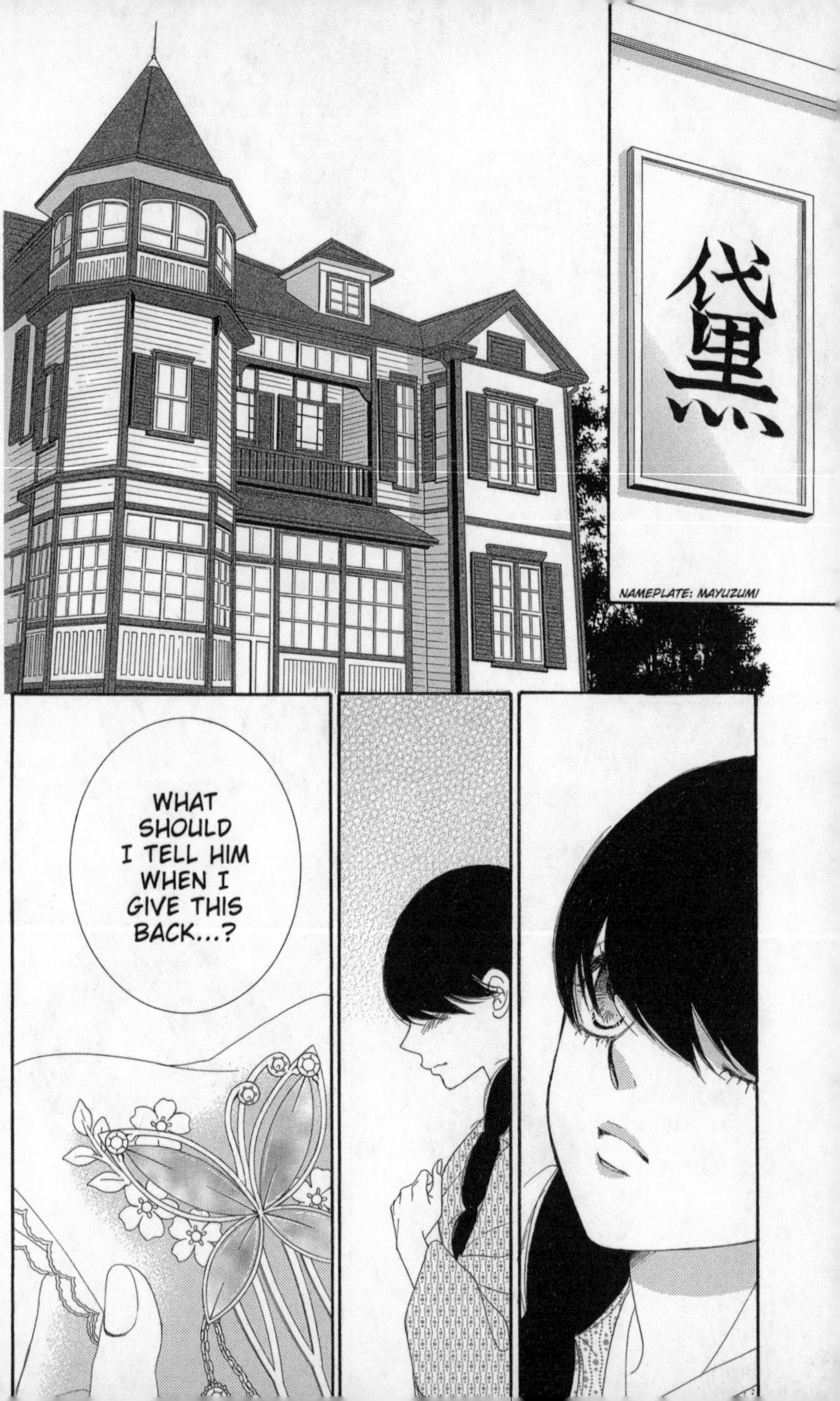
黛
NAMEPLATE: MAYUZUMI
WHAT SHOULD I TELL HIM WHEN I GIVE THIS BACK...?

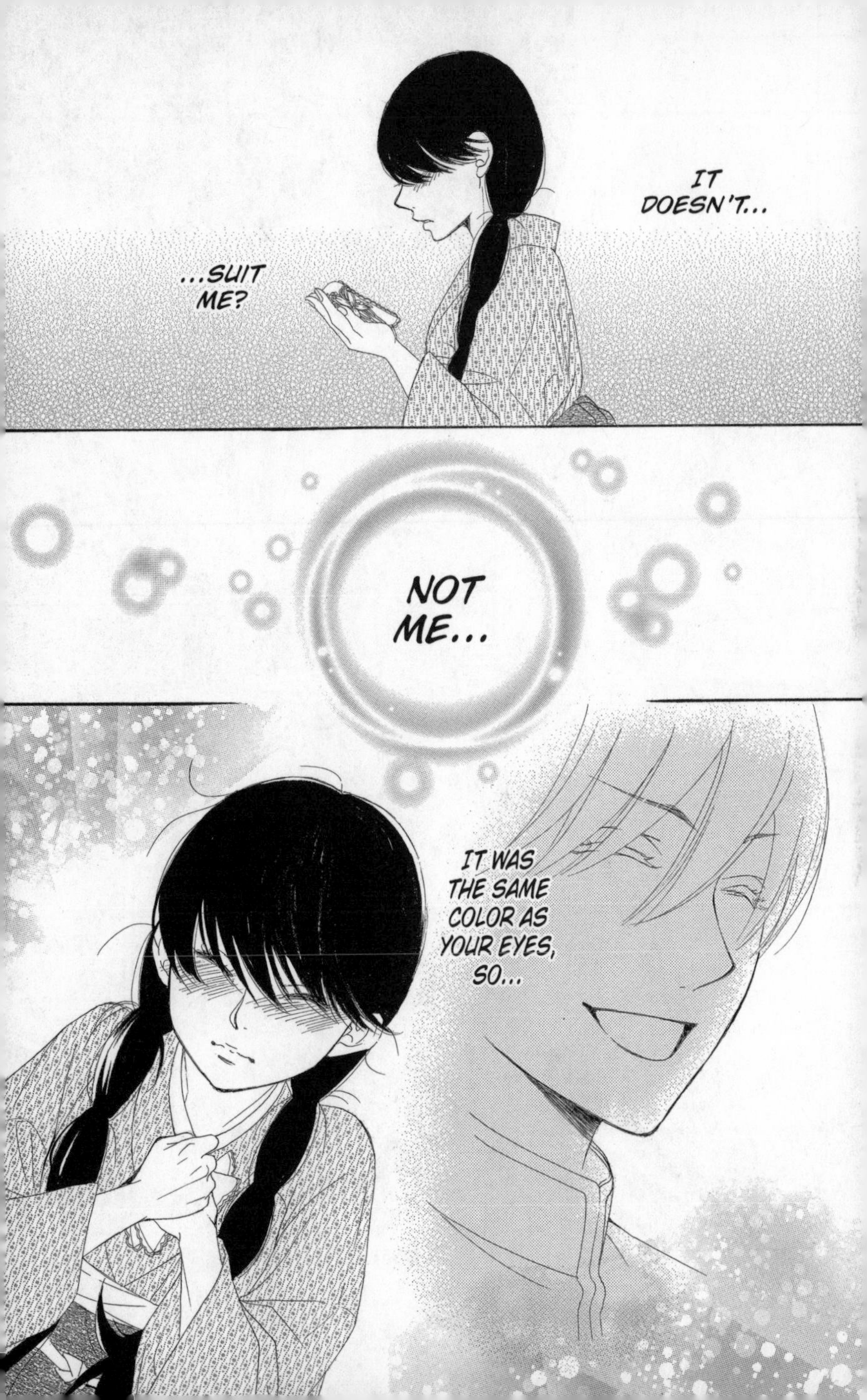
IT DOESN'T...
...SUIT ME?
NOT ME...
IT WAS THE SAME COLOR AS YOUR EYES, SO...

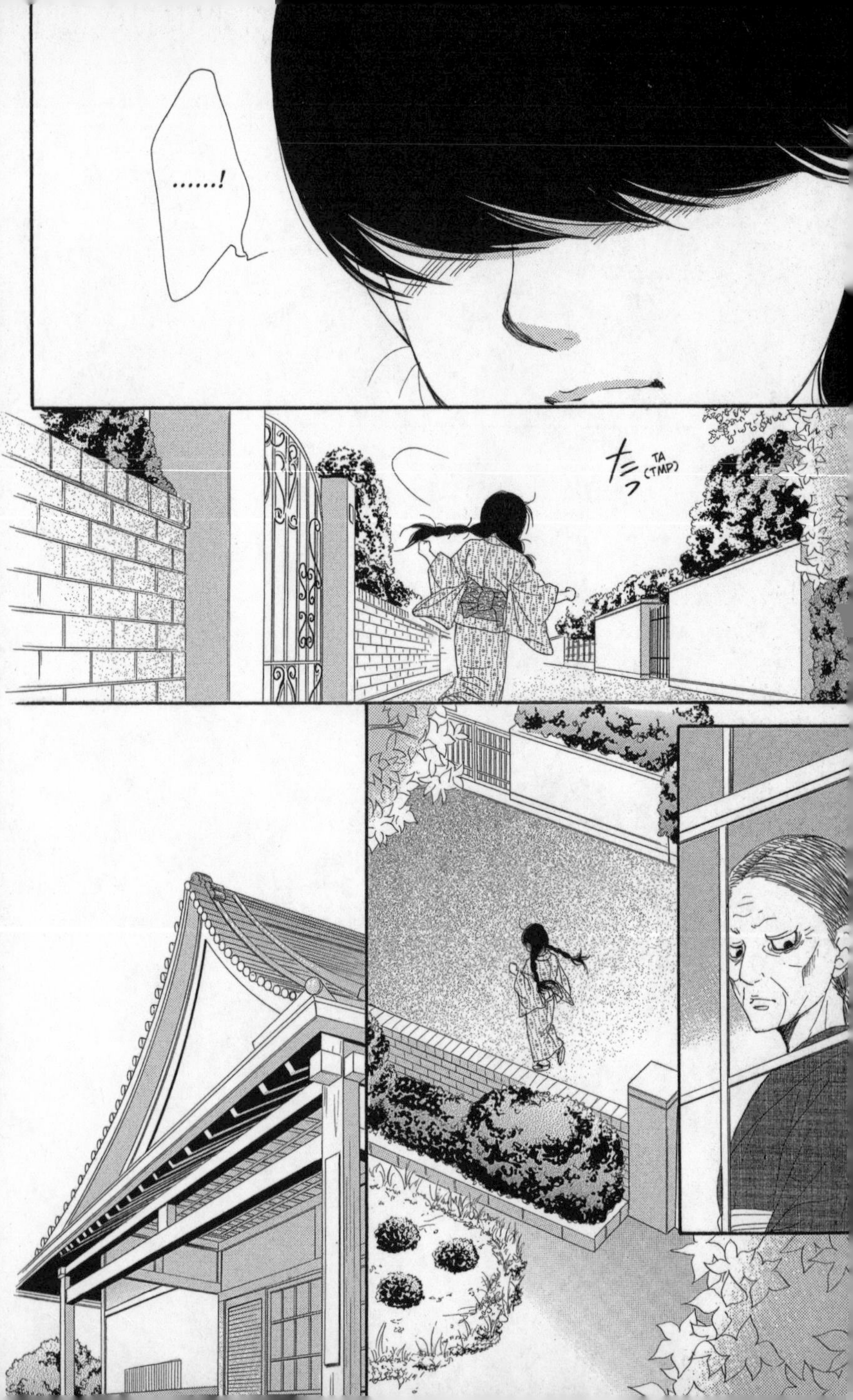
......!
たっ
TA (TMP)

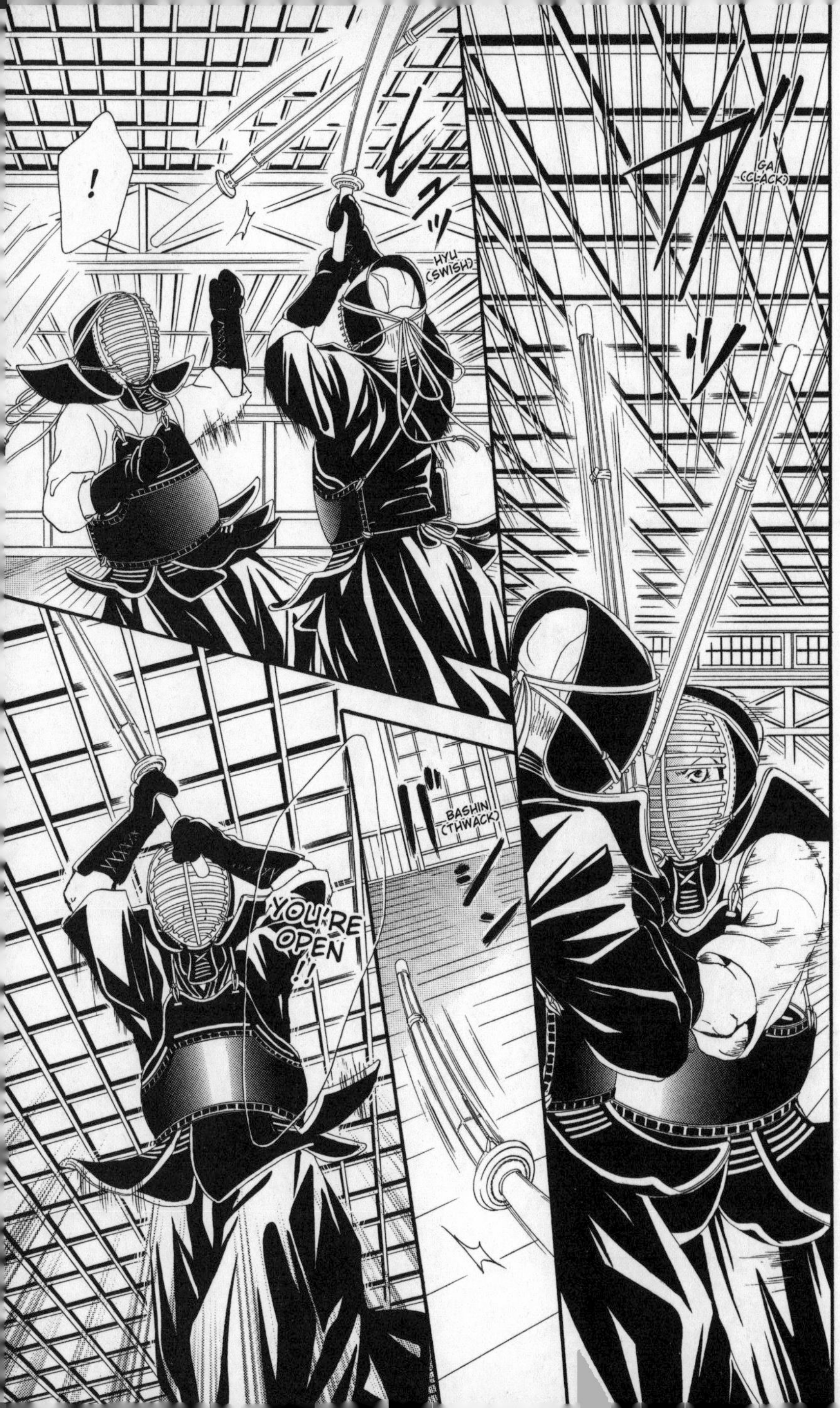
GA (CLACK)
!
HYU (SWISH)
BASHIN (THWACK)
YOU'RE OPEN!!

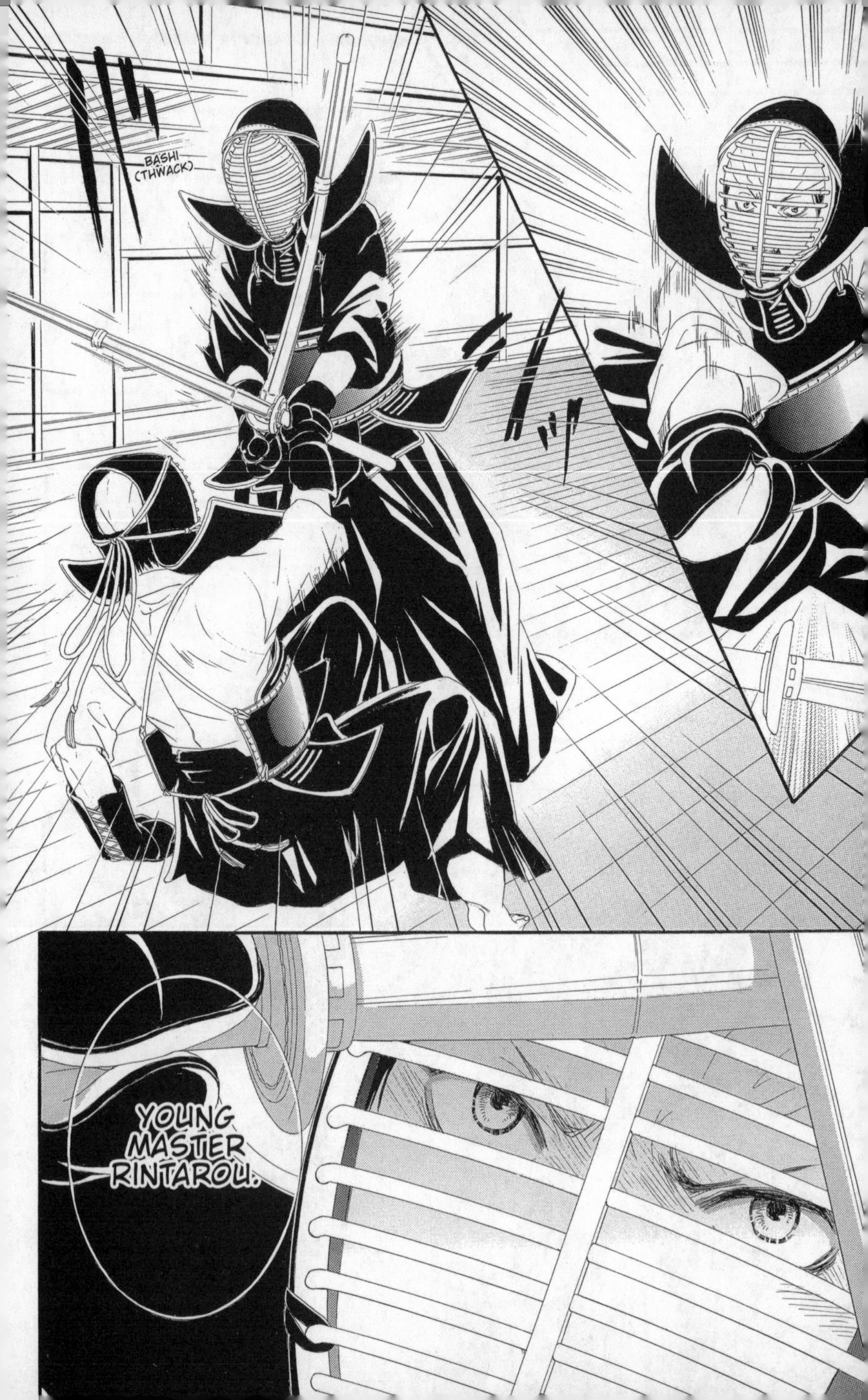
BASHI
(THWACK)
YOUNG MASTER RINTAROU.

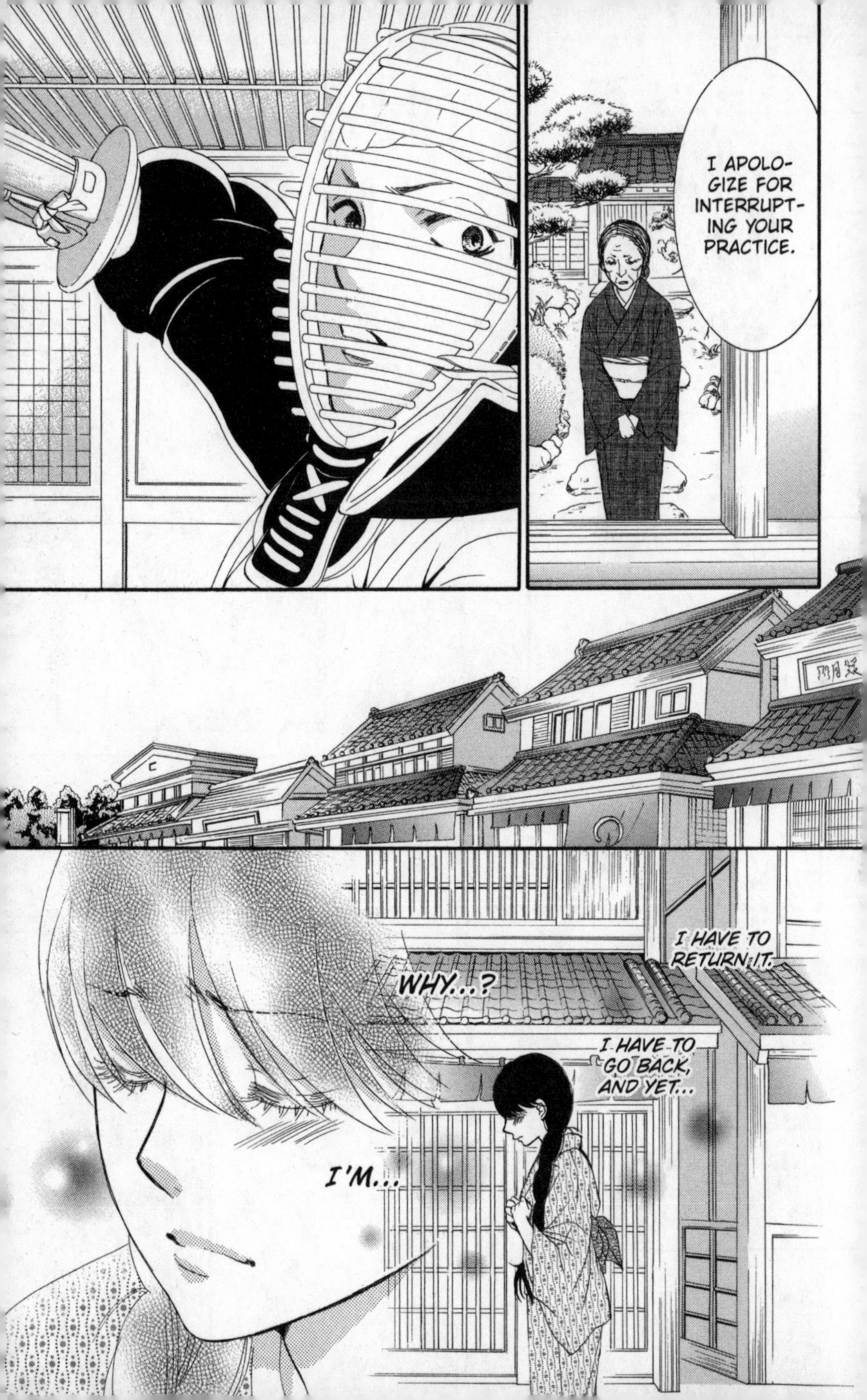
I APOLOGIZE FOR INTERRUPTING YOUR PRACTICE.
I HAVE TO RETURN IT.
WHY...?
I HAVE TO GO BACK, AND YET...
I'M...

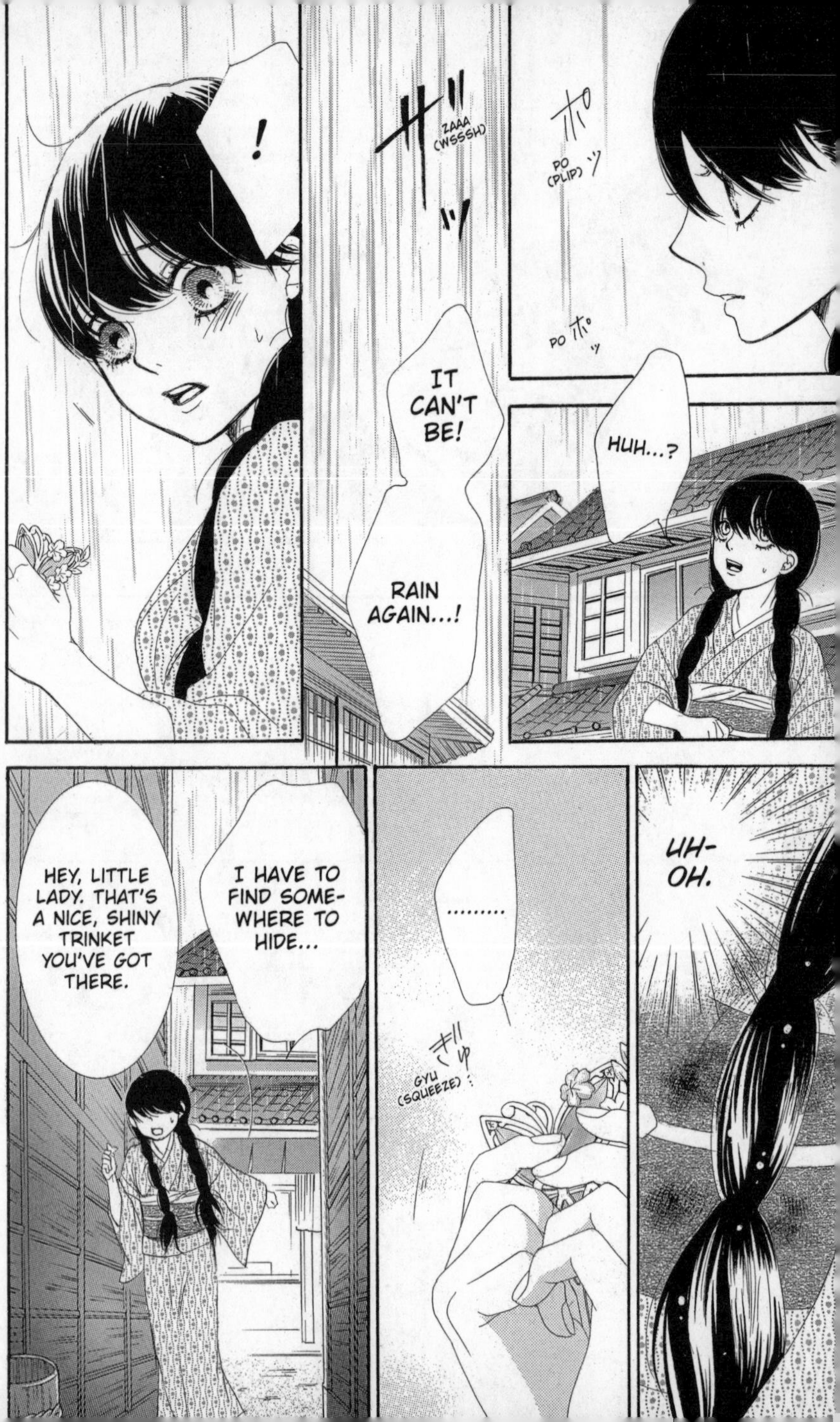

ポッ
PO (PLIP)
ポッ
PO
HUH...?
ザーッ
ZAAA (WSSSH)
!
IT CAN'T BE!
RAIN AGAIN...!
UH-OH.
....
ぎゅ
GYU (SQUEEZE)
I HAVE TO FIND SOME-WHERE TO HIDE...
HEY, LITTLE LADY. THAT'S A NICE, SHINY TRINKET YOU'VE GOT THERE.

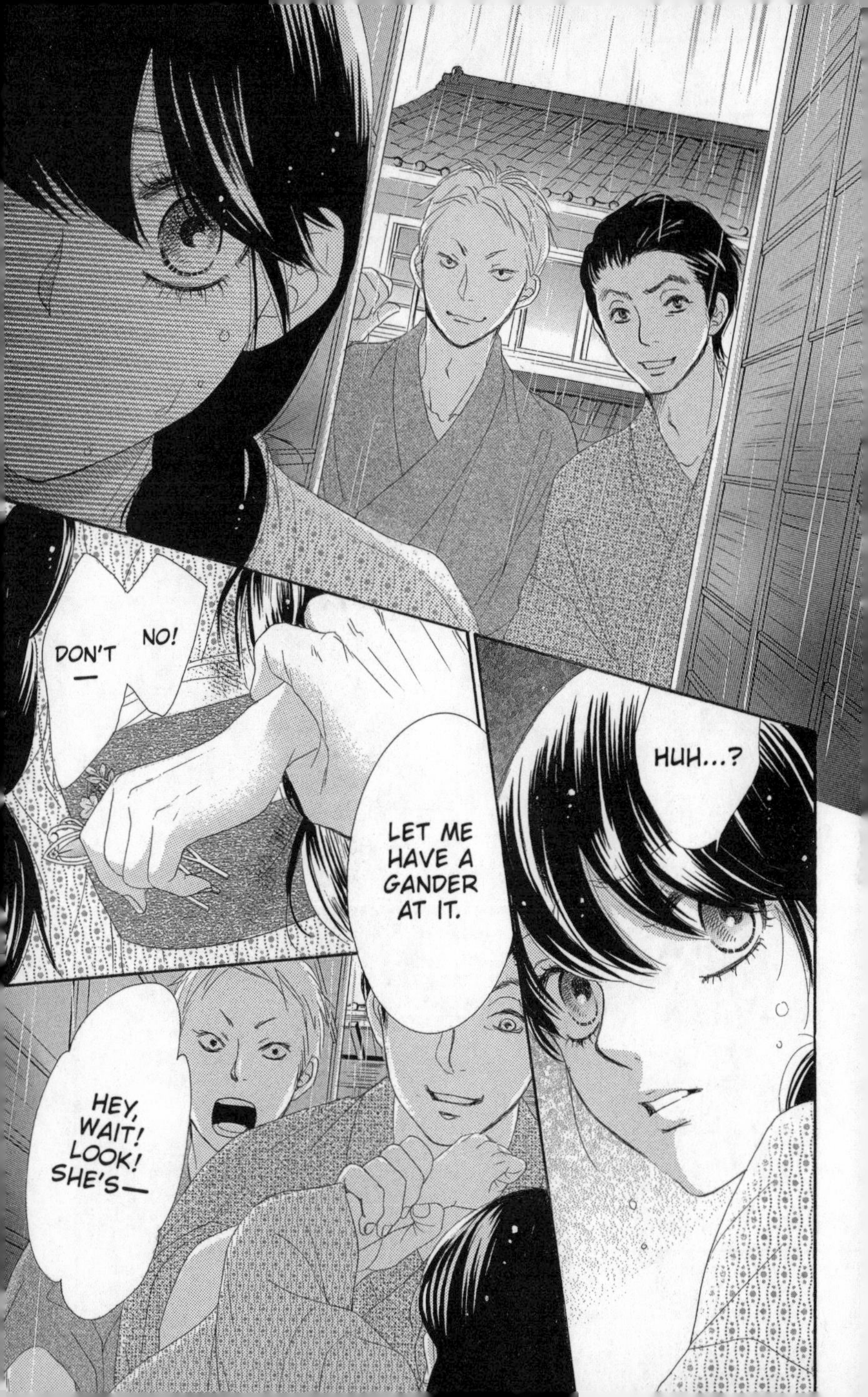
HUH...?
DON'T— NO!
LET ME HAVE A GANDER AT IT.
HEY, WAIT! LOOK! SHE'S—

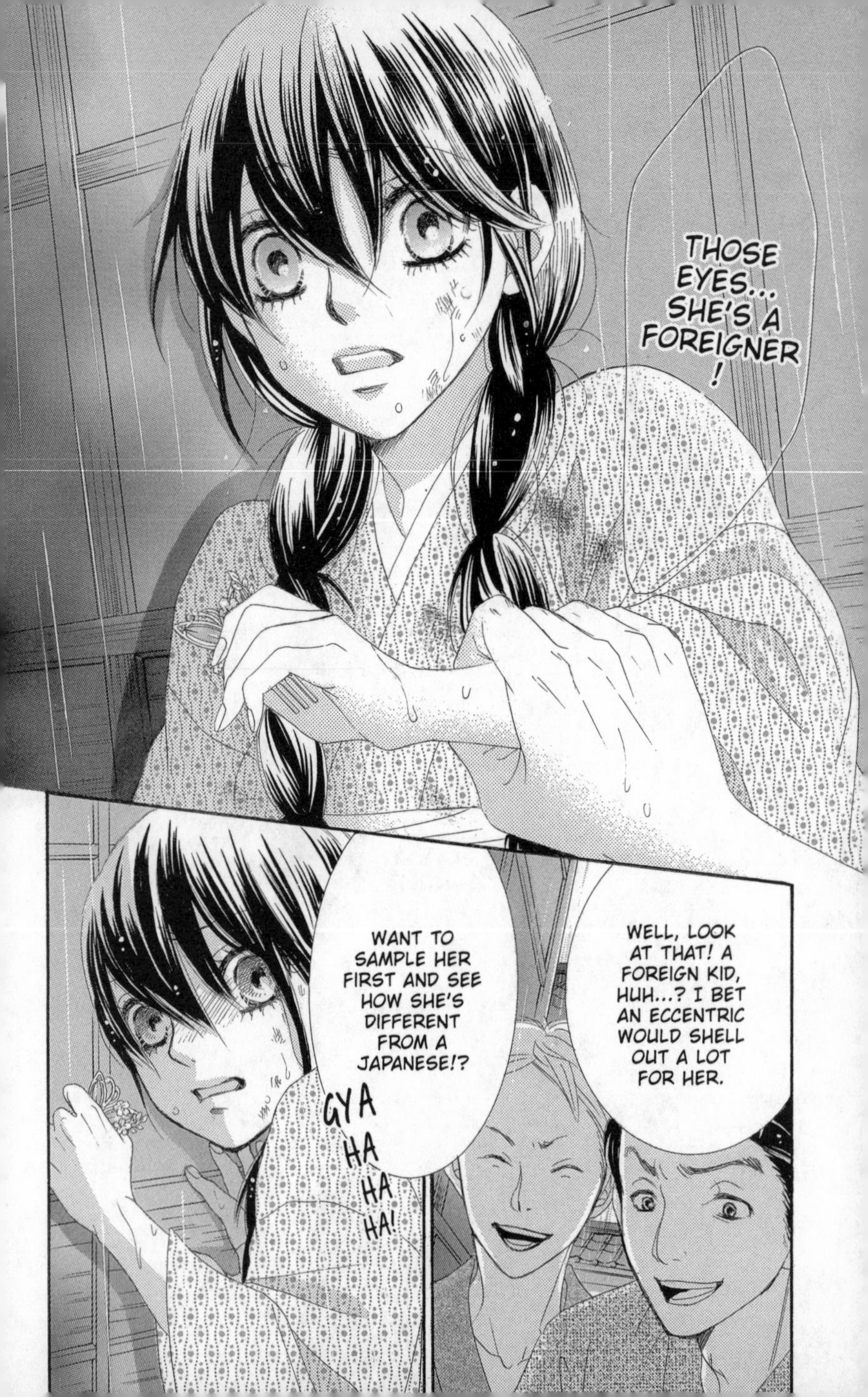
THOSE EYES... SHE'S A FOREIGNER!
WELL, LOOK AT THAT! A FOREIGN KID, HUH...? I BET AN ECCENTRIC WOULD SHELL OUT A LOT FOR HER.
WANT TO SAMPLE HER FIRST AND SEE HOW SHE'S DIFFERENT FROM A JAPANESE!?
GYA HA HA HA!

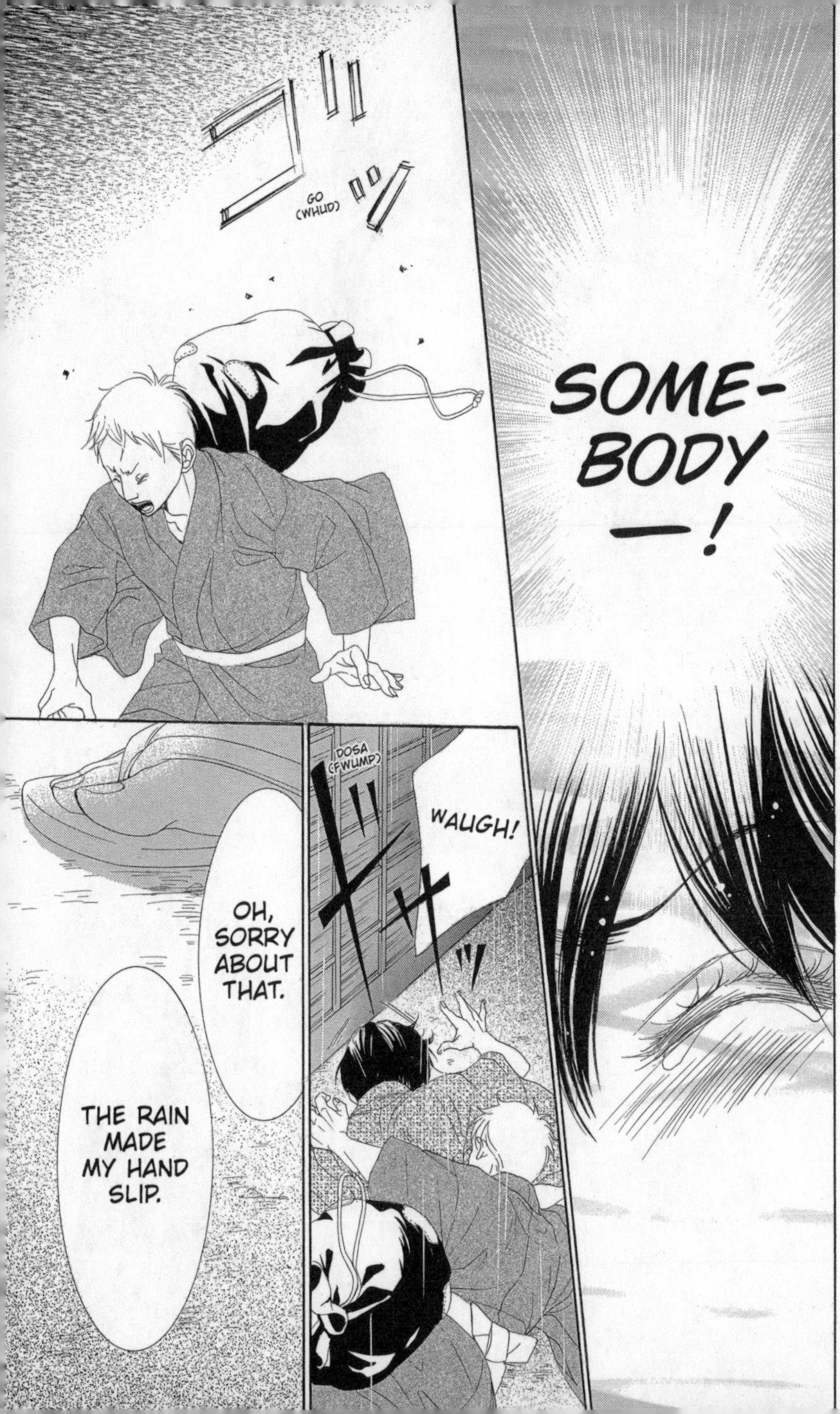
SOME-BODY—!
GO (WHUD)
DOSA (FWUMP)
WAUGH!
OH, SORRY ABOUT THAT.
THE RAIN MADE MY HAND SLIP.

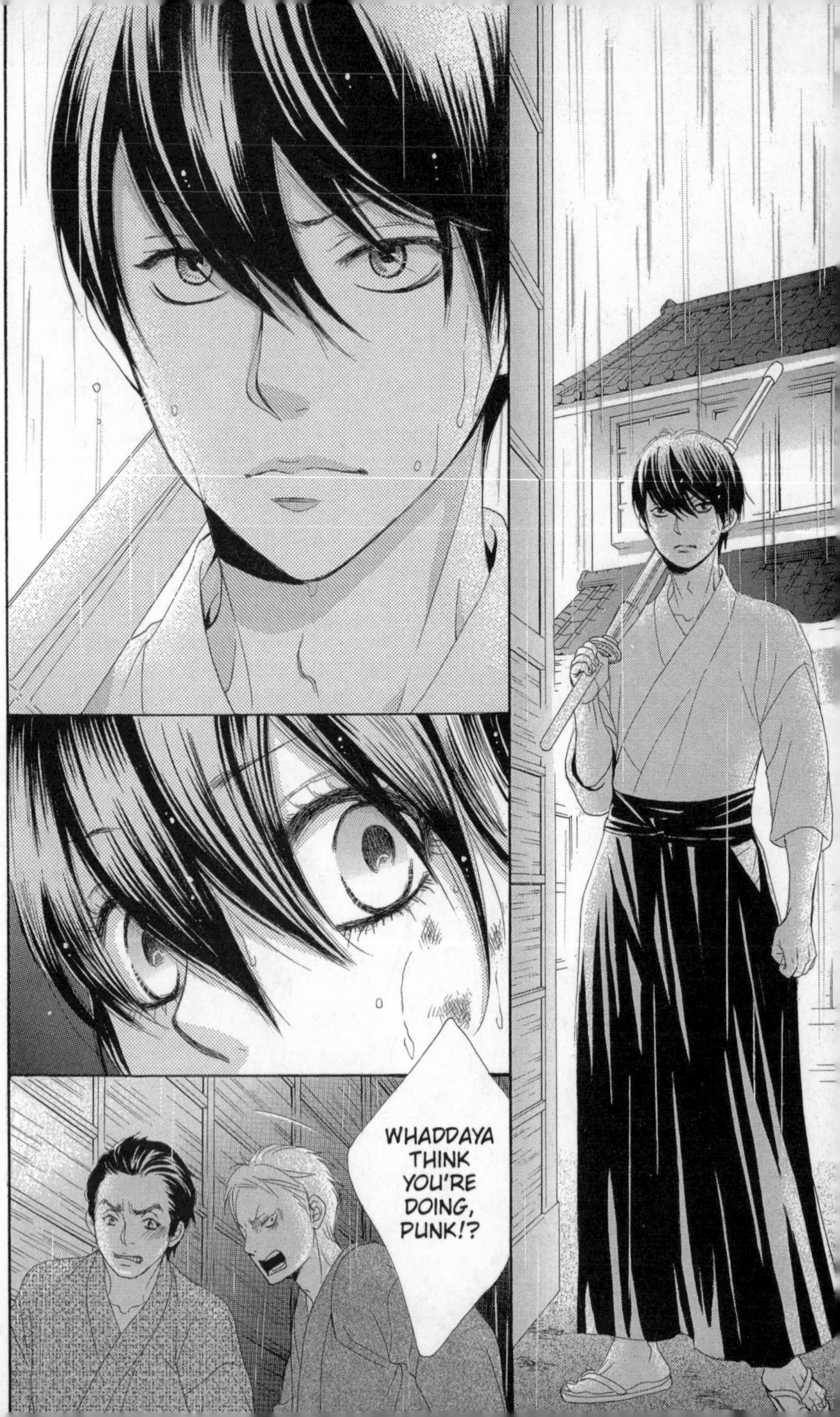
WHADDAYA THINK YOU'RE DOING, PUNK!?

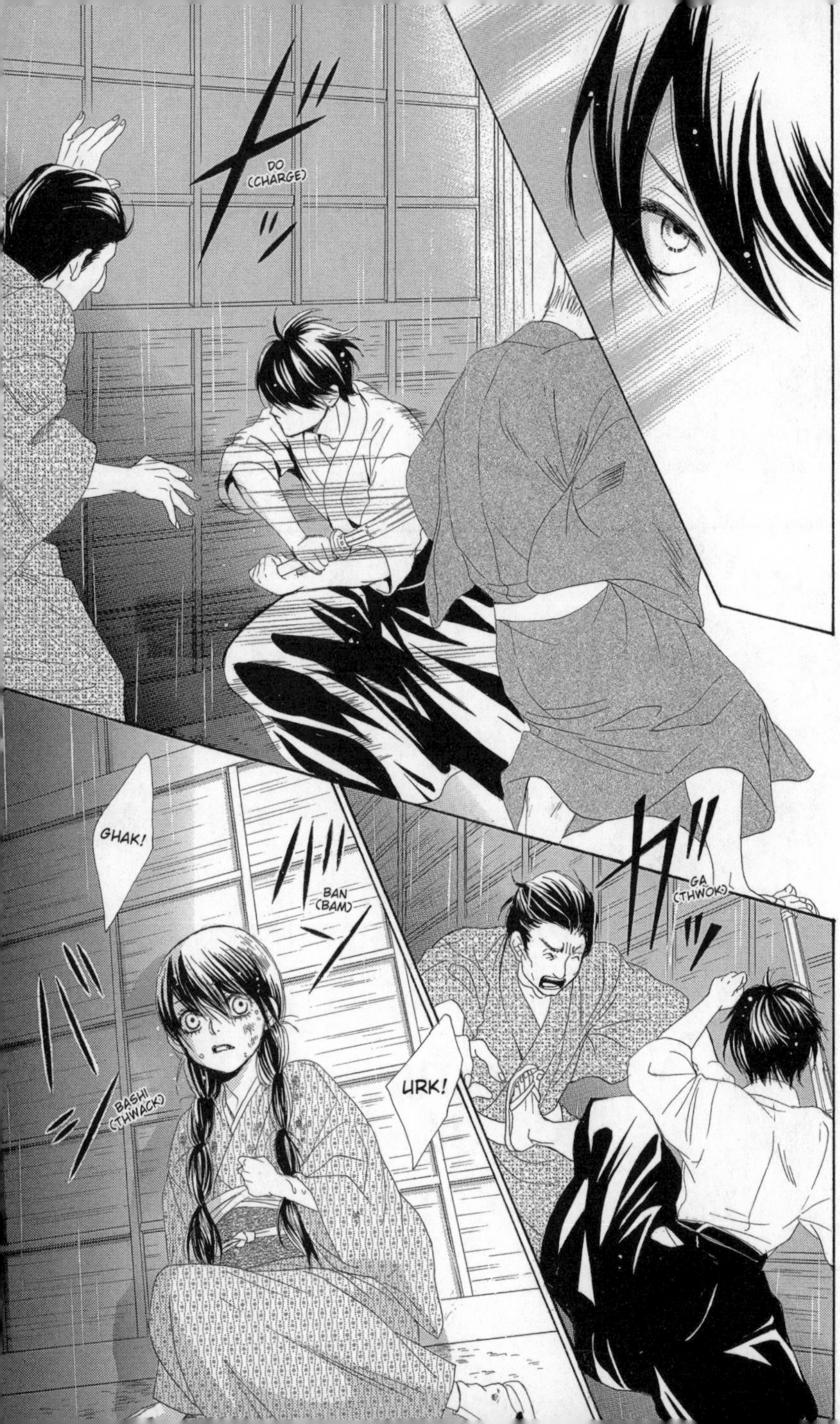
DO (CHARGE)
GA (THWOK)
URK!
BAN (BAM)
GHAK!
BASHI (THWACK)

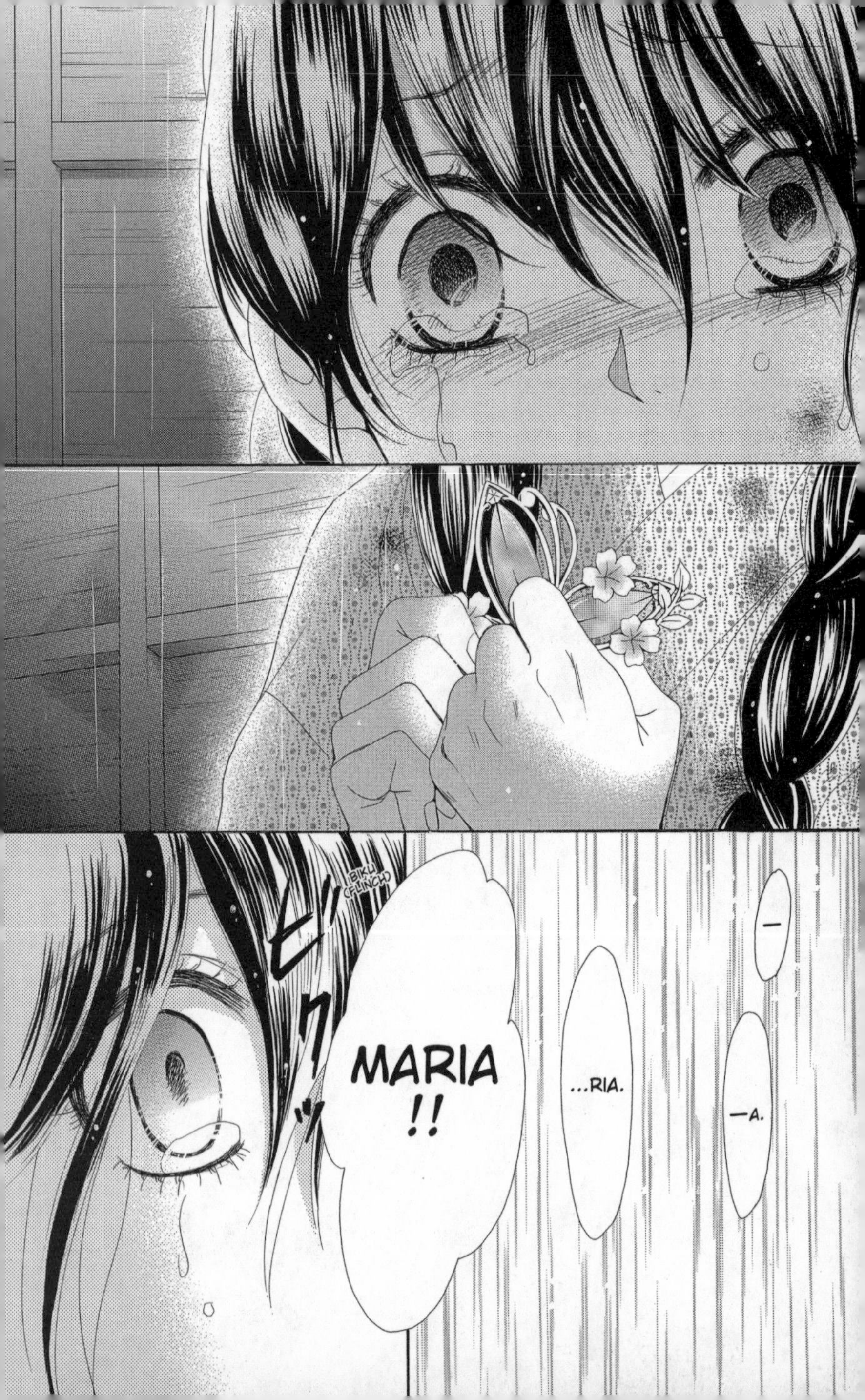
—
—A.
...RIA.
MARIA !!
BIKU (FLINCH)

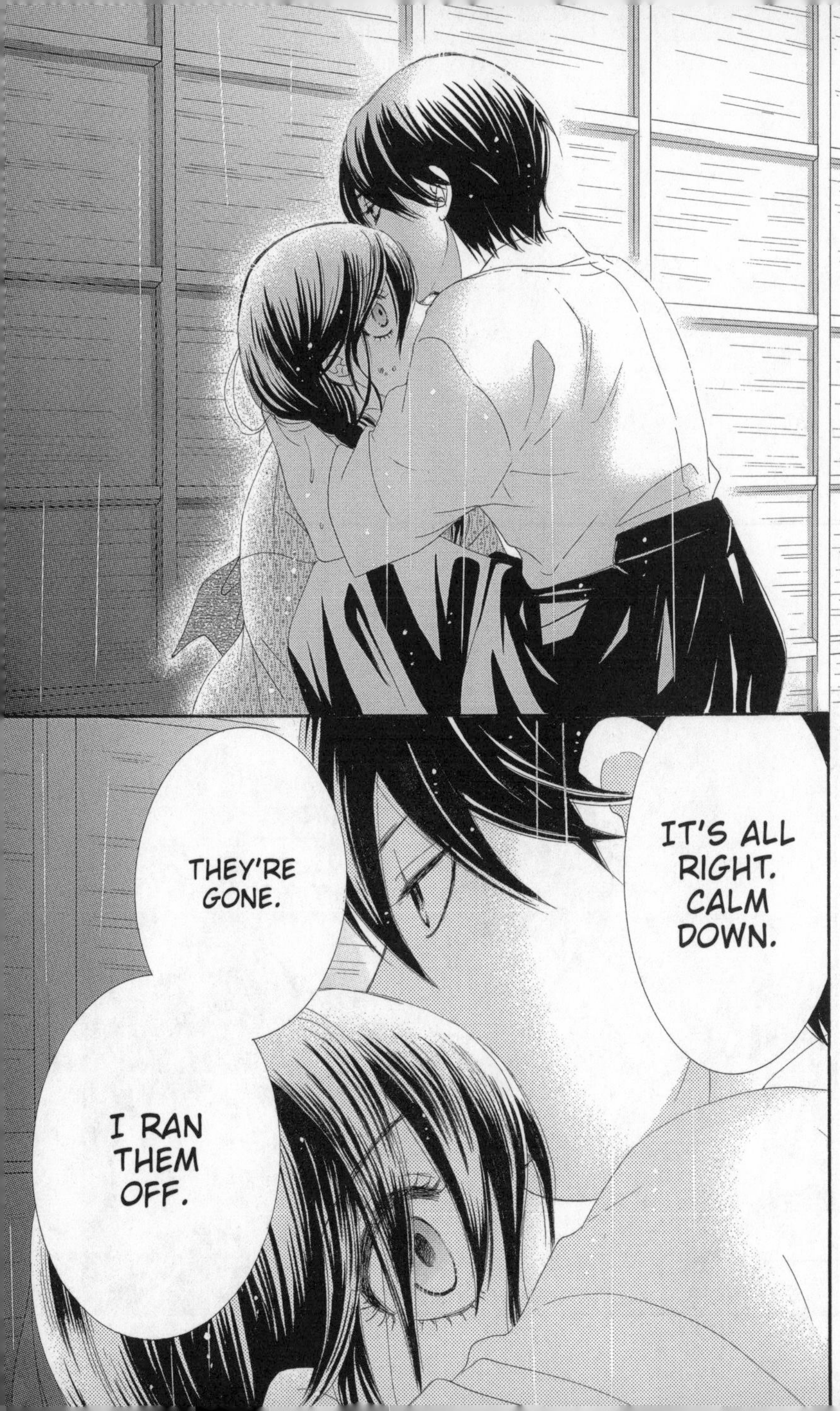
IT'S ALL RIGHT. CALM DOWN.
THEY'RE GONE.
I RAN THEM OFF.

GU
(SQUEEZE)

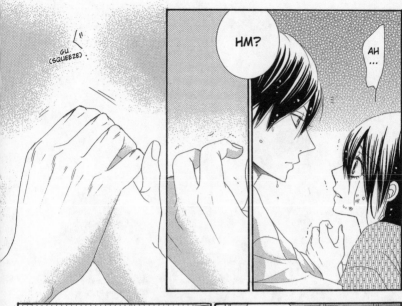

HM?

AH
...

AH!

YOUR
HANDS
ARE LIKE
ICE!

WHOA!
COLD!

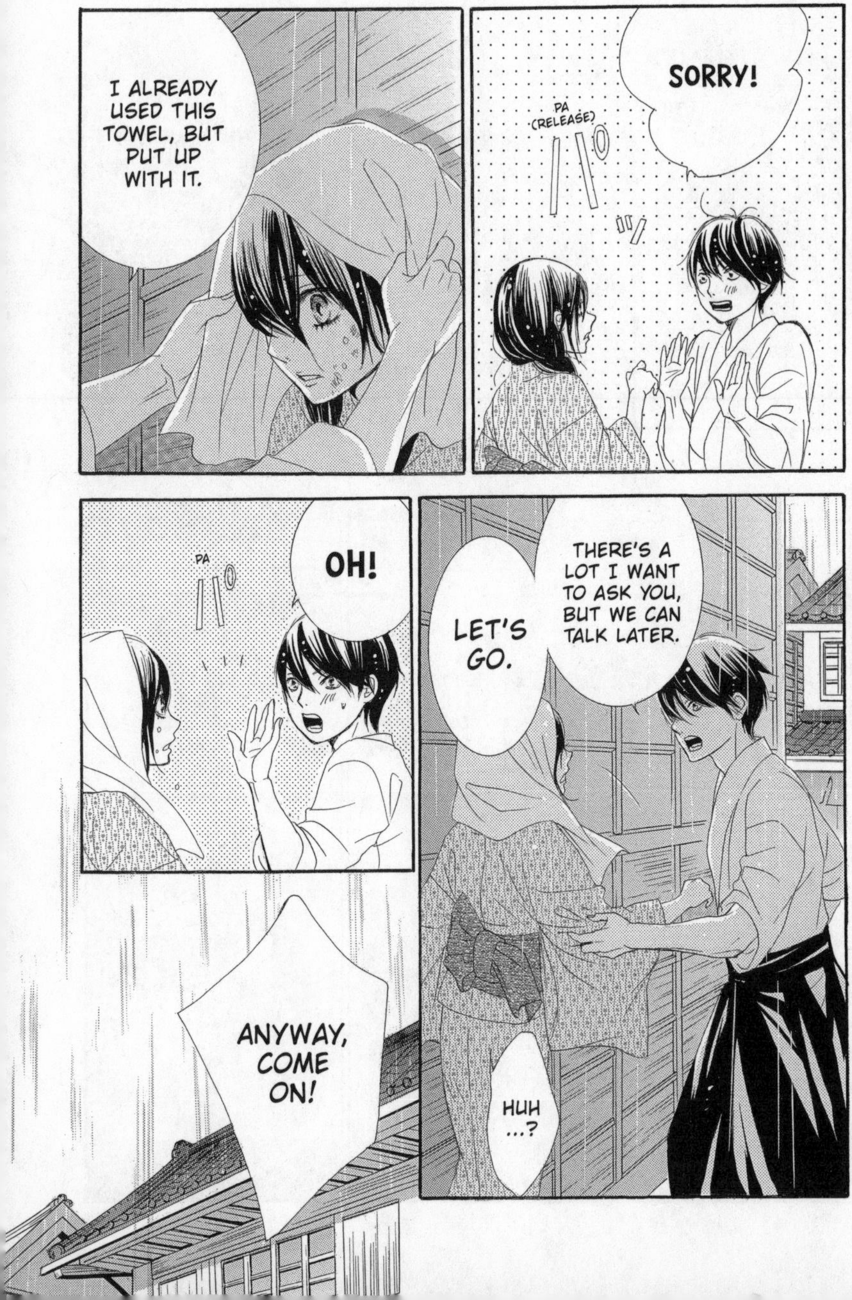
SORRY!
PA (RELEASE)
I ALREADY USED THIS TOWEL, BUT PUT UP WITH IT.
THERE'S A LOT I WANT TO ASK YOU, BUT WE CAN TALK LATER.
LET'S GO.
HUH ...?
OH!
PA
ANYWAY, COME ON!

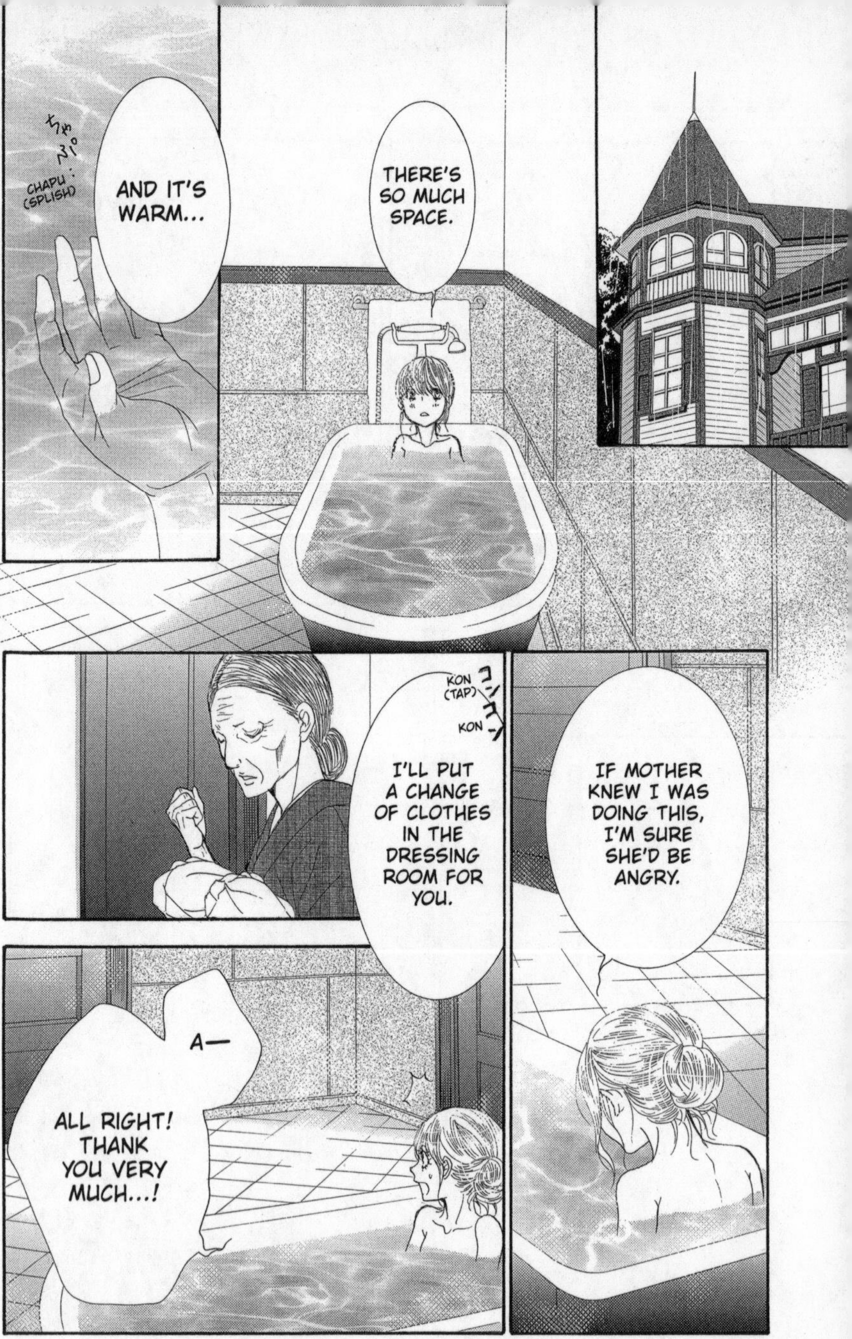
THERE'S SO MUCH SPACE.
ちゃぷ
CHAPU (SPLISH)
AND IT'S WARM...
IF MOTHER KNEW I WAS DOING THIS, I'M SURE SHE'D BE ANGRY.
KON (TAP) KON
I'LL PUT A CHANGE OF CLOTHES IN THE DRESSING ROOM FOR YOU.
A—
ALL RIGHT! THANK YOU VERY MUCH...!

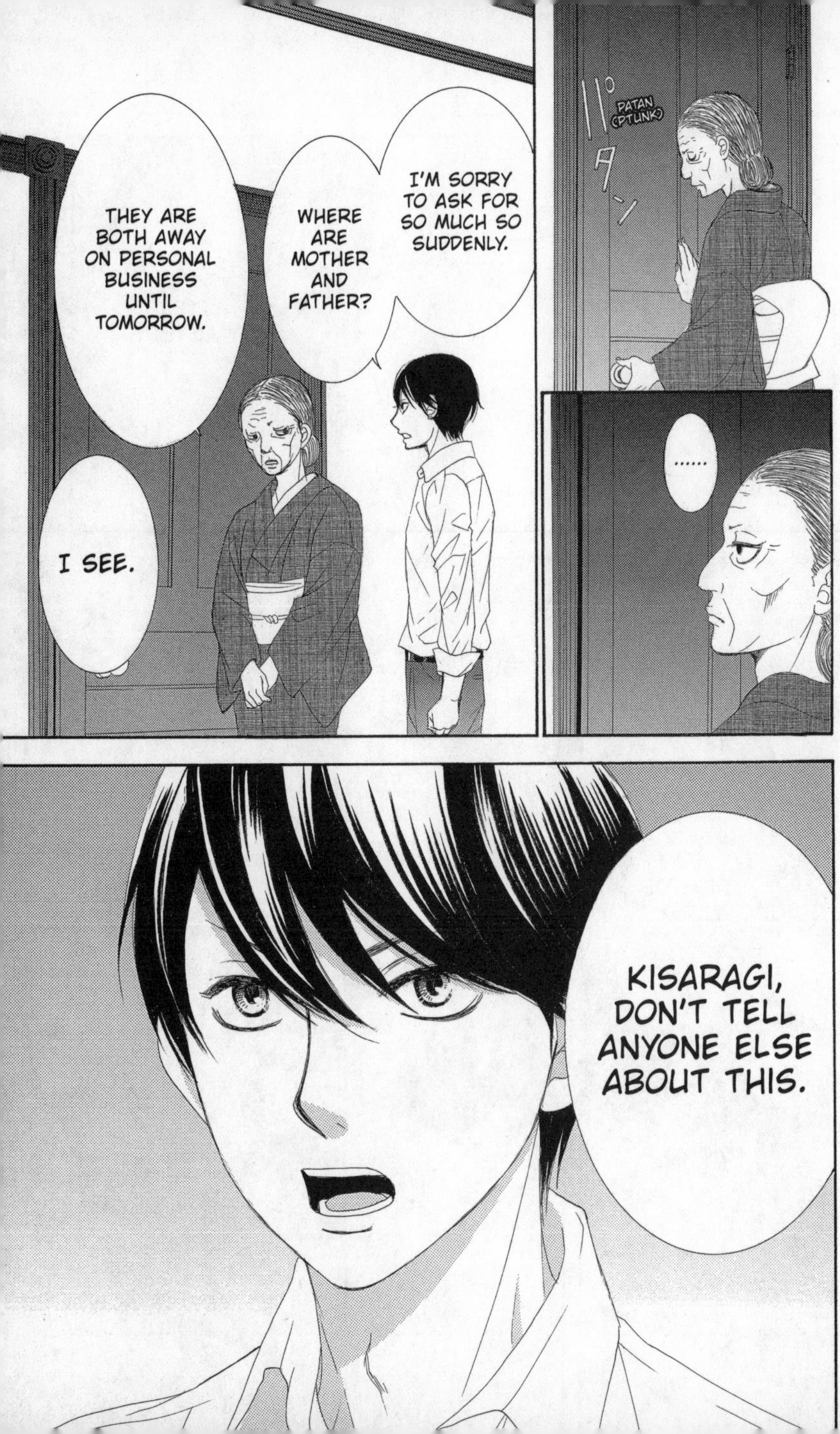
PATAN (PTUNK)
......
I'M SORRY TO ASK FOR SO MUCH SO SUDDENLY.
WHERE ARE MOTHER AND FATHER?
THEY ARE BOTH AWAY ON PERSONAL BUSINESS UNTIL TOMORROW.
I SEE.
KISARAGI, DON'T TELL ANYONE ELSE ABOUT THIS.

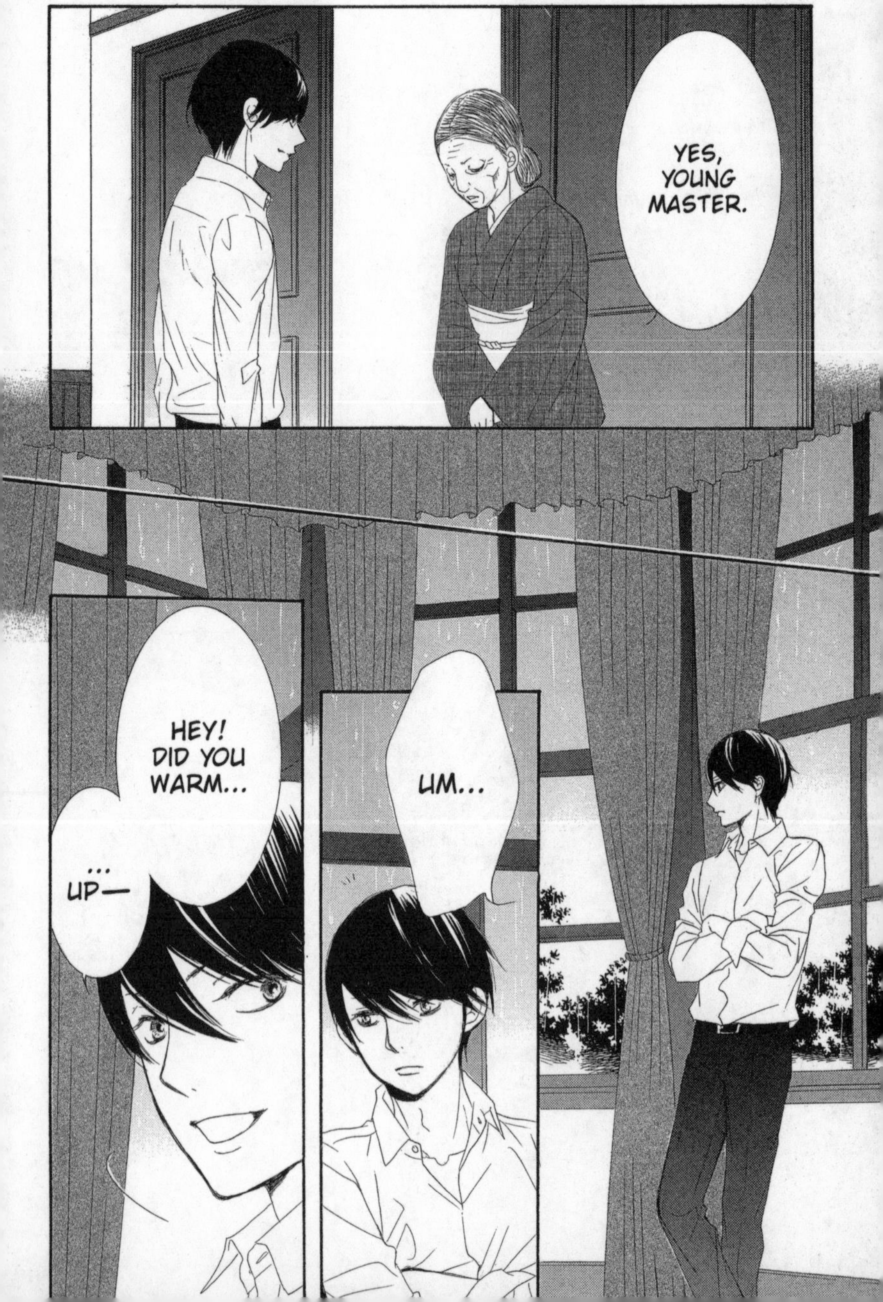
YES, YOUNG MASTER.
HEY! DID YOU WARM...
... UP—
UM...

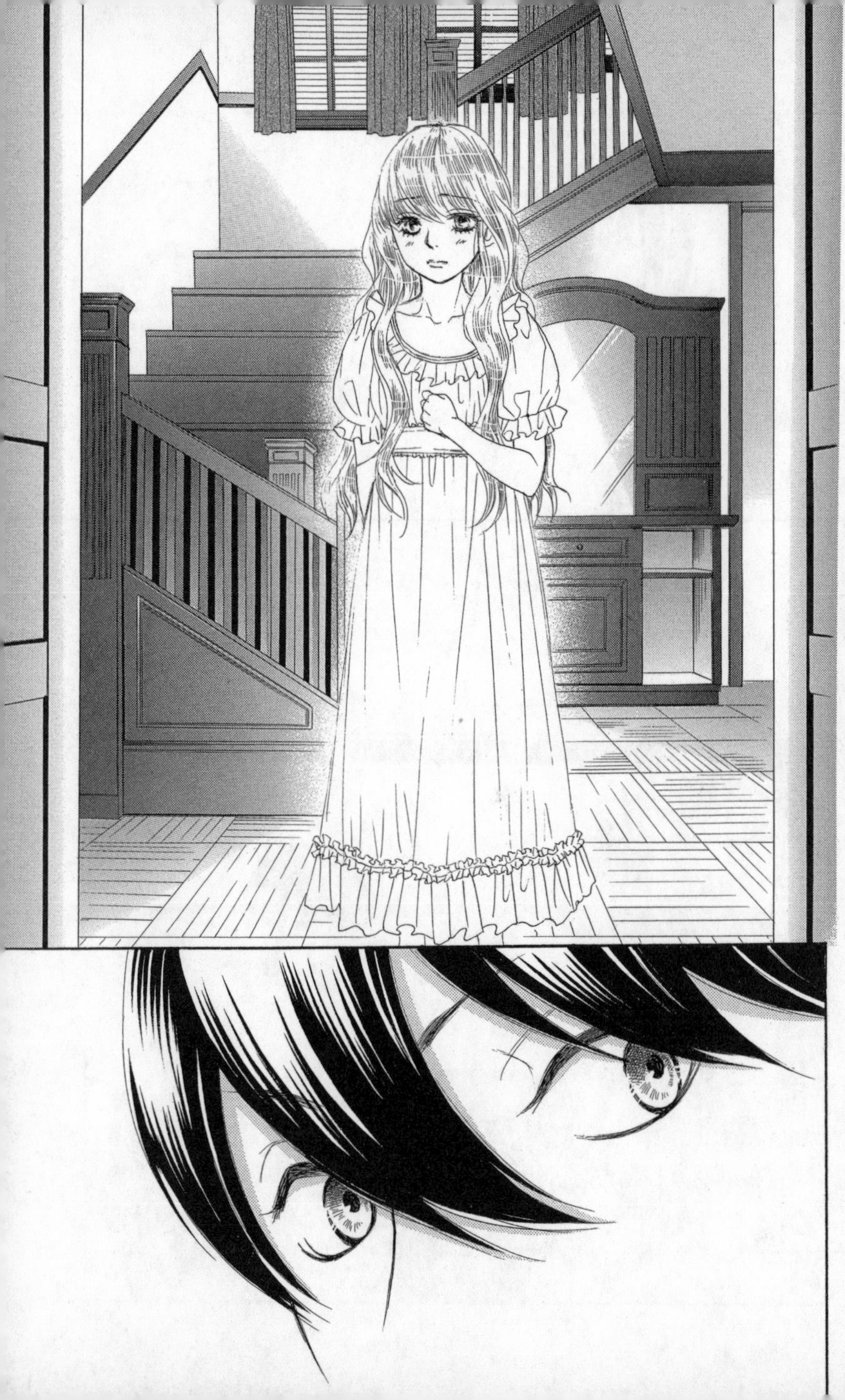

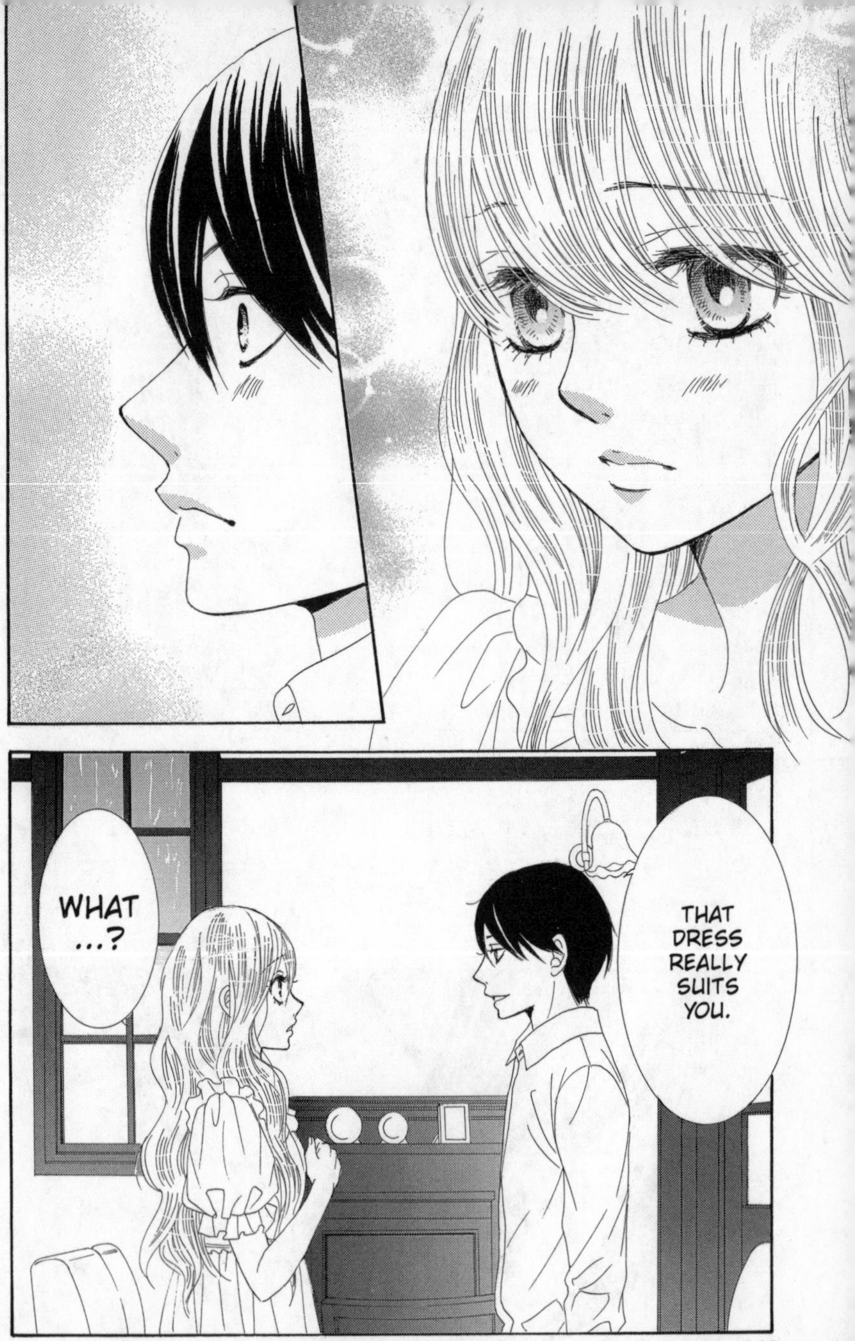
THAT DRESS REALLY SUITS YOU.
WHAT ...?

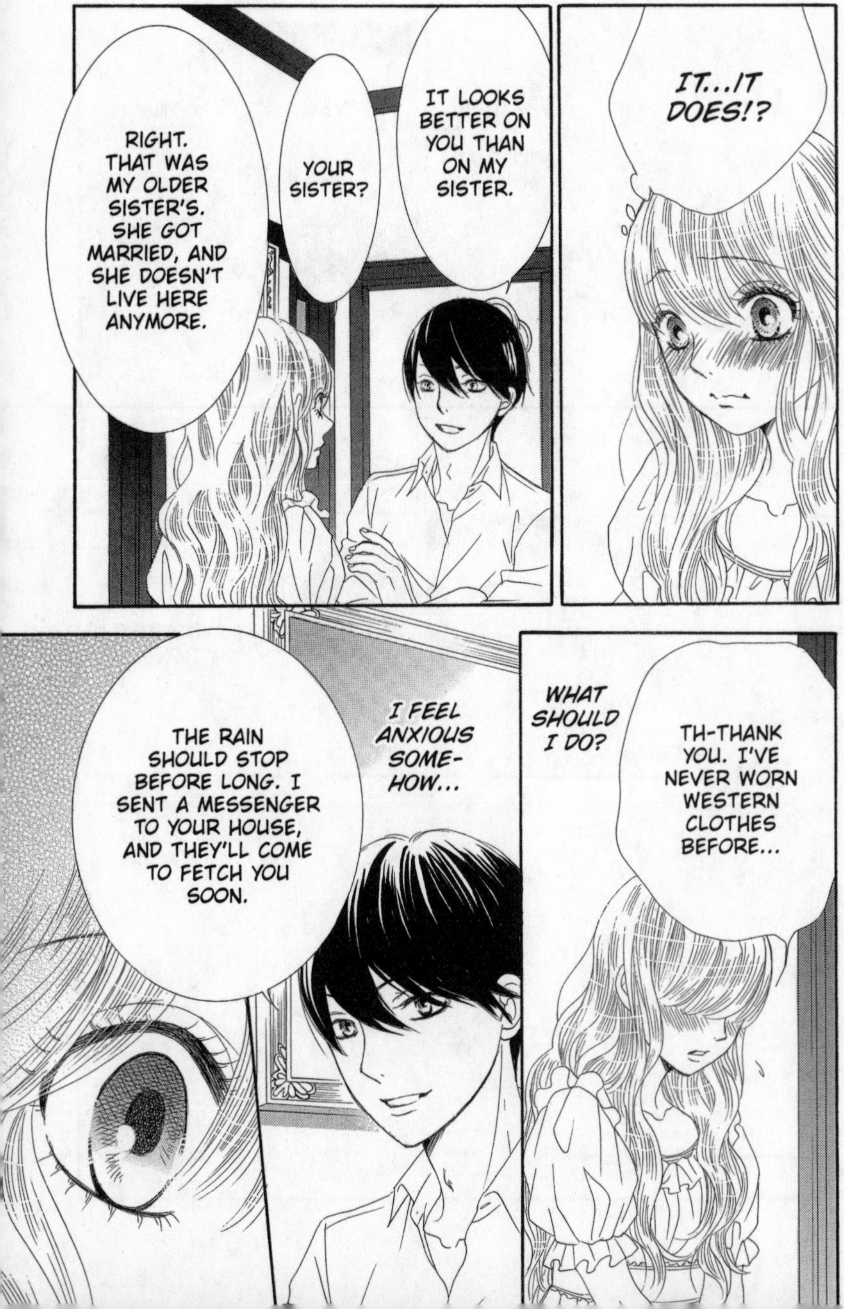
IT...IT DOES!?
IT LOOKS BETTER ON YOU THAN ON MY SISTER.
YOUR SISTER?
RIGHT. THAT WAS MY OLDER SISTER'S. SHE GOT MARRIED, AND SHE DOESN'T LIVE HERE ANYMORE.
TH-THANK YOU. I'VE NEVER WORN WESTERN CLOTHES BEFORE...
WHAT SHOULD I DO?
I FEEL ANXIOUS SOME-HOW...
THE RAIN SHOULD STOP BEFORE LONG. I SENT A MESSENGER TO YOUR HOUSE, AND THEY'LL COME TO FETCH YOU SOON.

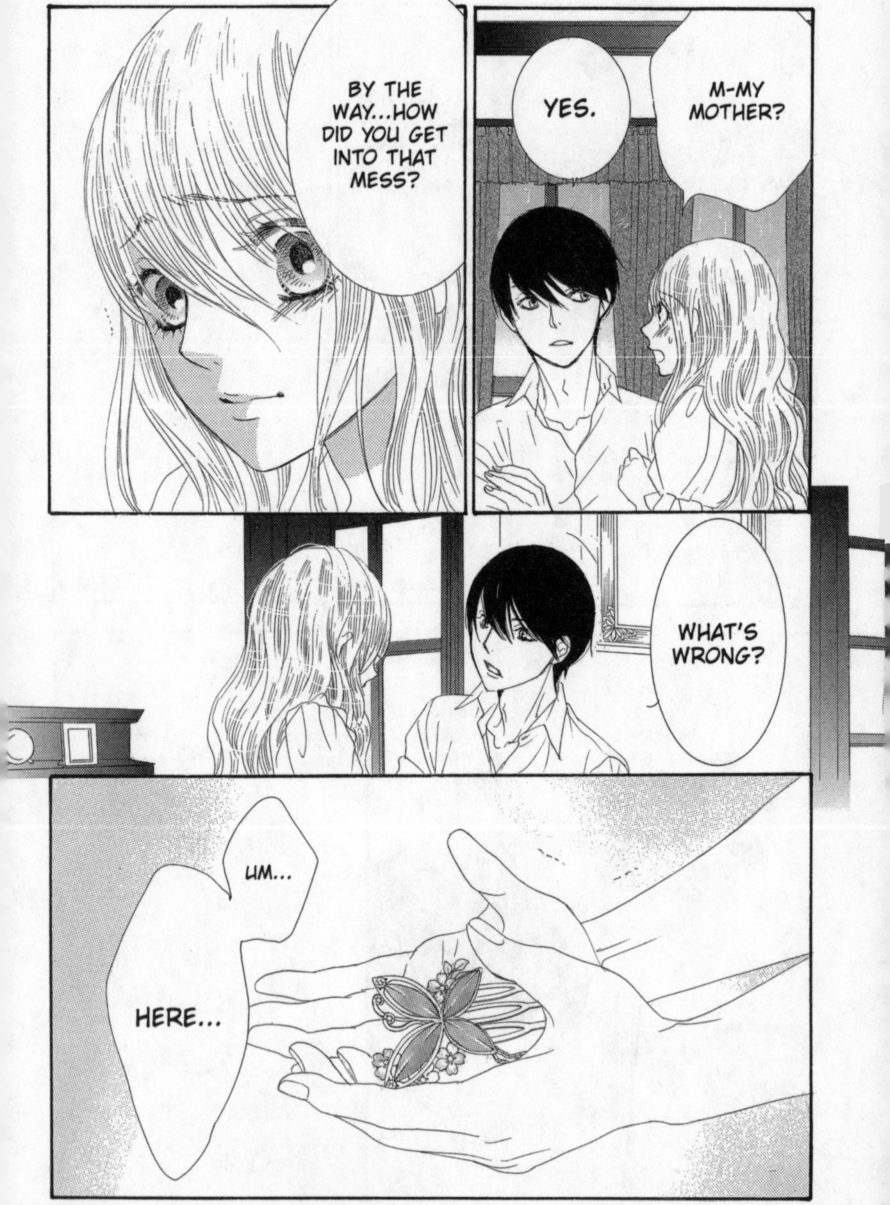
M-MY MOTHER?
YES.
BY THE WAY...HOW DID YOU GET INTO THAT MESS?
WHAT'S WRONG?
UM...
HERE...

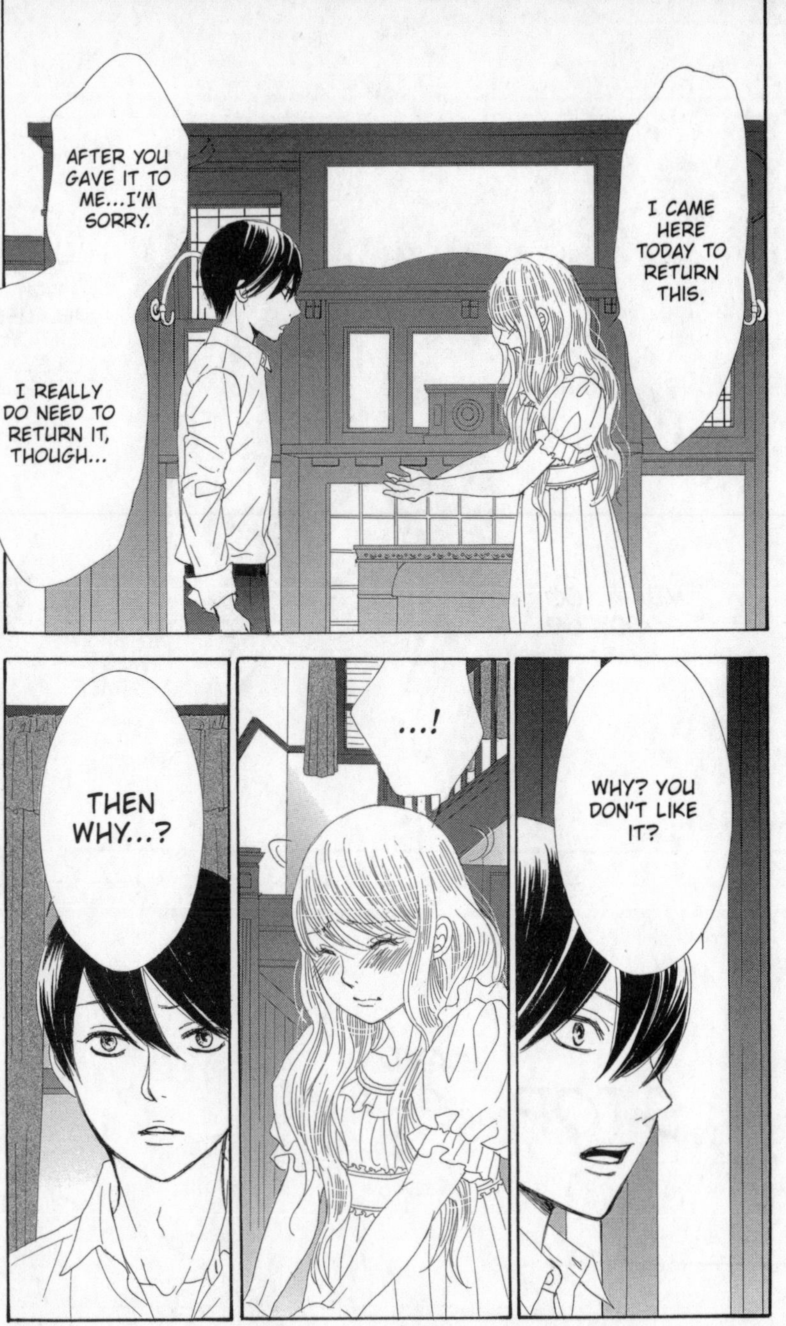
I CAME HERE TODAY TO RETURN THIS.
AFTER YOU GAVE IT TO ME...I'M SORRY.
I REALLY DO NEED TO RETURN IT, THOUGH...
WHY? YOU DON'T LIKE IT?
...!
THEN WHY...?

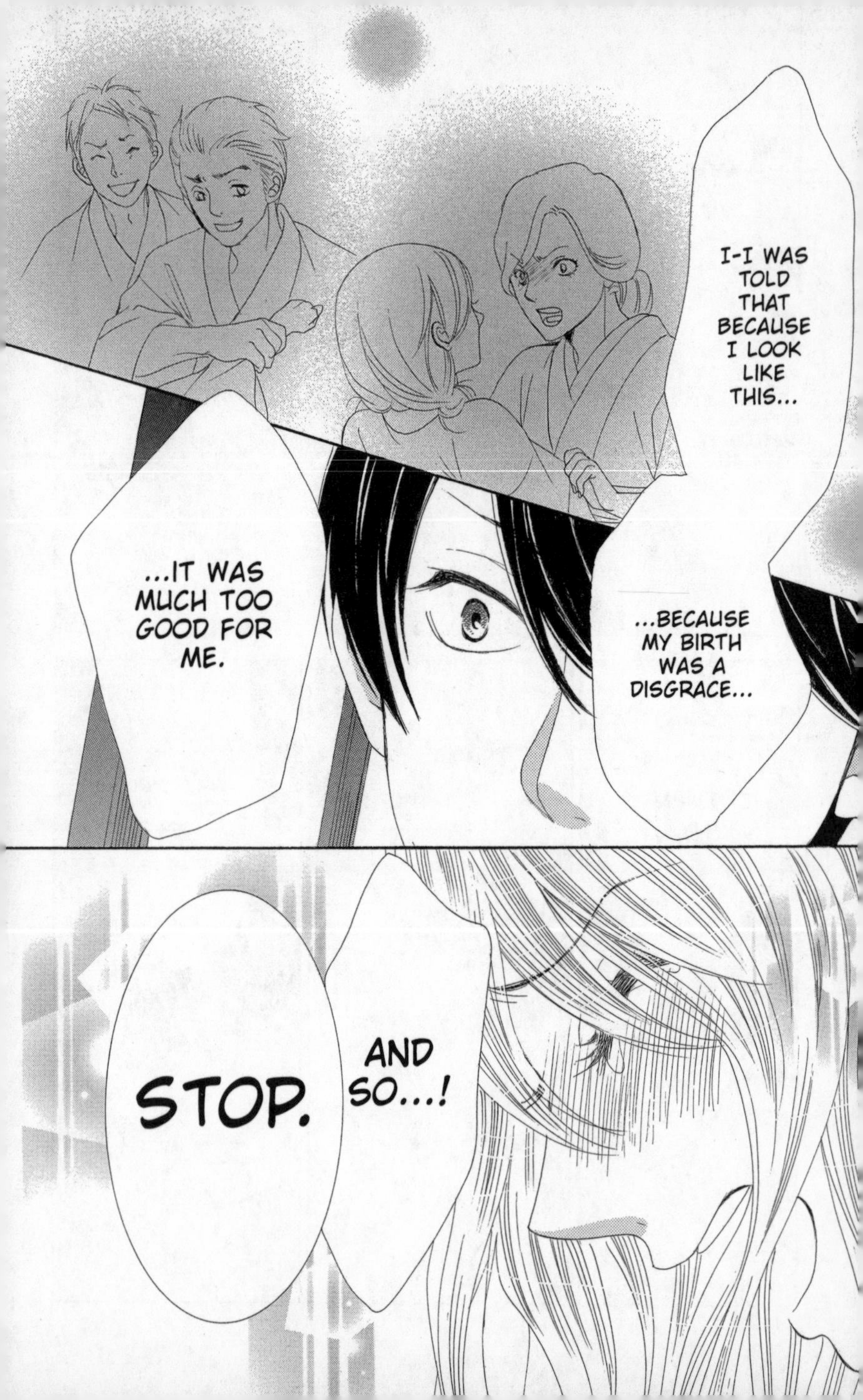
I-I WAS TOLD THAT BECAUSE I LOOK LIKE THIS...
...BECAUSE MY BIRTH WAS A DISGRACE...
...IT WAS MUCH TOO GOOD FOR ME.
AND SO...!
STOP.

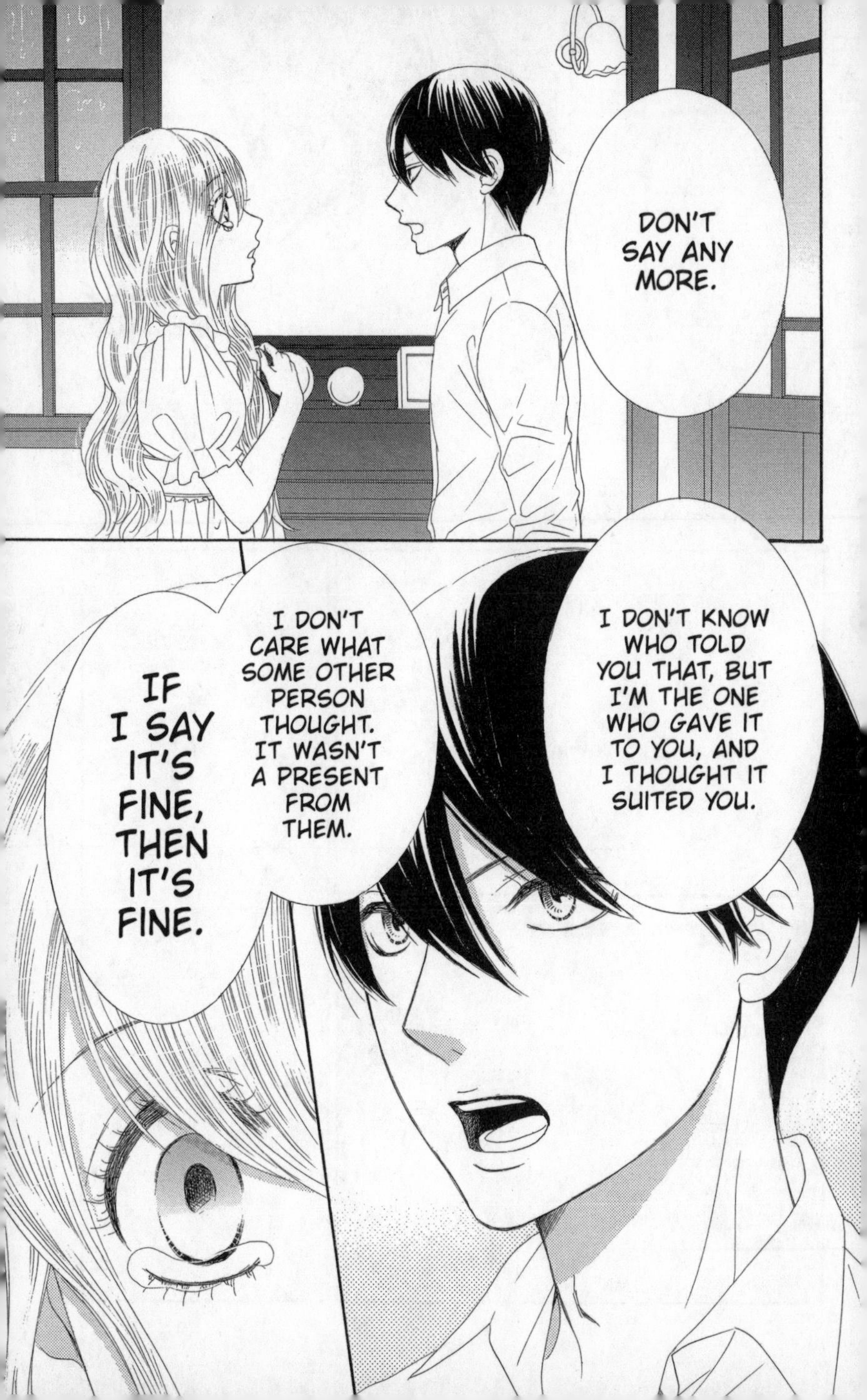
DON'T SAY ANY MORE.
I DON'T KNOW WHO TOLD YOU THAT, BUT I'M THE ONE WHO GAVE IT TO YOU, AND I THOUGHT IT SUITED YOU.
I DON'T CARE WHAT SOME OTHER PERSON THOUGHT. IT WASN'T A PRESENT FROM THEM.
IF I SAY IT'S FINE, THEN IT'S FINE.

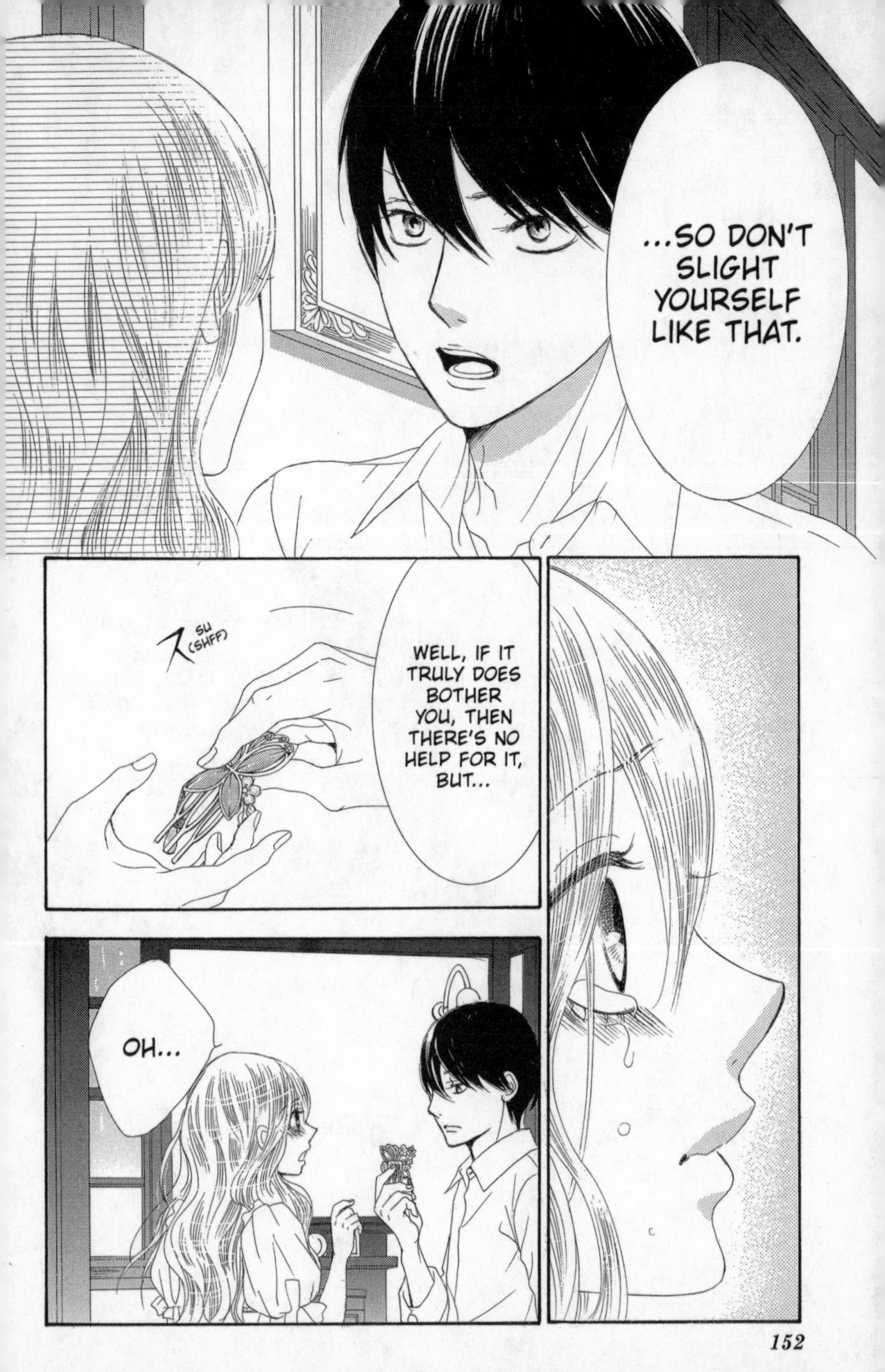
...SO DON'T SLIGHT YOURSELF LIKE THAT.
WELL, IF IT TRULY DOES BOTHER YOU, THEN THERE'S NO HELP FOR IT, BUT...
ス SU (SHFF)
OH...

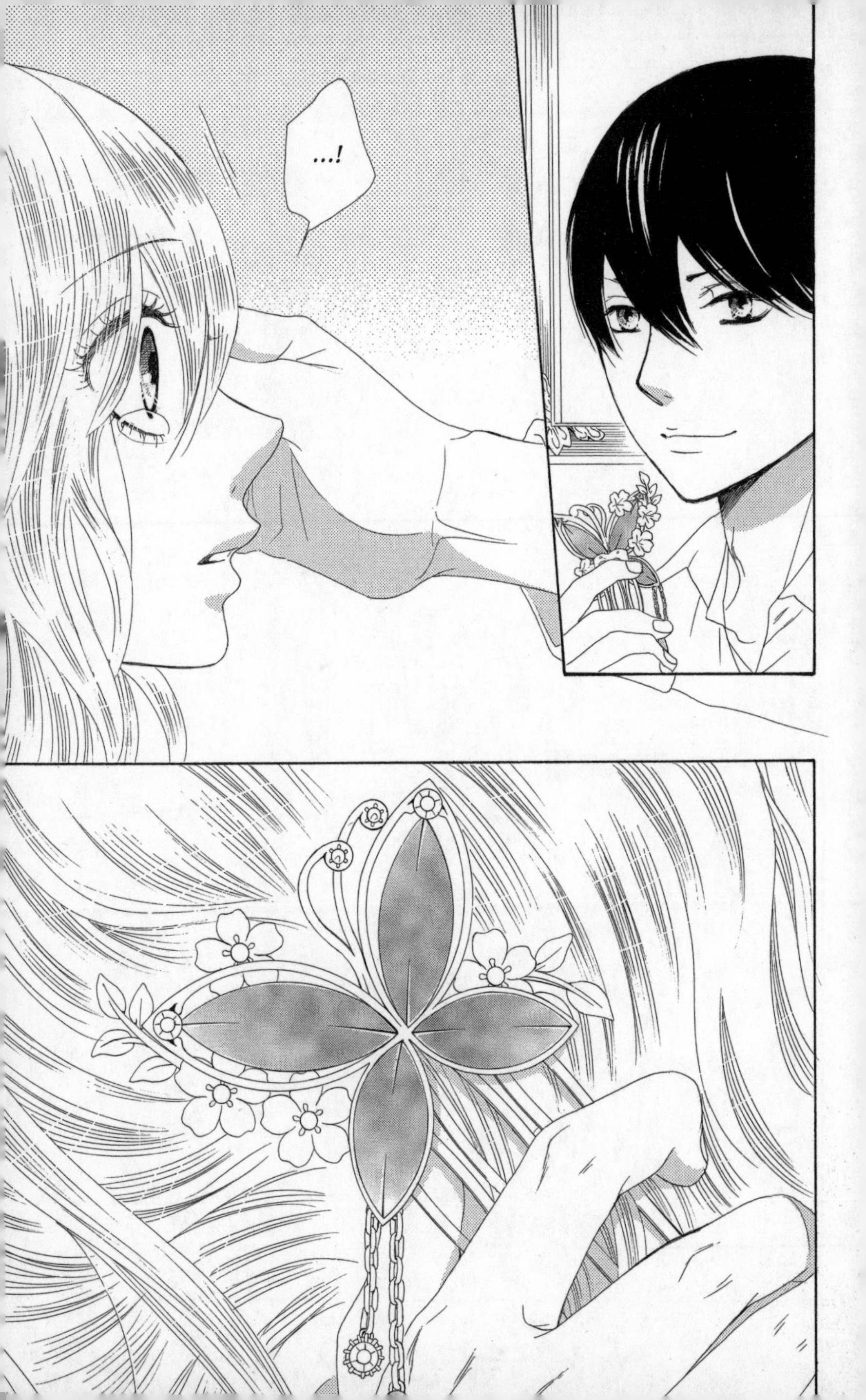
...!

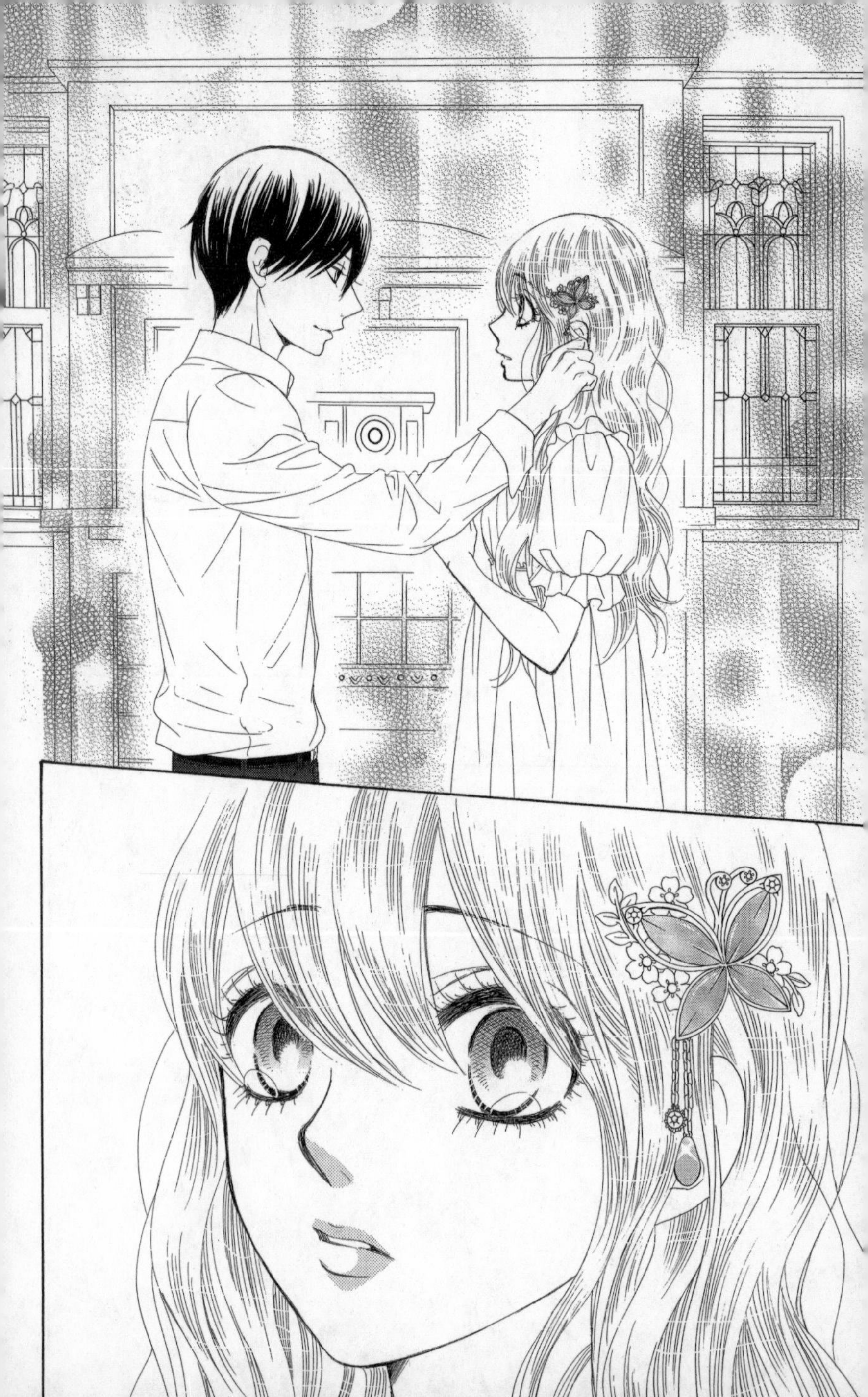

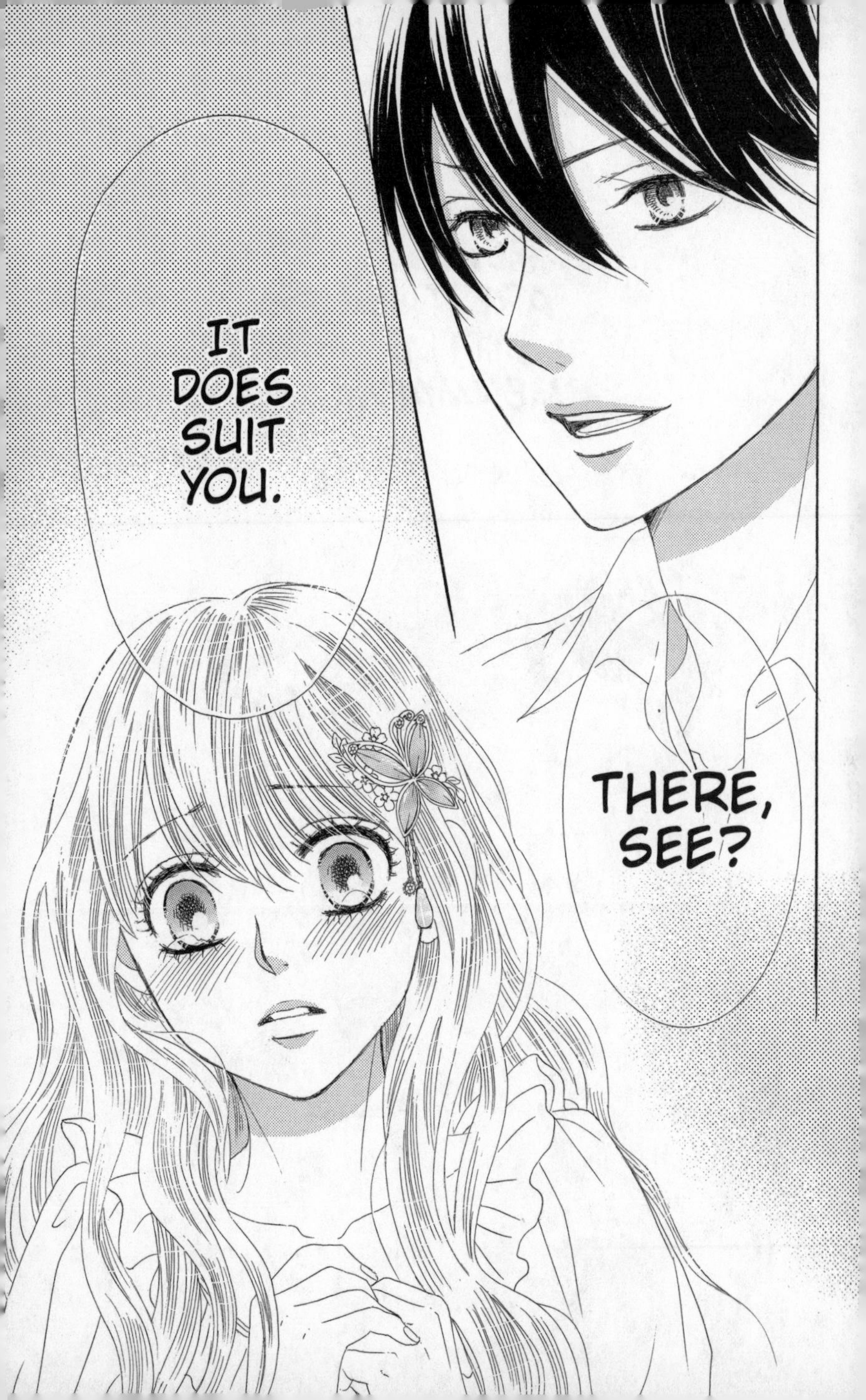
THERE, SEE?
IT DOES SUIT YOU.

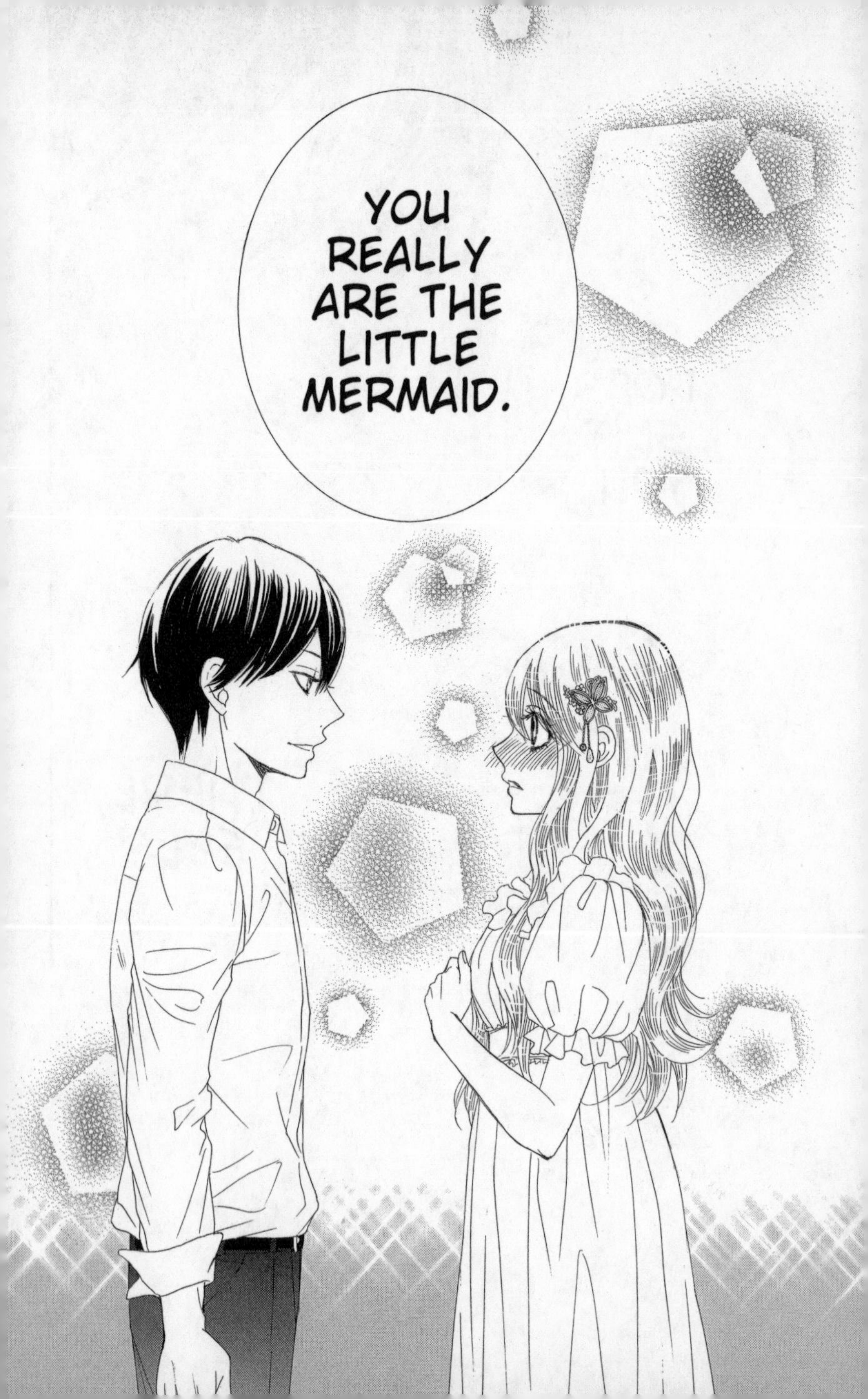
YOU REALLY ARE THE LITTLE MERMAID.

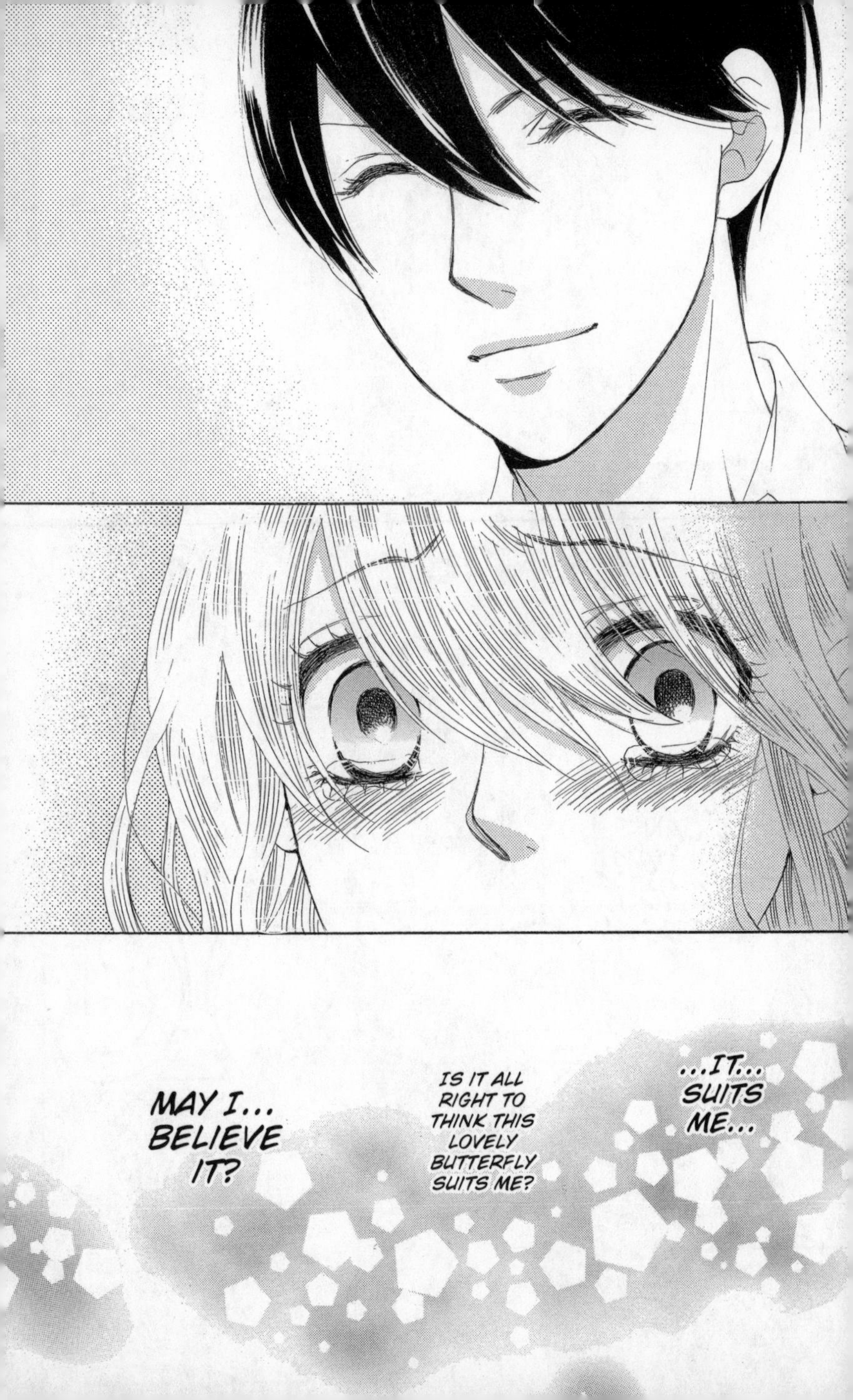
...IT... SUITS ME...
IS IT ALL RIGHT TO THINK THIS LOVELY BUTTERFLY SUITS ME?
MAY I... BELIEVE IT?

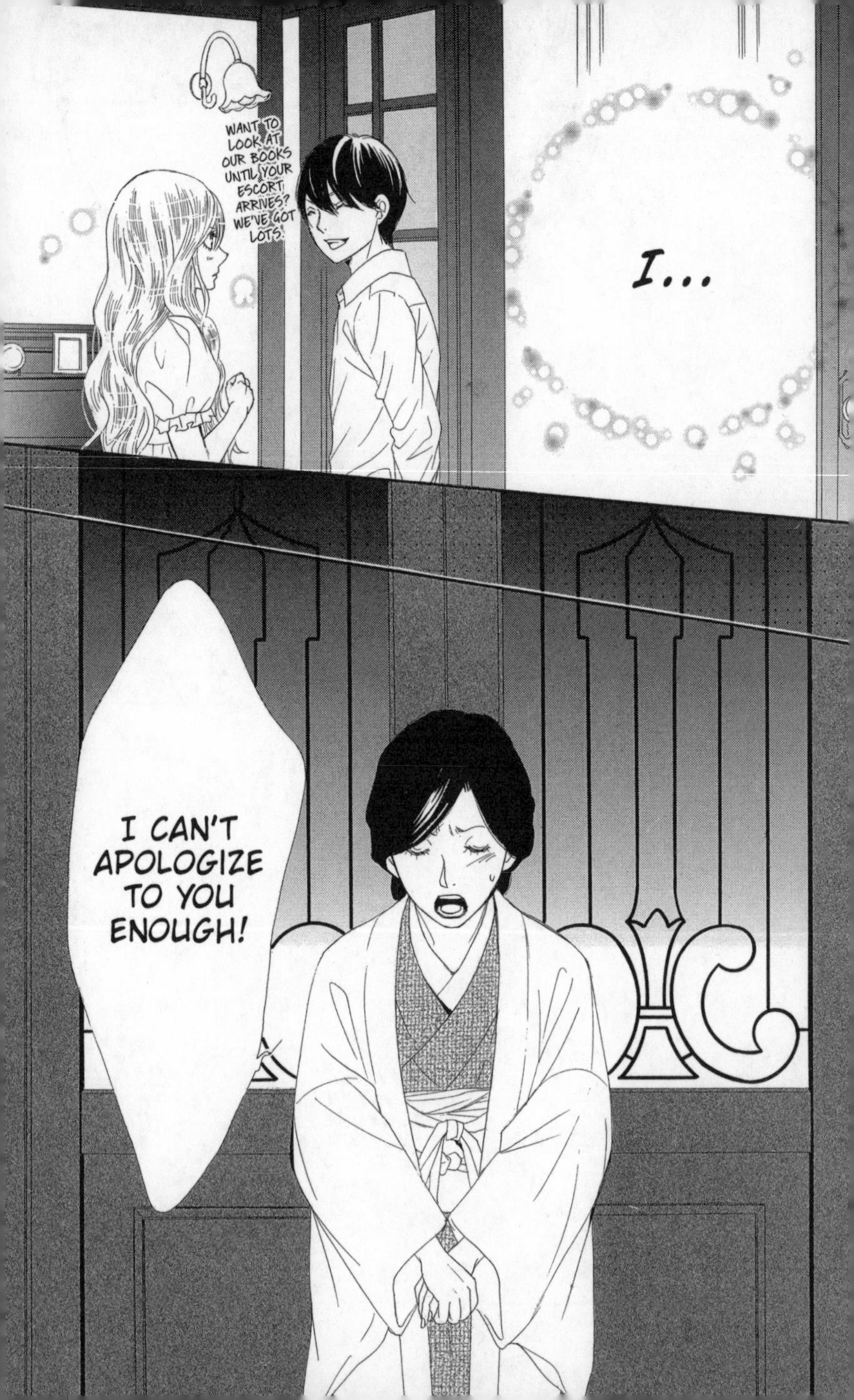
I...
WANT TO LOOK AT OUR BOOKS UNTIL YOUR ESCORT ARRIVES? WE'VE GOT LOTS.
I CAN'T APOLOGIZE TO YOU ENOUGH!

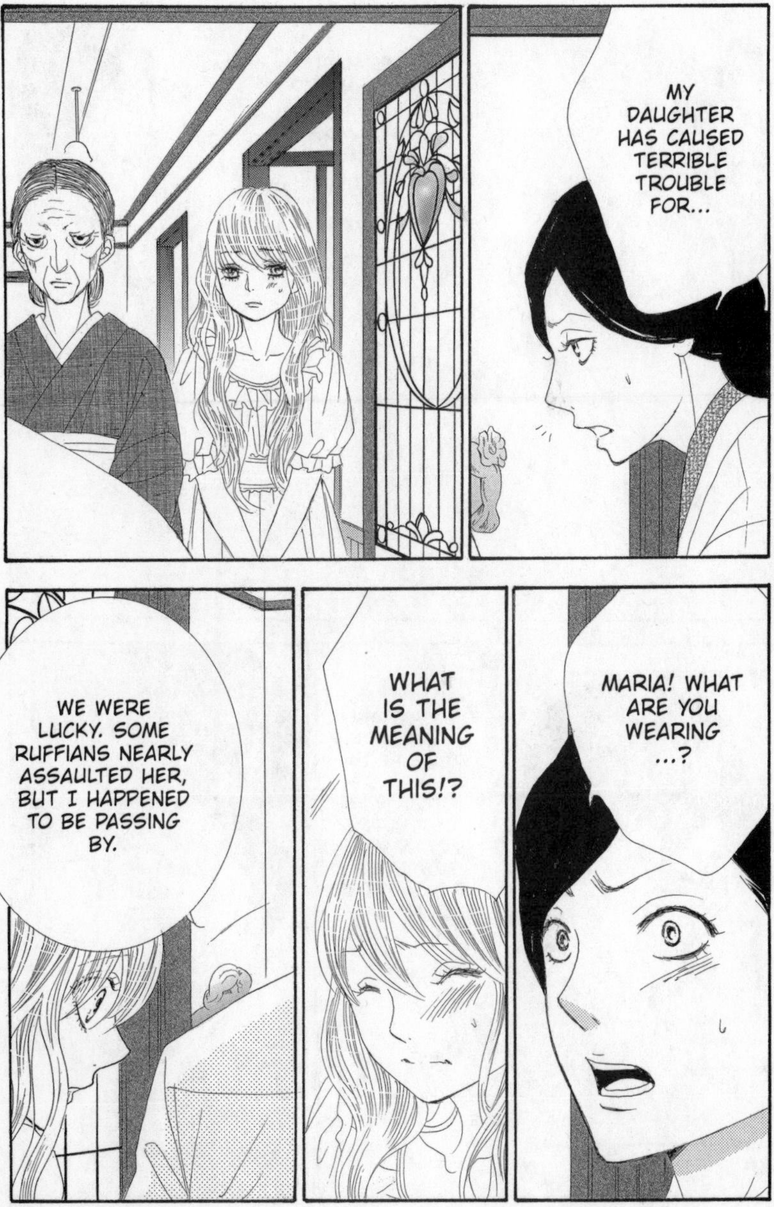
MY DAUGHTER HAS CAUSED TERRIBLE TROUBLE FOR...
MARIA! WHAT ARE YOU WEARING ...?
WHAT IS THE MEANING OF THIS!?
WE WERE LUCKY. SOME RUFFIANS NEARLY ASSAULTED HER, BUT I HAPPENED TO BE PASSING BY.

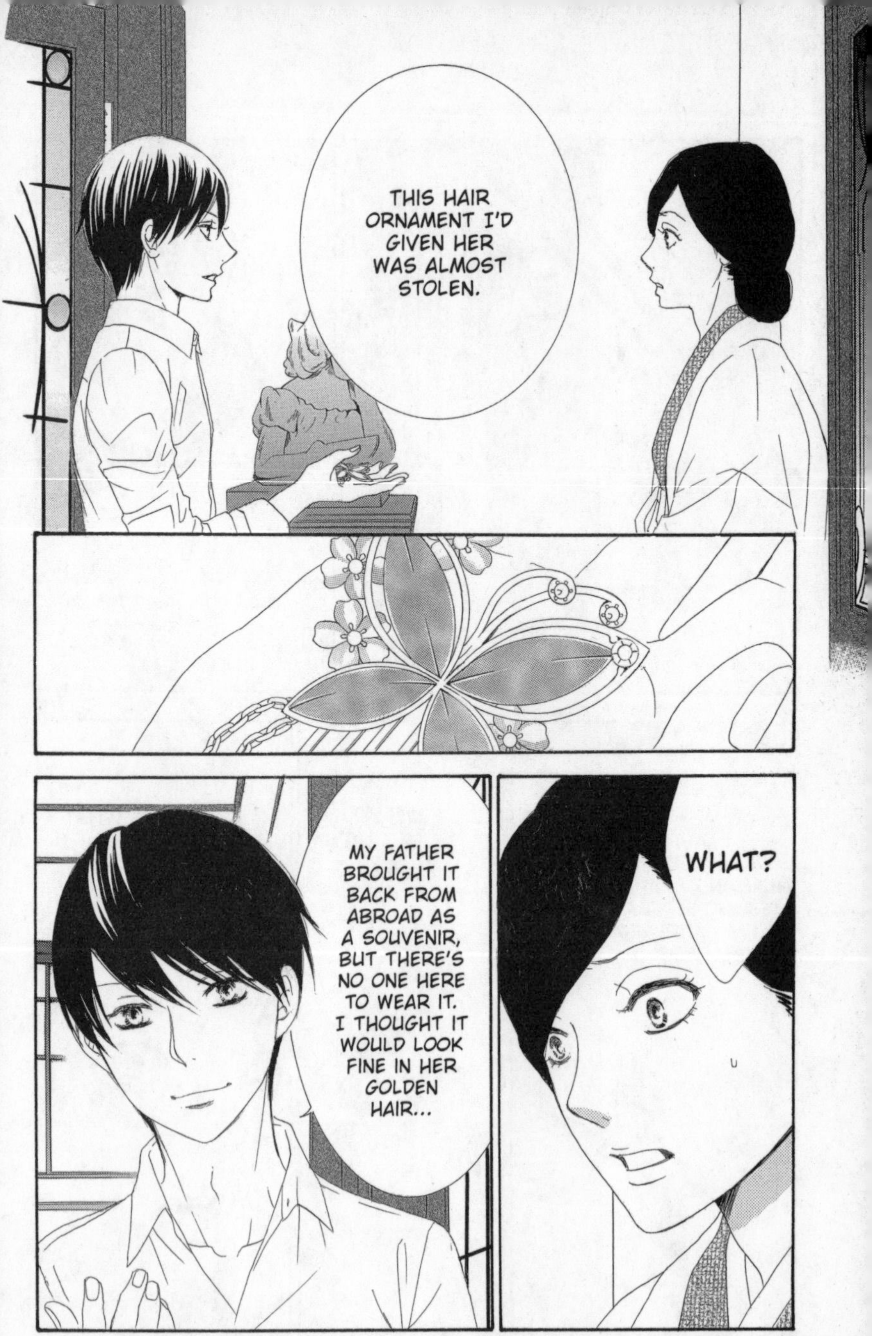
THIS HAIR ORNAMENT I'D GIVEN HER WAS ALMOST STOLEN.
WHAT?
MY FATHER BROUGHT IT BACK FROM ABROAD AS A SOUVENIR, BUT THERE'S NO ONE HERE TO WEAR IT. I THOUGHT IT WOULD LOOK FINE IN HER GOLDEN HAIR...

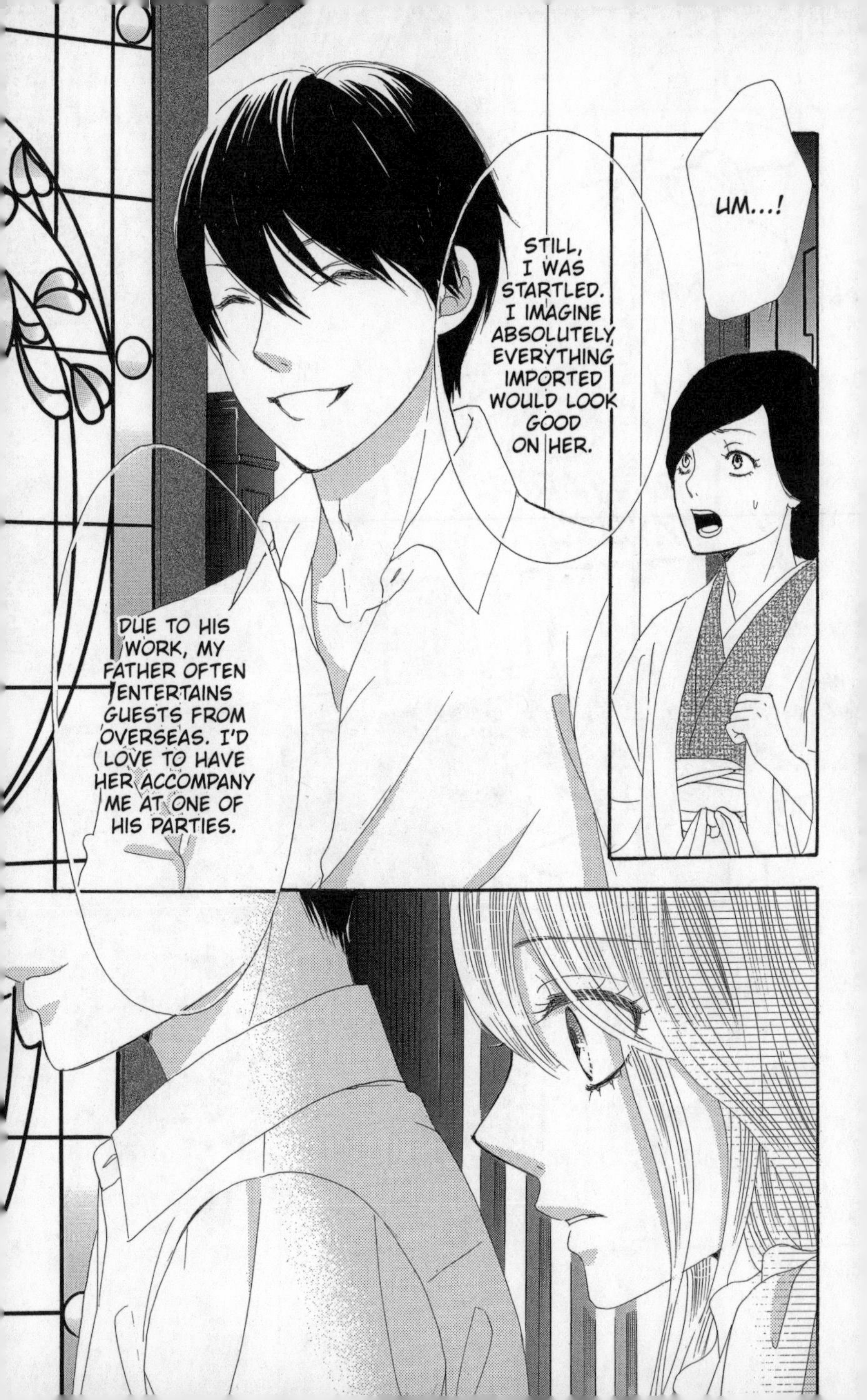
STILL, I WAS STARTLED. I IMAGINE ABSOLUTELY EVERYTHING IMPORTED WOULD LOOK GOOD ON HER.
DUE TO HIS WORK, MY FATHER OFTEN ENTERTAINS GUESTS FROM OVERSEAS. I'D LOVE TO HAVE HER ACCOMPANY ME AT ONE OF HIS PARTIES.
UM...!

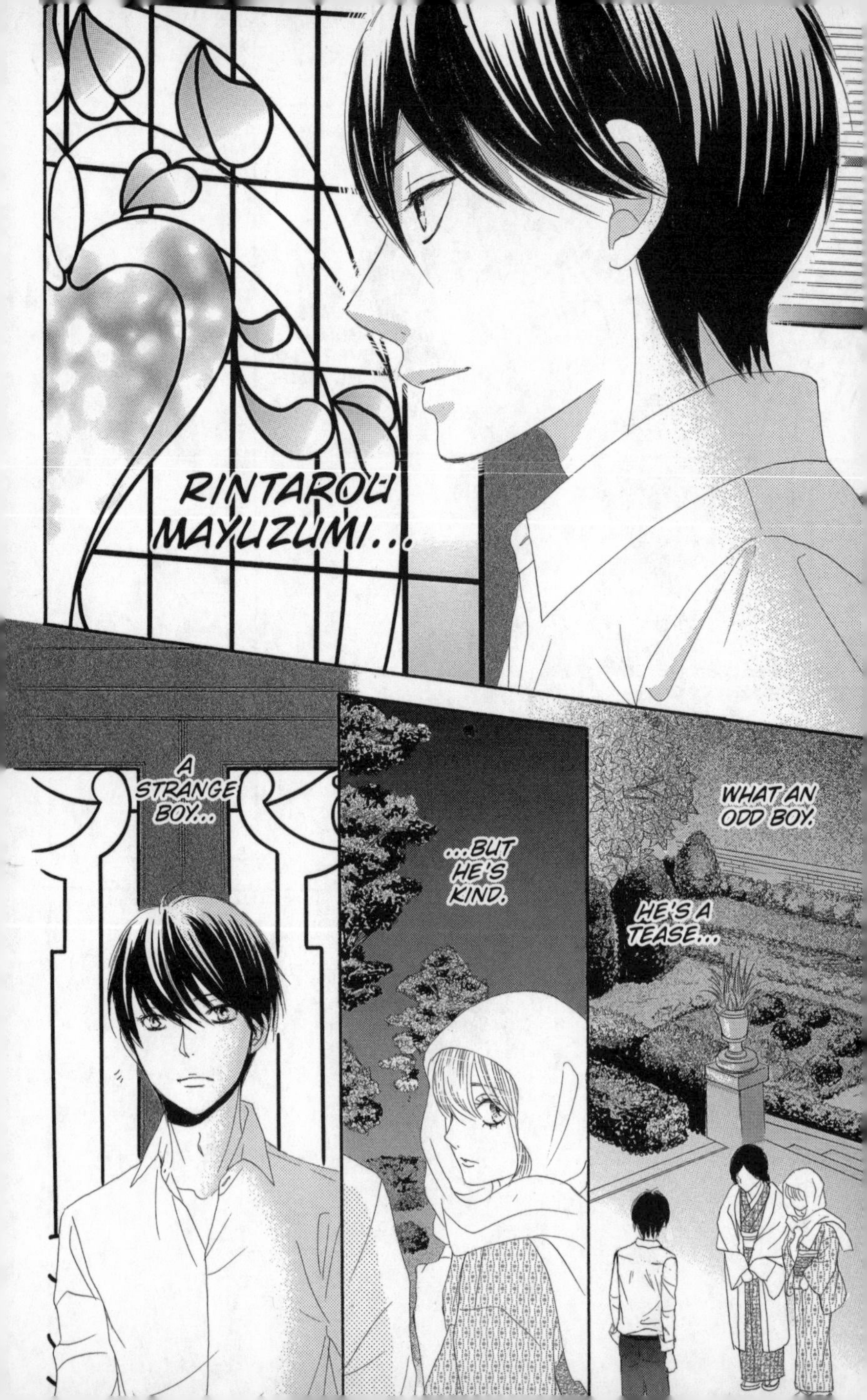
RINTAROU MAYUZUMI...
WHAT AN ODD BOY.
HE'S A TEASE...
...BUT HE'S KIND.
A STRANGE BOY...

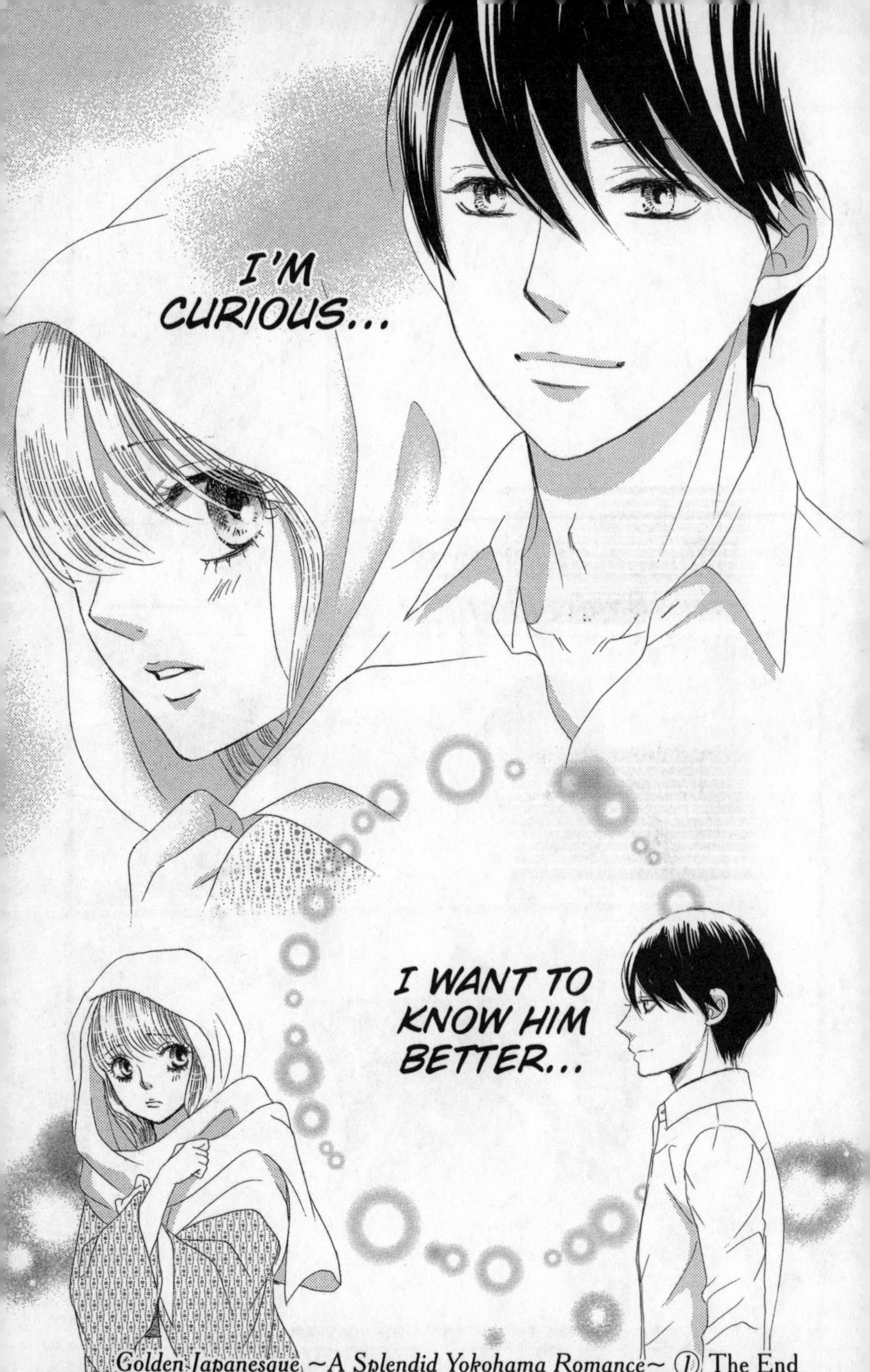
I'M CURIOUS...
I WANT TO KNOW HIM BETTER...

Golden Japanesque ~A Splendid Yokohama Romance~ ① The End

Preview of Next Volume

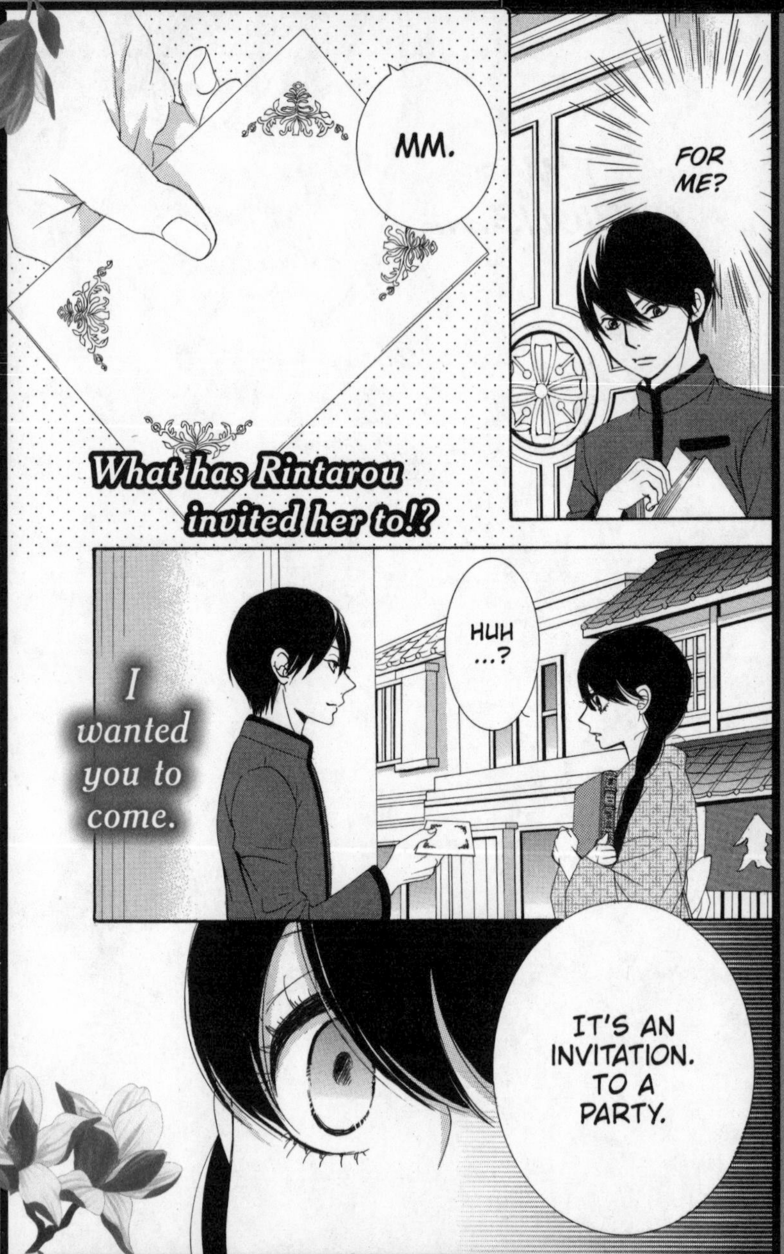
FOR ME?
MM.
What has Rintarou invited her to!?
HUH ...?
I wanted you to come.
IT'S AN INVITATION. TO A PARTY.

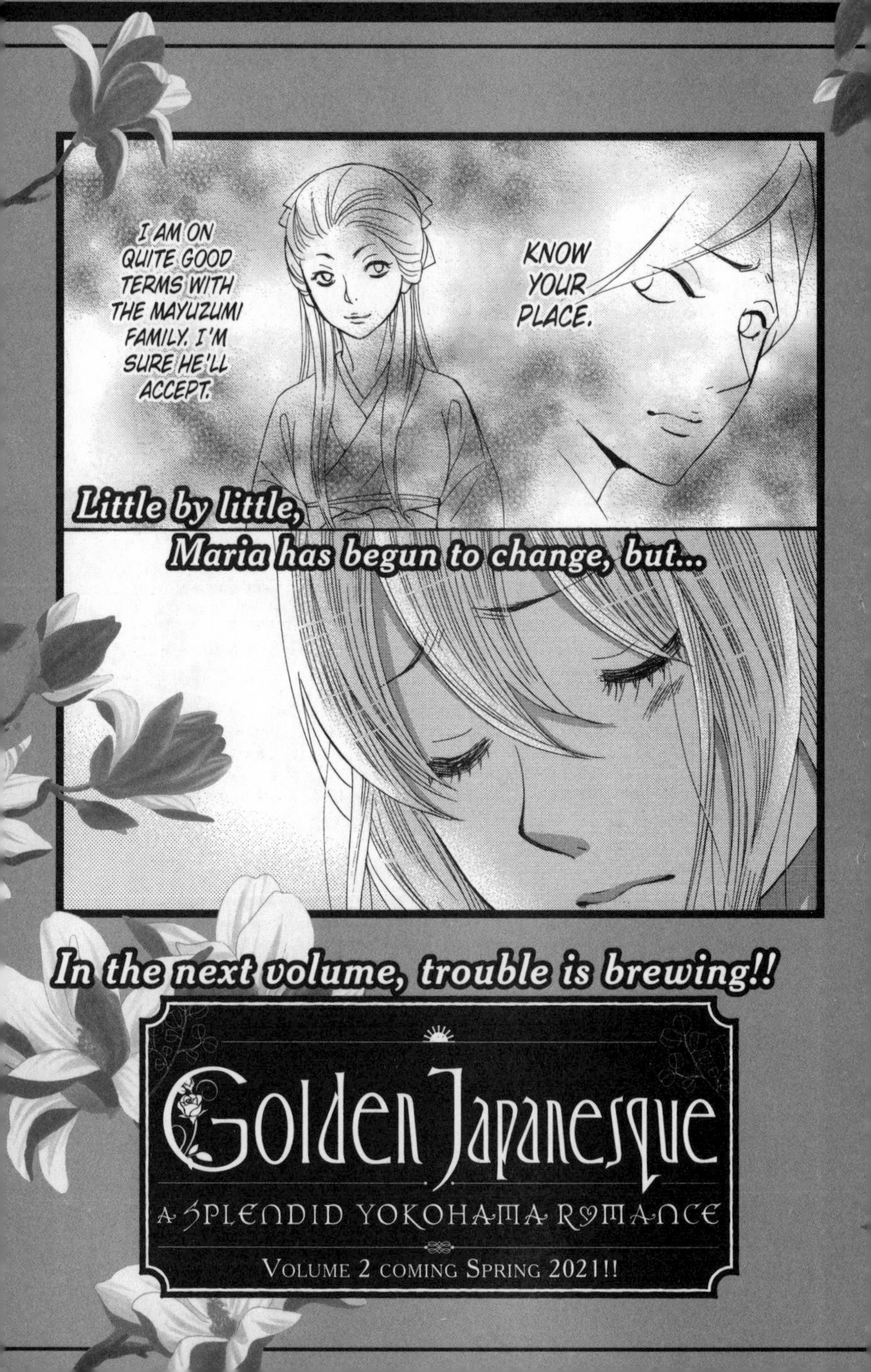
KNOW YOUR PLACE.
I AM ON QUITE GOOD TERMS WITH THE MAYUZUMI FAMILY. I'M SURE HE'LL ACCEPT.
Little by little, Maria has begun to change, but...
In the next volume, trouble is brewing!!
Golden Japanesque
A SPLENDID YOKOHAMA ROMANCE
VOLUME 2 COMING SPRING 2021!!

Translation Notes

GENERAL

no honorific: Indicates familiarity or closeness; if used without permission or reason, addressing someone in this manner would constitute an insult.

-san: The Japanese equivalent of Mr./Mrs./Miss. If a situation calls for politeness, this is the fail-safe honorific.

-sama: Conveys great respect; may also indicate that the social status of the speaker is lower than that of the addressee.

-shi: An impersonal honorific used in formal speech or writing, e.g., legal documents.

-dono: Roughly equivalent to "master" or "milord."

-kun: Used most often when referring to boys, this indicates affection or familiarity. Occasionally used by older men among their peers, but it may also be used by anyone referring to a person of lower standing.

-chan: An affectionate honorific indicating familiarity used mostly in reference to girls; also used in reference to cute persons or animals of either gender.

-(o)nii/(o)nee: Meaning "big brother"/ "big sister," it can also refer to those older but relatively close in age to the speaker. It can be combined with other honorifics, such as -san, -chan, or -sama.

-senpai: An honorific for describing someone with more immediate seniority, such as an upperclassman or senior club member.

Golden Japanesque is set in the Meiji era, which lasted from 1868 to 1912 and is known as a time of great Western influence in Japan. The era is named after the Meiji emperor, and it coincides with his reign. Referring to a given year in terms of an emperor's reign is typical in Japan—for example, Meiji Year 1 refers to 1868. The Meiji era is followed by Taisho (1912 to 1926), Showa (1926 to 1989), Heisei (1989 to 2019), and Reiwa (2019 to present).

Yokohama Port was opened to foreign trade in 1859.

The Japanese written language uses three different sets of characters in writing: *hiragana* and *katakana* (which are akin to alphabets) and *kanji* (Chinese characters). Achieving full literacy in Japanese requires mastering all three, with *kanji* being by far the most complex and difficult. However, it was even more challenging in the Meiji era, as that's when attempts to simplify and formalize the written language had only began to take place. Prior to then, written and spoken Japanese could also be incredibly different from each other.

PAGE 008

The **Hiraoka** sign, and many others in this manga, is written from right to left, instead of from left to right. Vertical writing in Japanese is read top to bottom and right to left, and for a long time, horizontal writing was treated the same way as vertical writing, with each "column" consisting of just one character. It could also be written from left to right, the way European languages are. The direction of horizontal writing wasn't standardized as from left to right until after World War II.

PAGE 011

In Japanese, the name **Maria** is written with *kanji*, so it is not meant to appear as an explicitly foreign-sounding name.

PAGE 017

Then nameplate here reads **Mayuzumi**. It's a fairly uncommon Japanese surname as well as a somewhat complex and unusual *kanji*, which is why Maria has trouble reading it.

PAGES 018–019

Maria actually says "*Hannya*" in Japanese for **demons**. The word refers to a Noh mask of a jealous female demon, and if you add horns to Kisaragi's head, her face really does resemble a Hannya mask.

PAGE 022

Maria can't read this text, but this is not typical Japanese. It's a style of writing known as *kanbun*, or "Chinese writing," specifically the *hakubun* type that exclusively uses *kanji* characters. The characters are ordered according to the rules of Chinese grammar, which means the reader has to mentally shuffle the words around a bit in order for them make sense in Japanese (or just read them in Chinese), and elements that would normally be written in *hiragana* are omitted. The text featured on this page is from "Regarding Demosthenes," or more specifically, the Japanese translation of a German work about the Greek philosopher. The translation was made in 1879 (Meiji Year 12) by a twenty-two-year-old Tokyo University medical faculty student named Enko Uchida.

PAGE 023

The **envelope** actually says "Year 2, Class 1, Rintarou Mayuzumi." Maria can only read the -tarou part because "Tarou" is an incredibly common Japanese name—similar to "John" in English.

PAGE 024

"Diiiiing" is Rintarou mimicking the sound effect of a metal bowl that's struck when offering prayers to the dead, because it looks as though Maria's attempting to send the book to him as an offering.

Translation Notes (Continued)

PAGE 029
The **mixed jelly dessert** is *anmitsu*, which is made with small cubes of white agar jelly, sweet red-bean paste, soft *mochi* (chewy rice cake), and slices of fruits, such as peaches, tangerines, pineapples, and cherries, with a sweet brown-sugar syrup poured over the top just before serving. The dessert dates back to the Meiji era, so it would have been fairly new at this point.

The **sweet-bean rice cake** is *daifuku*, which is made of sweet red-bean paste wrapped in sweetened *mochi*. In this particular variety, the *mochi* is studded with salted beans.

PAGE 032
"Sitting like a cat," in Japanese is *nekoze*, (literally "cat back"). It means "to stoop" or "to have a hunchback."

PAGE 038
Maria's hair isn't actually **red** but rather blond. Although the *kanji* used for the term is usually different, the Dutch were originally called "red-haired people" (*koumoujin*) in Japan, to differentiate them from the Portuguese and Spanish "southern barbarians" (*nanbanjin*). (The Dutch were traders and seen as relatively neutral; the Portuguese and Spanish were missionaries and were viewed less favorably.) After a certain point, "red-haired people" was a term applied to all Westerners (whether or not their hair was actually red).

PAGE 041
At this time, having **kanji** literacy was not necessarily taken for granted as it would be today for a teenage girl. Public education was just getting started in the Meiji era—in the 1870s, only 30 percent of eligible children were enrolled in elementary school, and of course those who weren't didn't go on to middle or high school.

PAGE 054
These candies are **konpeito**, and although they're a classic Japanese sweet at this point, they were originally brought to Japan by the Portuguese in the mid-1500s. *Konpeito* comes from the Portuguese word *confeito*, or "comfit." In the classic version, the only ingredients are sugar, water, and coloring, so their flavor is very simple. However, since these candies use so much sugar, they used to be something only the rich could afford. There's also the time element: They're made by covering a grain of coarse sugar in multiple coats of sugar syrup, and it used to take up to two months to make a batch. Even today, it takes one to two weeks.

PAGE 081
Youkai are supernatural creatures and monsters from Japanese folklore. They come in many different forms, from humanoid beings such as mermaids to shapeless entities.

PAGE 083
These **coins** are worth one *rin* each. A *rin* is an old unit of currency that was worth 1/1000 of a yen. In the 1870s, Maria would have needed about eight more *rin* to buy a red-bean bun, so this isn't a big tip—it's the rough equivalent of 40 or 50 cents today.

A Loner's Worst Nightmare: Human Interaction!

MY YOUTH R♥MANTIC COMEDY iS WRØNG, AS I EXPECTED

Wataru Watari
Illustration Ponkan⑧

MY YOUTH R♥MANTIC COMEDY iS WRØNG, AS I EXPECTED

Hachiman Hikigaya is a cynic. He believes "youth" is a crock—a sucker's game, an illusion woven from failure and hypocrisy. But when he turns in an essay for a school assignment espousing this view, he's sentenced to work in the Service Club, an organization dedicated to helping students with problems! Worse, the only other member of the club is the haughty Yukino Yukinoshita, a girl with beauty, brains, and the personality of a garbage fire. How will Hachiman the Cynic cope with a job that requires—*gasp!*—social skills?

Check out the manga too!

Yen Press

Two girls, a new school, and the beginning of a beautiful friendship.

Kiss & White Lily for My Dearest Girl

In middle school, Ayaka Shiramine was the perfect student: hard-working, with excellent grades and a great personality to match. As Ayaka enters high school she expects to still be on top, but one thing she didn't account for is her new classmate, the lazy yet genuine genius Yurine Kurosawa. What's in store for Ayaka and Yurine as they go through high school...together?

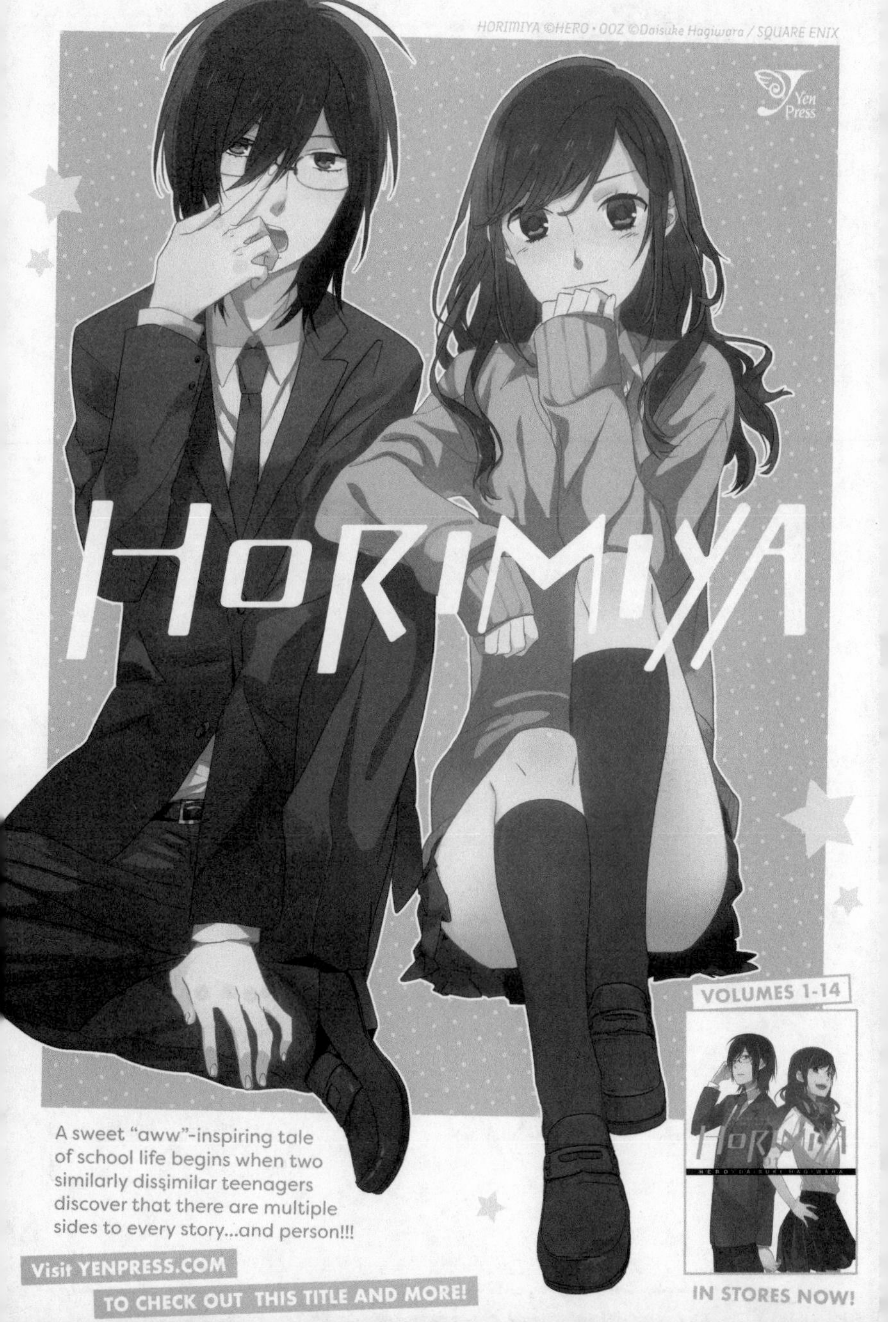
HORIMIYA ©HERO • OOZ ©Daisuke Hagiwara / SQUARE ENIX
Yen Press
HORIMIYA
VOLUMES 1-14
A sweet "aww"-inspiring tale of school life begins when two similarly dissimilar teenagers discover that there are multiple sides to every story...and person!!!
Visit YENPRESS.COM
TO CHECK OUT THIS TITLE AND MORE!
IN STORES NOW!

Golden Japanesque
A SPLENDID YOKOHAMA ROMANCE

KAHO MIYASAKA 1

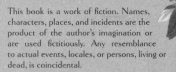

Translation/Adaptation:
TAYLOR ENGEL

Lettering:
LYS BLAKESLEE

KINIRO JAPANESQUE
-YOKOHAMA KARENTAN- vol.1 by Kaho MIYASAKA
© 2019 Kaho MIYASAKA
All rights reserved.
Original Japanese edition published by SHOGAKUKAN.
English translation rights in the United States of America, Canada, the United Kingdom, Ireland, Australia and New Zealand arranged with SHOGAKUKAN through Tuttle-Mori Agency, Inc.

English translation © 2021 by Yen Press, LLC

Yen Press
150 West 30th Street, 19th Floor
New York, NY 10001

Visit us at yenpress.com
facebook.com/yenpress
twitter.com/yenpress
yenpress.tumblr.com
instagram.com/yenpress

First Yen Press Edition: January 2021

Yen Press is an imprint of Yen Press, LLC.
The Yen Press name and logo are trademarks of Yen Press, LLC.

The publisher is not responsible for websites (or their content) that are not owned by the publisher.

Library of Congress Control Number:
2020948881

ISBN: 978-1-9753-1977-9

10 9 8 7 6 5 4 3 2 1

BVG

Printed in the United States of America